Thinking About Social Thinking

ANTONY FLEW is Professor Emeritus of Philosophy in the University of Reading. He has for the last six years served part-time as a Distinguished Research Fellow in the Social Philosophy and Policy Center, Bowling Green State University, Ohio. His books include the classic *Thinking About Thinking* (also available from Fontana Press), *An Introduction to Western Philosophy, Darwinian Evolution, A Rational Animal, The Politics of Procrustes: Contradictions of Enforced Equality,* and his Gifford Lectures on *The Logic of Mortality.*

Thinking About Social Thinking

Escaping Deception,
Resisting Self-deception

SECOND EDITION

Antony Flew

FontanaPress
An Imprint of HarperCollinsPublishers

Fontana Press
An Imprint of HarperCollins *Publishers*,
77–85 Fulham Palace Road,
Hammersmith, London W6 8JB

First published by Basil Blackwell Ltd 1985
This Second Edition published by Fontana Press 1991
9 8 7 6 5 4 3 2 1

ISBN 0 00 686218 7

Set in Baskerville

Printed in Great Britain by
HarperCollins Manufacturing Glasgow

'What about a bit of parental authority and discipline?',
suggested Sir Humphrey. I told him not to be silly.
'If you could make her listen to reason . . . ' volunteered
Bernard.
I explained to him that she is a Sociology student.
'Oh I see,' he said sadly.

J. Lynn and A. Jay (Eds.)
*Yes Minister: The Diaries of a
Cabinet Minister*, p. 145.

CONTENTS

1 The Need for Honesty

Some years before the First World War, a Parisian periodical asked some of the most prominent French figures in the various branches of what we would now call the social sciences, and which were known at that time in France as *les sciences morales*, about what they regarded as the most essential method in their field. While other respondents sent back learned methodological disquisitions Georges Sorel replied in one word, 'honesty'.

Stanislav Andreski,
Social Sciences as Sorcery, p. 232.

This book is a comprehensively revised, substantially re-shaped, and somewhat extended version of my *Thinking About Social Thinking* (Oxford: Blackwell, 1985). The object of this radical reconstruction – which has among other things included the complete rewriting of what were the initial and the final chapters, the division into two each of what were the second and the fourth, and a major extension of the latter – was to produce what should now be seen as a somewhat more advanced companion volume to my *Thinking About Thinking: Or do I sincerely want to be right?* (London: Collins/Fontana, 1975, Seventh Impression 1989). The publisher's blurb on that book describes it as "a primer to how . . . if we sincerely want to think better and straighter, we can."

The predecessor of the present *Thinking About Social Thinking* was offered as, in the first place, an essay in the philosophy of the social sciences, intended to be serviceable as a set book for courses such as are already taken by many whose main studies are in either philosophy or sociology, and which surely should be required of all those who aspire to become any sort of social scientist. This successor is, I believe, equally well if not better suited for that purpose.

For instance: to assist systematic revisers, as well as those who occasionally need to remind themselves of something said in a previous chapter, it too contains a fairly exhaustive Index of Notions as well as the usual Index of Names. Again, it too makes unusually frequent reference to some of those whose prime claim to fame is as philosophers. But, Aristotle, for instance, also has a strong claim as the founder of political science. For, besides producing his *Politics*, with its extensive and always astringent critique of the political proposals made by Plato in *The Republic* and *The Laws*, Aristotle both wrote his own study of *The Constitution of Athens* and inspired or cajoled pupils and associates to produce similar studies of the constitutions of over one hundred and fifty other Greek city-states.

None of this, however, is out of place in a book primarily directed at a much wider public. For what is the philosophy of the social sciences if not an exercise in *Thinking About Social Thinking*? That intended wider public consists in would-be discriminating consumers of presently available and possible future findings of the social sciences; rather than in would-be future producers of such findings.

1   What is to be done

There is a great need for such a companion volume to *Thinking About Thinking*. It is a need which arises from peculiarities of the subject matter of the social or, as they used to be called, the moral sciences, and from consequent peculiarities in their present condition. The most widely read and, some would say, the most scurrilous of British Sunday newspapers once advertised its scope in the slogan: "All human life is here!" The same could rather more truly be said of the social sciences. For these studies are in their different ways all concerned with all the behaviour of, and with interactions between, members of our kind of creatures.

It is for this reason that the actual or alleged findings of achieved research, and the potential findings of the further research which might and perhaps ought to be done, often have or appear to have a crucial bearing upon matters not of purely specialist but of more general concern. These actual or possible findings have or seem to have practical implications not only for public questions of social and political policy, but also for such more private matters as marriage, divorce and the upbringing of children.

This means that even if and when the putative experts are unanimously agreed upon the robustness of findings reported, responsible and independent-minded adults will nevertheless want to insist on making up their own minds, in the light of their own judgements and values, about the correct interpretations and the proper applications of these findings. The purpose of the present book is to help such people to equip themselves to do just that.

A survey of the present condition of the social sciences, as compared with the physical and the biological, has led one prominent practitioner to label them "*developing* subjects" – a mischievous allusion to the established euphemisms under which countries formerly put down as backward are now politely rated under-developed or, more optimistically, developing (Anderson 1980, p. 55: here, as always later, except where due notice is given, the emphasis in quotations is that of the original text). Others conducting similar reviews have been inclined to refuse to award what they consider the diploma label 'science' to any social or political studies.

There are two differences between the social and the natural sciences which go far to explain the unsatisfactory condition of the former. The first and less interesting is the greater complexity of human beings. We are, so far as we know, creatures of the most complex kind to be found in the Universe. The second is more interesting, and much more important. It is that we are fellow creatures of those studied. It is, therefore, difficult or perhaps downright impossible for us to avoid having sometimes very strong and often potentially distracting preferences: preferences, that is, not only for what we should wish to be true of particular social phenomena and categories of social phenomena; but also, sometimes, because of our own involvements in these phenomena, preferences for what we should like (some) other people to believe (even if falsely) about (some) such phenomena.

Of course in every field investigators will naturally hope and wish to prove that their own hypotheses are as such correct, and will therefore feel at least some temptation to ignore or dismiss evidence either suggesting or showing that in truth they are not. The social sciences, which are throughout taken to include practically important researches into the actual effects of implemented social and political policies, are peculiar in that the investigators may be almost irresistibly tempted to align and ally with some of the subjects under investigation; and, hence, against others. Such alignments and alliances generate temptations: temptations not to discover truths unwelcome to us about these people, or truths which would be unwelcome to them; or, when and if such truths have been discovered, temptations to conceal these truths from at least some other people.

It would be hard indeed to make a partisan commitment of that kind to one set of subatomic particles as against another. But it is scarcely possible consistently to maintain a complete and perfect detachment from every human conflict. Fortunately such total and inhuman detachment, even if it were attainable, is neither necessary nor desirable. It is quite sufficient, yet at the same time quite sufficiently difficult, to discipline ourselves: to discipline ourselves so that we begin every inquiry by asking what we would ourselves wish to be the case; and so that, having first answered this question, we then go on systematically to suspect all work suggesting that it is.

This, as we shall show in Chapter 2, is a matter of good faith. One distinctive feature of *Thinking About Thinking* is its insistence that when we are in fact deceived most often this is at least in part because we wish to be. Hence the existential challenge embodied in the subtitle. The present rather more advanced and specialized sequel similarly sees self-deception as the main enemy; and self-discipline, therefore, as the main need.

2 Simple, and not quite so simple honesty

Suppose now that someone gives vent to utterances which others, whether rightly or wrongly, consider to be perverse, contrary to manifest fact, scandalous, immoral or in some other way beyond the pale. Then, in these permissive and latitudinarian days, someone else is almost bound to come forward with the eirenic suggestion that, whatever else might be said to their discredit, both the beliefs expressed in those utterances, and the believer, must be allowed to have been totally sincere.

To this complacently charitable response it would be as appropriate as uncommon to respond in turn that such a concession constitutes a paradigm case of praising with faint damns. For, to anyone seized of the enormous possibilities of wishful thinking, of self-persuasion and of self-deception, to allow that the speaker was at least guiltless of plain, conscious, calculated mendacity can scarcely appear generous. Neither can the fulfilment of so universal and absolute an obligation serve as the basis for awarding any kind of diploma. To warrant that we need something more; perhaps that the speaker's pronouncements were, however mistaken, an outcome of a sincere and open-minded search for the truth; or that he is already obeying his proposed practical imperatives, however unacceptable to us, at some self-sacrificial cost.

Certainly Georges Sorel (1847–1922) in our motto quotation was calling for honesty in more than the most narrow and minimal understanding. Yet it still needs to be noted, before going after more, that even the minimum is not always supplied – not even in the physical and medical sciences. For instance: some years ago *The Economist* reported, along with many other cases, under the headline 'The Professor is a fraud', how "a highly respected worker in the field of cancer research was exposed as having painted black areas on experimental mice to simulate the results he desired", and that the "federal food and drug administration had to move against one of the country's leading cardiologists,

a professor of medicine at the University of California at
Irvine, for reporting false results with patients".

(i)

At that time (21 January 1984) the most notorious recent
British case of alleged direct and deliberate falsification of
tests in the moral sciences was that of the then recently
deceased Sir Cyril Burt. This was a matter of falsification
in the everyday rather than the philosophical sense of 'falsification'; the sense in which to falsify is to misrepresent the true
as false or the false as true, rather than to show to be false.
On the front page of its issue of 24 October 1976, under
the headline 'Crucial data faked by eminent psychologist',
the *Sunday Times* (London) proclaimed "the most sensational
charge of scientific fraud this century . . . Leading scientists
are convinced that Burt published false data and invented
crucial facts to support his controversial theory that intelligence is largely inherited."

This contention was and remains controversial because
of its incompatibility with a very fiercely and very widely
cherished assumption: "the assumption of equal inherited
ability as something which . . . does not require experimental
evidence . . . , and which it is politically wicked to question". In the same 1977 Presidential Address to the British
Association for the Advancement of Science Sir Andrew
Huxley went on to complain: "There is in fact a taboo
on openminded investigation . . . at least as strong as the
resistance in Darwin's day to questioning the authority of
the Bible." (For an illuminating review of this IQ controversy, and of its treatment in the US news media, compare
Snyderman and Rothman 1990.)

From that first breaking of the story, and for many years
thereafter, it was generally assumed that the case against Burt
had been proved. But a recent, extremely comprehensive
study of *The Burt Affair* (Joynson 1989) puts things in a
different light. The case for the prosecution now appears far
too weak to secure a conviction. So on sound Common Law

principles Burt must be presumed personally innocent, even while his reported findings may as such remain suspect.

Suppose Burt did in fact fake his figures. Then is the consequence that that "controversial theory" is totally discredited? No, because the findings Burt reported are neither unparalleled nor crucial. On the contrary: "they were sufficiently similar to those reported earlier . . . to be generally accepted as genuine . . . " (Joynson 1989, p. 28). For instance: already in the twenties there had been those reported in *Crime as Destiny: A Study of Criminal Twins* (Lange 1931). This work is especially remarkable because it was emphatically endorsed by a man who was both Britain's leading geneticist and for several years a member of the Executive Committee of its Communist Party (Haldane 1937). To his credit, and unlike so many other secular scientists, Haldane was apparently never tempted into prejudiced insistence that the facts about the relations between human heredity and environment must be as perhaps they would have been had the Universe been created, and he its Creator.

(ii)

Even if Burt did have to be put down as a liar and a cheat, it would remain true that, in the moral as in the natural sciences, the direct falsification of results is exceedingly rare. What is much more common is a failure or a refusal to take account of contrary evidence; a failure which can in extreme cases shade over into downright suppression.

What should long since have become the stock, textbook example comes in the first volume of *Capital* (Marx 1867), the only one which the author himself saw through the press. One of the main contentions of that book, one of the main predictions supposedly generated by the theoretical system which it propounded, was what later came to be called the Immiseration Thesis. As originally set out in the *Communist Manifesto* (Marx and Engels 1848), this was that, under capitalism, the representative proletarian, "instead of rising with the progress of industry, sinks deeper and deeper *below the condition of his own class.* He becomes a pauper, and pauperism develops more rapidly than population and wealth" (p. 93: emphasis added). That thesis was taken to warrant the further claim that "the bourgeoisie [i.e., the capitalist class – AF], therefore, produces above all . . . its own gravediggers. Its fall and the victory of the proletariat are equally inevitable" (p. 94).

Capital was the book long promised to provide scientific proof for these apocalyptic claims. (Just how long and how it had been promised Schwartzschild 1948 makes very clear.) *Capital* contained a far fuller account of the development predicted: "Along with the constantly diminishing number of magnates of capital . . . grows the mass of misery, oppression, slavery, degradation, exploitation; but with this too grows the revolt of the working-class, a class always increasing in numbers, and disciplined, united, organized by the very mechanism of the process of capitalist production itself . . .. The knell of capitalist private property sounds. The expropriators are expropriated" (I, p. 763).

Unfortunately for the theories of Marx, although fortunately for those more practically concerned, in the country in which he was living, and the one which on his view was leading along a road which others must follow, wages were in real terms actually rising; and had been for many years past. So what to do?

An honest scientist would have had at the very least to recognize this objection as a difficulty, a difficulty which must eventually be met in full if his theory was to be saved. Darwin, to whom Engels later dared to compare his lifelong friend, by his scrupulous treatment of objections in *The Origin of Species*, provided a model of scientific integrity (Flew 1984, I 4 and III 3). That, however, was not the method of Marx. *Capital* takes no note at all of an apparently devastating objection. And whereas it gives other runs of British statistics up to 1865 or 1866, those for the movement of wages stop at 1850. In the second edition, which again Marx himself was able to see through the press, all the other runs are brought up to date, but that of wage movements still stops at 1850.

It was in his obituary address at the graveside in London's Highgate Cemetery that Engels famously compared Marx to Darwin: "Just as Darwin discovered the law of development of organic nature, so Marx discovered the law of development of human history." This first part concluded with the claim: "*So war dieser Mann der Wissenschaft*" [Such was this man of science]. In the second part Engels went on to insist that Marx had been always and above all the revolutionary. It was because that second claim was so true that Marx was so willing to suppress and to misrepresent.

In a double-edged tribute to *Marx as Politician* the author describes "*The Civil War in France*, argued with his superb disdain for the facts", as "the last of Marx's polemical masterpieces" (Felix 1983, p. 175). Judging by measures of political influence rather than by the standards of historical scholarship, it was indeed an extraordinary achievement. For though Marx himself, in a letter of 22 February 1881 to Ferdinand Nieuwenhuis, admitted that the Paris Commune of 1871 "was in no sense socialist, nor could it have been" this book succeeded in persuading almost everyone – friend and foe alike – that really it had been the first Communist coup, providing a paradigm case of a "dictatorship of the proletariat".

One clear and memorable example of that "superb disdain for the facts" is the assertion that all elected Councillors and appointed functionaries had "to do their jobs at workingmen's wages". The truth was that the 6000 franc annual wage which the Deputies of the Commune voted for themselves and set as a maximum for state officials was nearly twelve times the amount being paid to members of the National Guard defending Paris (Wolfe 1967, Ch. 8; and compare Felix 1983, pp. 166ff.). *So war dieser Mann der Wissenschaft*!

2   The Call for Criticism

What a man had rather were true, that he more readily
believes.

Francis Bacon, *Novum Organum*, I, 49.

Men mark when they hit, not when they miss.

Francis Bacon, *de Augmentis Scientarum*. V, 4.

Our own contemporaries provide numerous examples, if
not perhaps of equally monstrous misrepresentation, then
certainly of studious ignoring of obviously relevant yet to
them unwelcome facts. For instance – an instance taken more
or less at random from a bulging file – in a volume of essays
setting out to examine the achievement of the 1974–9 Labour
administrations in producing "far greater economic equality
– in income, wealth and living standards", and to reveal what
all of the professional social scientist contributors considered
to be the deplorable inadequacy of this achievement, none
of these contributors brought themselves to mention the top
rates of taxation introduced in 1974 by Chancellor Denis
Healey in his first budget. These top rates – a partial fulfilment of his promise, thunderously applauded at the 1973
Party conference, "to make the rich howl in agony" – were,
starting from what were by EEC standards low thresholds, 83
per cent on earned and 98 per cent on investment income.
One economist contributor, without either making or referring to any attempt to show either that these rates were not
high or not in fact paid, simply dismissed what he called "the
myth that the top 20 percent of household incomes . . . are
highly taxed" (Bosanquet and Townsend 1980, p. 41).

Whenever some intelligent and well-informed person is
guilty of any such intellectual misdemeanour the most constructive response is to seize every opportunity of pointing out
that so competent a person would not, surely, resort to such

illicit means of persuasion if only they were able to deploy a respectable case; a case honestly and straightforwardly establishing whatever it is that they wish to establish.

Similarly we ought, both when confronted with sneering misrepresentations of positions dear to us, and when ourselves inclined similarly to misrepresent the positions of opponents, to try hard to remember that all such distortings may reasonably be construed as tantamount to confessions that the positions actually held by the person or persons thus misrepresented cannot in truth be so easily refuted.

In a book such as this that first employment of the word 'refute' must not be allowed to pass without a warning that 'refute' should never be abused as a mere synonym for 'deny'. If I allow that she refuted the proposition p, then I am associating myself with her claim, not merely to have said, but also to have shown, that p is indeed false (Flew 1975, Sections 1.54 and 1.55). We should also notice here that, in the vocabulary of philosophers and logicians, as opposed to that of businesspersons and playboys, a proposition is whatever can significantly be said to be either true or false.

1   Sincere purposing, and monitoring progress

There is much more still to be made of Sorel's reply. The first essential is to grasp the simple, fundamental truth about logically necessary connections between sincerity of purpose and the constant, alert monitoring of success or failure in the achievement of sincerely pursued purposes. For sincerity in the pursuit of any purpose whatsoever absolutely presupposes a strong concern to discover whether and how far that purpose has been and is being achieved. Furthermore, if and in so far as the agent becomes aware that it has not been or is not being achieved, and unless there is a readiness to attempt alternative and hopefully more promising tactics, we cannot truly say, even if it was originally a sincere commitment, that that purpose still continues as the same commitment pursued with the same sincerity as before.

Suppose, for instance, that someone is so old-fashioned as to proclaim a Quest for the Holy Grail. And suppose then that, almost before the fanfares have died, they settle for the first antique-seeming mug offered by the first fluent rogue in the local bazaar. We surely have to say that this neglect of any systematic inquiry, this total lack of interest in either the true history of the purchase put in the place of honour on the mantelpiece or the evidence that perhaps the real thing does survive somewhere, all conspire together to show that, whatever else they may have been after, it certainly was not to unearth and acquire the vessel actually employed in the original Last Supper; if such there was.

Again, since many find it hard to accept that a point so down-to-earth can be enforced by an illustration so far-fetched, consider two more pedestrian alternatives. Suppose someone professes to be in business in order, no doubt among other things, to turn a profit; or suppose that the captain of a cricket team says that he is playing, no doubt again among other things, in order to win. Then what credence could we give to these professions if there is no care to keep, in the one case, accounts and, in the other, the score. The French philosopher-mathematician René Descartes (1596–1650) used to say that he preferred to judge what people sincerely believe by what they do rather than by what they say. The same shrewd principle applies equally well to the determination of true intentions and actual purposes.

The next step is to relate these logically necessary connections to recommendations made by Sir Karl Popper (1902–). These proposals, developed in *The Open Society and its Enemies* in 1945, refer to both theoretical science and practical policy. In each case Popperian methodology can be seen as the direct and necessary outcome of sincerity in the appropriate purposes. It is the more worthwhile to represent these recommendations in this way in as much as he himself seems never to have done so. His apparent reluctance, and the consequent failure to deploy what is perhaps the most powerful supporting argument, are probably to be explained by reference to a generous yet unrealistic unwillingness to recognize discreditable distractions or even sheer bad faith in any of his academic opponents.

The aim of all theoretical science is truth. If that is what we are sincerely seeking, then we have to adopt what Popper calls the critical approach. For people who truly want to discover the truth, like knights who with pure hearts and single minds seek the Holy Grail, cannot and will not embrace unexamined candidates. They must and will be ever ready to test, and test and test again. And in the present context criticism just is this sort of testing.

It is testing by raising and pressing relevant questions. Are there, for a start, any inconsistencies within or between the propositions propounded? And are these propositions all compatible with whatever else we know or believe that we know? It is of course precisely in as much as critics are sincerely seeking the truth that they refuse to tolerate contradictions. For though two contradictory propositions may both be false they cannot, being mutually contradictory, both be true. So the sincere truth-seeker urgently requires to discover which, if either, actually is true (Flew 1975, 1.19).

Suppose now that the claims made are both internally consistent and consistent with everything which is already known. Then we have to ask: 'What else follows from the theory or hypothesis proposed, and how are we to set about discovering whether these further consequences do in fact obtain?'

Paradoxically Popper maintains that, having started by making bold conjectures – conjectures apparently fitting all available facts while also carrying extensive implications of what else must be the case if these bold conjectures are correct – scientists should then seek strenuously to falsify those conjectures; that is, to show that they are, after all, false. He insists that the proper method of science, whether natural or social, is that of *Conjectures and Refutations* (Popper 1963).

Honest inquirers, therefore, though they will naturally want their own theories and their own hypotheses to turn out to have been correct, must to the extent that they are indeed sincere truth-seekers necessarily labour to show that all theories and hypotheses proposed – most especially their own – are after all false. Suppose that one nevertheless survives the most rigorous and comprehensive criticism. Then, however temporarily, the hopes of its sponsors are fulfilled. On the other hand, when a promising theory or hypothesis is falsified its sponsors can console themselves with the thought that the strenuous testing culminating in this conclusion must surely have advanced research. So the successor theory or hypothesis should be, if not the final truth, at least significantly nearer to it.

The reason for seeking not confirming instances but falsifications is, in the oft-quoted words of Francis Bacon (1561–1626), "that the force of the negative instance is greater". For conclusively to falsify any unrestricted universal generalization – any proposition, that is, of the form 'All so-and-sos, without restriction of time or place, are such-and-such' – it is sufficient to produce a single counter-example, a single case, that is, of a so-and-so which is not a such-and-such. It is, however, impossible equally conclusively to verify a proposition of this form. For, provided that these 'All so-and-sos' are not restricted to only 'All so-and-sos' in such-and-such a place or during such-and-such a period', there remains always, no matter how many so-and-sos are found to be such and such, at least the theoretical if not the live practical possibility of eventually discovering a counter-example.

2 An anthropological object-lesson

The stronger the desires of investigators that some particular proposition or system of propositions should turn out to be true, the more formidable are the dangers of wishful-thinking and self-deception, and the greater the consequent need for the critical approach, the approach searching for falsification rather than confirmation. Consider, for example, the prime anthropological scandal of the eighties.

It was in 1928 that Margaret Mead (1901–78), who was

later to become throughout North America the doyenne of
that discipline, first published her all-time anthropological
bestseller *Coming of Age in Samoa*. Fifty-five years were to
pass before Professor Derek Freeman of the Australian
National University was able to deploy his entirely decisive
demonstrations: that every one of Mead's major general
claims about the Samoans was not just wrong but diamet-
rically wrong; and, what is for us much more significant,
that they could have been known to be so on the basis of
sources freely available at the time of her fieldwork. But,
being committed to confirming principles and prejudices
shared with her charismatic teacher Franz Boas, Mead never
even attempted to use other sources (Freeman 1983). Verily,
to quote the famous nineteenth-century preacher Charles
Haddon Spurgeon, "A lie travels round the world while
truth is putting on her boots"!

While Mead assured her readers, for instance, that
"Samoans never hate enough to want to kill anybody", and
that "The idea of forceful rape or any sexual act to which
both partners do not give themselves freely is completely
foreign to the Samoan mind", the criminal records of
the then colonial power show that, on the appropriate
international comparisons, both murder and rape were
exceptionally common (Ibid., pp. 162 and 244). Whereas
she insisted that in Samoan society "competition is muted
and controlled" other and closer observers – of whom there
have been several since the European discovery of these
islands – appear to agree with the Samoans themselves that
"omnipresent competitiveness is liable to break . . . into
open contention and conflict" (Ibid., p. 142 and Ch. 10
passim).

Again, Mead maintained that premarital sex was for young
Samoans the "pastime *par excellence*", and that girls deferred
marriage "through as many years of casual love-making as
possible" (Ibid., p. 226). It is, of course, this claim, alluringly
presented, to which we may attribute the wide and continuing popular appeal of *Coming of Age in Samoa*. (It certainly
constituted the book's main attraction to the present author,

when as a very young man he read it in the first Pelican paperback edition!) Yet the perhaps disappointing truth is that Samoan society during the period of Mead's residence was profoundly and traditionally Christian, with if anything quite unusually effective inhibitions on the premarital abandonment of virginity (Freeman 1983, Chs. 12 and 16).

Mead's false findings were, it seems, exclusively derived from misinformation supplied by mischievous adolescent informants – misinformation congenially confirming the extreme environmentalist preconceptions instilled by her supervisor-guru Franz Boas. (An extreme environmentalist, in this context, is someone maintaining that we are in all things completely creatures of our several environments.) These twenty-five misinformants visited Mead in the house where she roomed with an American missionary family: she was unwilling to endure the hubbub, and the un-American diet, of standard Samoan accommodation.

When confronted long afterwards by indignant Samoans telling her how wrong she had been, or by the contradictory findings of fieldworkers who had thrown themselves more generously into the life of the people they were supposed to be studying, she resolutely refused to correct or withdraw anything, much less to make an effort to undeceive some of the innumerable readers whom she had herself self-deludingly deceived. Instead, in Prefaces to the 1949, 1961 and 1973 editions of *Coming of Age in Samoa*, she insisted, in a characteristic outburst of obscurantist relativism, that it "must remain, as all anthropological works must remain, exactly as it was written, true to what I saw in Samoa and what I was able to convey of what I saw, true to the state of our knowledge of human behaviour as it was in the mid-1920s; true to our hopes and fears for the future of the world". (Quoted Freeman 1983, pp. 113–14; and compare p. 327 and passim.)

It will soon be possible to compare Freeman 1992 or 1993. This second book is to relate the depressingly instructive tale of how the first was received by many of his anthropological colleagues. For Freeman seems to have been treated as a pariah by the American Anthropological Association. Or, since this shunning was inspired by a corrupt kind of professional loyalty, perhaps the apt words are 'scab' or 'blackleg' rather than 'pariah'. Freeman also supplies a deal of further evidence about Samoan life and customs – including a sworn statement from one of Mead's surviving misinformants, explaining that they were all engaged in a traditional competition in fictive composition. Apparently it never occurred to them that their American visitor could be so ignorant of local customs and so eager to believe, any more than it ever occurred to her that they might delight in stuffing her up with the spicy stories she was so hungry to hear.

3   Great social 'experiments'

Whereas the single aim of theoretical science is truth, the purposes of practical policies, and of the institutions established for the implementation of those policies, and the fulfilment of those purposes, are as multifarious as human desires. Yet parallel considerations apply here too. If, therefore, you want to claim that it was in order to secure some particular goods that a policy was originally introduced, and that those are still the objectives for which it continues to be sustained, then you have to show that both the people who first introduced the policy, and the people who now support and sustain that policy and its related institutions, were, and are, keen to monitor success or failure by that same stated standard.

This insistence can help us to understand Popper's advocacy of what he distinguishes as piecemeal, reformist, social engineering – as opposed to the wholesale, Utopian, revolutionary alternative. Popper's advocacy here is consequence and expression of his sincere and rational concern for the welfare of the subjects of such social engineering – the, so to speak, socially engineered. For Popper's crucial objection to the wholesale Utopian variety precisely is that this must make impossible the effective monitoring of success or failure in achieving the goods supposedly intended by the social engineers. It therefore makes it equally impossible for them to recognize and to learn from their mistakes; and then to apply the lessons learnt to the amendment of their policies. So there is an obvious Popperian answer to a frequently pressed question: 'Just how wide-ranging and upsetting does a programme have to be before its implementation ceases to count as piecemeal, and begins to rate as wholesale, social engineering?'

It is: 'Just so soon as it becomes impossible effectively to monitor success or failure, and to make cybernetic corrections of perceived mistakes.' Popper himself says: " . . . the reconstruction of society is a big undertaking which must cause considerable inconvenience to many and for a considerable span of time. Accordingly, the Utopian engineer will have to be deaf to many complaints: in fact it will be part of his business to suppress unreasonable objections. (He will say, like Lenin, 'You can't make an omelette without breaking eggs.' But with it, he must invariably suppress "reasonable criticism also" (Popper 1945, I p. 160).

(i)

In this perspective it is easy to see how inept it was to describe the enormous exercises of social engineering made possible by the Bolshevik October coup as features of 'that great social experiment in Russia' – notwithstanding that these were in the twenties and the thirties frequently so described. With reference to the compulsory and almost unbelievably mass-murderous collectivization of agriculture, for instance (Conquest 1986), there was absolutely no willingness to change course when and as it became clear that, whatever its other attractions to the ruling class and party, collectivization had been and remains an economic disaster.

Since, both in the USSR and in numerous other countries subjected to similar regimes, such exercises have been executed in the name of what calls itself Scientific Socialism, it becomes very much to the point to quote Popper's counterclaim – that the critical approach would "lead to the happy

situation where politicians begin to look out for their own
mistakes instead of trying . . . to prove that they have always
been right. This – and not Utopian planning or historical
prophecy – would mean the introduction of scientific method
into politics, *since the whole secret of scientific method is a readiness
to learn from mistakes"* (1945, I p. 163: emphasis added).

(ii)

The word 'politician' must not of course here be construed as
referring only to professional politicians. We all, by supporting or opposing particular political and social policies, expose
ourselves to similar temptations, and sometimes succumb.
How, after all, could there be demagogues if there were
not voters ready to make demagoguery pay, by rewarding
it with their votes? The present moral, therefore, is a moral
for us all.

The Comprehensive Revolution in the UK provides what
can be an instructive example of a drastic and extensive
change imposed in a similarly dogmatic, inflexible, and
unenquiring way; although in this case the imposition was
of course totally non-violent and democratically legitimate.
For the first ten or fifteen years after World War II almost
all Britain's state-maintained secondary schools were of two
types: either selective, so-called Grammar Schools; or else
non-selective Secondary Modern Schools. The aim of the
revolution, by now largely fulfilled, was to transform the
whole lot into non-selective neighbourhood schools. The
militants of this revolution have always insisted too that
it could not be considered to have been fully accomplished
until all existing independent secondary schools had been
somehow assimilated into a total and homogeneous state
education monopoly. Although the label employed has been
'Comprehensive School', and although the name of John
Dewey (1859–1952) was scarcely ever mentioned, the model
surely was his "common school" (Shaw 1983).

Since the Comprehensive Revolution. like the Glorious
Revolution of 1688–9, was effected through Parliament we

do well to quote from the operative resolution passed by the House of Commons in 1965. This started from "the need to raise educational standards at all levels"; regretted "that the realization of this objective is impeded by the separation of children into different types of secondary schools"; and went on to suggest that the impediment was deficiencies in the selection process – the notorious eleven plus examinations which, being a human system and therefore necessarily imperfect, undoubtedly misselected many of the children subject to its operation.

Given that the stated aim was thus "to raise educational standards at all levels", the intelligent but still entirely innocent stranger would have assumed: either that there already was a completely comprehensive, national system of independently assessed, criteria-related examinations; or, if not, that the belated establishment of such a system would be seen as the first essential element in this or any other project for radical reform.

To make adequate and reliable monitoring of progress or regress possible the crucial tests and examinations must be both independently assessed and criteria-related: independently assessed because teachers exclusively responsible for examining their own pupils are – in violation of one of the fundamental principles of natural justice – serving as judges in what are necessarily in part their own causes; and criteria-related because the norm-related alternative, with equal necessity, invalidates all direct year on year comparisons. (In criteria-related tests and examinations the examiners are trying, as far as possible, to award the same marks or grades to the same qualities and quantities of work in successive years, whereas in the norm-related alternative they attempt to ensure that in every successive year roughly the same proportions of all candidates get the same marks or grades.)

The expectations of our imaginary stranger would of course have been disappointed. Perhaps in the long term the passing of the Education Reform Act of 1988 will have the effect of establishing such a completely comprehensive system of independently assessed, criteria-related tests and examinations. But at the time of writing no such system is actually in place. At the launching of the Comprehensive Revolution and for many years thereafter no such system was ever even contemplated. For anyone generally concerned to improve the quality of thinking in this area the remarkable fact is that in the UK there is no such system, and never has been. What is still more remarkable is that this most remarkable fact is itself so rarely remarked. Nor are its important consequences often noticed.

One is that what is by any measure one of the country's biggest industries does not and cannot provide the kind and amount of information about production and productivity which is elsewhere normally both demanded and available. This gross deficiency of information encourages the widespread but wholly unwarranted equation of resource input with education output. Ministers of rival political parties boast of, in real terms, increasing expenditure per pupil head, and proceed to take it for granted that – at least under their own superior administration – this has guaranteed a corresponding increase in pupil learning.

Another important consequence is that under some Local Education Authorities (LEAs) as many as half of all those too many who leave school at the first legal opportunity leave without any reliable written evidence to show how much or how little they have benefited from their ten years of compulsory and tax-financed education – and hence without any convincing evidence of employability. Again, when official committees are set up to investigate and report on putative problems of illiteracy or innumeracy they cannot refer to the findings of tests universally taken. Instead they have to begin their deliberations by scratching around for materials from which to guesstimate the extent of the evils upon which they are directed to recommend (Flew 1987, pp. 107–8).

Had an adequate system of tests and examinations been in place during the Comprehensive Revolution it would have been possible to read off the answer to the question whether it was in fact raising "educational standards at all levels" more or less directly from the published results of those adequate tests and examinations. But as things actually were the most widely taken examinations were for the Certificate of Secondary Education (CSE) and for the General Certificate of Education (GCE) at O (Ordinary) or A (Advanced) levels. These examinations were intended to cater for only the top 60 per cent of the ability range. And in 1962, as the revolution was beginning, the word had gone out from the then Secondary Schools Examinations Council that these examinations should be norm- rather than criteria-related. This recommendation should surely provoke the traditional Roman lawyer's question: 'Cui bono?' [Who benefits?].

It was only after a bitterly contested clause in the 1980 Education Act compelled the regular school by school publication of the results achieved in these examinations that it became possible to base a study of the impact of the revolution upon these results. And even this would have been impossible had there not still been a few LEAs holding out in diehard defence of the old regime. It is an index of the importance both of collective interests and of the control of information in this area that the National Union of Teachers (NUT), the largest of the teachers' unions, proclaimed its "total opposition" to that publication clause in the 1980 Act. Apart from a general concern about the possibilities of misinterpretation, the NUT particularly feared publication would provoke the construction of "league tables" and consequent competition – to increase the effectiveness of the teaching of its teacher members!

After the Department of Education and Science (DES), which had by then become wholeheartedly committed to the Comprehensive Revolution (S. Williams 1981, p. 184), had refused to channel any tax money into relevant research, the unofficial National Council for Educational Standards (NCES) managed to finance an unprecedentedly exhaustive study. Its conclusion, which the authors themselves chose to print in block capitals, was: "that substantially higher O-level, CSE and A-level examination results are to be expected for pupils in a fully selective system of schools compared with pupils in a fully comprehensive system .... This finding applies to all the indices of examination success which we studied and, according to our data, is as robust as the generally accepted finding that examination results are highly correlated with social class" (Marks, Cox and Pomian-Srzednicki 1983, p. 61).

Our concern here is not, or not primarily, with the correctness or incorrectness of these findings but with their reception. There was uproar, including much personal abuse directed at the researchers. The main charge was that their work had, in a document which as unofficial outsiders they themselves were not permitted to see, been 'rubbished' by the professional statisticians of the DES. Although the researchers eventually got a sight of that document, and although the DES statisticians in a consequent face-to-face discussion were quickly persuaded honestly to admit that the mistake had been theirs, and although later the most contested of the original findings was quietly corroborated by other researchers working within the DES, the protracted and almost wholly hostile press campaign succeeded in concealing from any wider public the rubbishing of the rubbishers. (For a full account of this remarkable and in many ways disturbing affair see Cox and Marks 1988; and compare Flew 1987, Ch. 2.)

To us the relevance of all this lies in the fact that, apparently, none of the most vociferous vilifiers of that NCES work has ever allowed a discovery that the central finding is as robust as could reasonably be expected to in any way affect their own commitment to maintaining and extending the revolution. There have, for instance, been no calls for a halt – at least until further research reveals that the strongholds of selection are not, after all, achieving substantially better educational results. This surely shows that, whatever the original motivation, it cannot now be, simply and solely, that of the Parliamentary resolution.

In this case reluctance to admit and to learn from a mistake is not the only alternative explanation for this refusal to accept and to act on such findings. No doubt with many people that is a large part or even the whole of the story. But there are others among the militants for whom 'comprehension' is either a good in itself and/or a means to other and non-educational ends (Flew 1987, pp. 27 and 59). For them failure to achieve promised increases in attainment may be at best a matter of indifference or at worst an acceptable cost.

Much has been said about distracting "preferences . . . for what we should wish to be true". It is time to point to "preferences for what we should like (some) other people to believe (even if falsely) . . . " For everyone strongly committed to the comprehensive ideal, but more or less indifferent to increases or decreases in individual achievement, must know that there are others who care a lot – especially about the achievements of their own children. So they have reason to wish those others to be, however mistakenly, persuaded that the Comprehensive Revolution is being accomplished at no substantial cost in forgone learning achievement.

Whatever may be the truth about the actual effects of that revolution one research worker was right, both as a sincere social scientist and as a morally responsible citizen, to be scandalized by the failure, indeed the refusal, systematically to monitor those consequences. This was, he argued, scientifically unjustifiable "because, without adequate up-to-date information we can only discuss the issue in terms of prejudice. Morally unjustifiable also because, without such enquiries and information, we are, in effect, asking parents to endorse our convictions, beliefs and prejudices either for or against comprehensive education, without the opportunity of making their own judgment . . . " (Neave 1979).

4   Breaking the spell of the welfare state

By 'welfare state' is meant the tax-financed, state provision of health, education and welfare services. Since all the advanced democratic countries devote substantial shares of their total national incomes to such provision, we need most urgently a comparable amount of critical thinking about the relevant

institutions and the activities and inactivities of those who –
shall we say? – person them.

When the Social Affairs Unit (SAU) was founded the
stated aim was "to break the spell of the welfare state".
The contention was that it *"distributes the burden of proof
unfairly* .... *It ... consumes public money, and it is its obligation to prove that it is not wasting it* ... " So the proper
function of the external critic is "to ... prick, chide and
goad a self-satisfied web of self-perpetuating bureaucracy
into giving an account of itself ... " (Anderson 1981,
pp. 25–6). For, as the previous section will have reminded
us, it is all too easy for those professionally involved in these
institutions to obstruct any independent investigations which
may succeed in getting started; or, failing that, at least to seem
thoroughly to discredit their findings. The insiders can, and
will, reply to every objection – often quite truly – that the
outsiders are out of touch, or, misinformed and out of date:
nothing was ever wrong or, if it was, it is already being put
right (Anderson 1980, Ch. 1).

To this already strong case we can now add arguments
drawn from the first section of the present chapter. Professionals sincerely and single-mindedly devoted to producing
the relevant services will have no difficulty in meeting the
SAU challenge: not only because, as insiders, they enjoy the
insiders' privileged access to information; but also because,
as sincerely devoted professionals, they will already have
been making every effort to monitor the effectiveness of
their own performance. And, furthermore, the same sincere
commitment ensures that they have been constantly concerned not only to maintain but also to improve productivity.
For people dedicated to the production of any kind of good
cannot but study to economize; that is to say, deploy to
maximum effect whatever resources may from time to time
become available to them.

(i)

It is tempting to draw out further implications of these ideas for the provision of secondary education in the UK. For in what is still the standard *Introduction to the Economics of Education* the author, employing the indisputably inadequate available measures of outputs, calculated his way to the disquieting conclusion that productivity actually "declined at an annual rate of at least 2 per cent a year over the thirteen year period" of his study (Blaug 1970, p. 276; and compare Flew 1991a).

But let us instead glance now at what calls itself the "community mental health movement" in the USA. This consists in all who – as its members certainly would wish us to say – person programmes launched under the Community Mental Health Centers Act of 1963. This was passed in response to a Message to the Congress on 'Mental Health and Mental Retardation', dated 5 February 1963. President Kennedy made it absolutely clear what good results were desired. Demanding "a bold new approach" he emphasized that "prevention is far more desirable for all concerned" than cure. Without himself specifying any illustrative examples, he called for "selective specific programs directed at known causes".

Fifteen or more years later a collective of contributors, all of whom are members of this movement and who therefore have, it must be added, strong and obvious personal stakes in the continuation and expansion of these programmes, published what was announced as the first of a series of *Annual Reviews of Community Mental Health* (Price and others 1980).

Judging by the contents, and still more by what it does not contain, no one expected it to be studied by any critical outsider. For with this book – as with Sherlock Holmes and the dog barking during the night – the most remarkable thing is what does not happen. Nowhere from beginning to end does there occur one single reference, whether direct or indirect, to any evidence that any of these programmes has actually succeeded in reducing the incidence of mental retardation or mental illness; or even in holding it down below the higher level to which it might perhaps otherwise have been expected to rise.

Had there in fact been any such demonstrated successes, we can be sure that this book would have been full of allusions to them. And, furthermore, everyone who had joined and was remaining in 'the movement' with the prime intention of helping to prevent or cure such manifestly evil afflictions would now be rejoicing in the successes already achieved; while anyone proposing fresh initiatives towards similar ends would have been eager to learn and to apply the lessons to be drawn from those past achievements.

The unlovely truth is, however, quite otherwise. These proud "prevention professionals", professing carers and compassionists though they be, do not, it seems, feel constrained even to pretend to have fulfilled any part of the beneficent (do-gooding) mandate with which they were charged. Yet they are no whit disturbed by what, for all that they themselves have to say to the contrary, appears to have been their expensive and total failure actually to prevent any specifiable and determinate evils.

Instead – with some sideswipes against certain notoriously callous and uncaring Conservatives, suspected of contemplating what to all these people would be cruel cuts in both their programme and, indirectly, their individual budgets – some of them now propose, with no awkward self-questioning about past failures, so to reinterpret the expressions 'mental disease', 'mental disorder', and 'mental retardation', as to facilitate demands for (yet more) further funding and extra staff. This and this alone, they suggest, will enable another and more ambitious kind of good to be done; albeit with equally little reason offered for believing that they will have any more success in attaining these different though no doubt equally worthy objectives.

In the perspective of the present chapter the most revealing as well as the most scandalous feature of the entire *Annual* is the form taken by a solitary statement of the need for some systematic monitoring of success and failure. Except for this rare moment of illumination all the contributors are inclined blindly to identify (their) stated intentions with (their) actual achievements.

Nowhere in this *Annual* is there so much as a hint that some monitoring of actual success or failure is essential to the doing of a decent and progressively improving job. Instead the sole reference to this task points in a quite different direction. A trio of contributors makes what has so far proved to be, from the standpoint of the "community mental health movement in the United States", a quite unwarrantably pessimistic statement: " . . . it is our strong conviction that prevention proponents will lose the political battle for funding without good data – capable of documenting the effectiveness and social utility of prevention programs" (Ibid., pp. 7 and 288).

(ii)

Very similar things may and need to be said about the social work world in the UK. One, and still the only properly critical, review is full of material revealing an almost universal unwillingness to monitor results. Thus, referring to a major official report, the joint authors note how "The Committee mention without comment that an irritant to many doctors is the lack of interest of many workers in the social services, and even among academics, in evaluating the results of their work" (Brewer and Lait 1980, p. 24). Although they make a point of adding that they themselves share the irritation of the doctors, neither these authors nor the Committee brings out the shocking significance of this indifference. It is, as we are now in a position to see all too clearly, that many such professional benefactors (literally, do-gooders) are not in fact much interested in what and how much good they are actually doing. How else can we account for the chorus of complaints about failures either to make reports or to keep records (Brewer and Lait 1980, pp. 65–6 and passim).

This nasty suggestion is, alas, confirmed by later observations. For instance: referring to one extremely unrepresentative social worker attending a lecture about the findings of one of the few available monitoring studies, the same authors write: "Sheldon was greatly disturbed by the ineffectiveness . . . which the study revealed. But he goes on to say: 'I was much more worried (and still am) by the complacent smiles of colleagues all around me.' He characterizes the typical response among social workers to demonstrations of their ineffectiveness as: 'let's pretend nothing of importance has happened' " (p. 184).

This lack of interest in effectiveness and results, and the failure to produce more studies both of the effectiveness of social work and of the actual relevance and utility of the courses of training now required of those hoping to secure employment in such work, have to be related to very direct interests in not discovering and/or not making public what are feared or known to be the true answers to these important questions.

For the people who most naturally might in some sense be expected to undertake research into anything to do with social work, and in one obvious way the best qualified people, are the members of the university and polytechnic departments established or expanded in order to run these allegedly invaluable training courses. With appropriate alterations the same applies to Departments, Institutes and Colleges of Education, and to research into any aspect of the educational system, as well as to other academic sectors and to their respective objects. For university teachers have indeed traditionally been hired on the understanding that they will devote roughly half their working hours to teaching and roughly half to research, presumably in some area not too remote from that of their teaching. (Apropos three year Bachelor of Education courses, the requirement for which gives the teachers' unions welcome grounds to claim professional salaries, I recall the occasion when the Senior Tutor of the University of Keele told a shamefacedly assenting Senate; "You have made your B.Ed., and now you must lie about it!")

Suppose now, what is in fact the case, that there are excellent reasons to suspect that the established courses are, as training for social work, at best useless and at worst counterproductive (Brewer and Lait 1980, Ch. 2 and passim). Then we shall scarcely expect to detect enthusiasm for penetrating investigations among those who make their livings from Departments of Social Work: few people are willing to risk researching themselves out of a job. We ought to be similarly uneasy when we find, as we so often do, that most of those either appointed to the relevant official committees or selected by the media to offer expert opinion on these matters are similarly interested parties.

(iii)

Finally, to round off the chapter, consider how, and speculate why, a magnificent opportunity to research the effects and effectiveness of social work came to be wasted. The London borough of Tower Hamlets had been – as North Americans say – struck by its 275 rank-and-file social workers. They stayed out for ten months. Unlike most, this strike seems not greatly to have inconvenienced anyone. Certainly there were no TV news flashes of desperate 'clients' fighting their way through howling picket lines to secure the services of whatever social workers were still social working.

At the end of the day the Department of Health and Social Security (DHSS) directed, not some outside organization, but the London Region Social Work Service, to produce *The Effect on Clients of Industrial Action in the London Borough of Tower Hamlets: An Investigation*. People often protest the practice of making some internal police organization responsible for the investigation of alleged police misdemeanours. The principle behind such protests is sound, and should surely be applied more widely.

This Tower Hamlets strike provided a rare and wonderful research opportunity. 'Clients' neglected during the ten months of the strike constituted an ideal control group to set against the experimental group of those not so neglected in some subsequent ten months. It would not have been callous researchers who were proposing to deprive the 'clients' of what might or might not be valuable services; but, instead, those 'caring' social workers who had already done so. The wasting of this research opportunity deserves to become – and is hereby becoming – a textbook example.

The report, apparently accepted without protest either from the Minister himself or from the concerned Department, should leave the critical reader in no doubts about the general quality of the investigation. One single feature, however, is alone totally discrediting. For the two appointed to investigate – who "individualize and personalize" themselves by adding their signatures in facsimile at the end – were asked to find out the effects *on the clients*. Believe it or not, they do not claim to have asked for the views of even one (Lait 1980, pp. 63–8). So who, if anyone, truly wanted to know?

3   Our Reasons for Acting

I say the following about the Whole ... Man is that
which we all know.

Democritus of Abdera: Fragment 165,
in H. Diels, *Fragmente der Vorsokratiker*

Perhaps the simplest and most psychologically satisfying
explanation of any observed phenomenon is that it happened that way because someone wanted it to happen
that way.

Thomas Sowell, *Knowledge and Decisions*, p. 97

Scientists or would-be scientists approaching a fresh subject
area are like emigrants about to set foot upon an unknown
continent. If that continent happens to be uninhabited, then
– as Milton said of Adam and Eve after the expulsion from
Eden – "The world [is] all before them, where to choose."
But suppose that already there are indigenous settlers and
settlements. Then our immigrants will have either to search
out vacant lots in the interstices of existing habitation, or else
to find means to dispossess some of the previous occupants.
In this respect the investigatory fields of the social sciences
resemble the already partly settled continent. For, unlike
the stars above, people offer and have every right to offer
both descriptions and explanations of at least some of their
own movements. The aspiring social scientist has, therefore,
either to show that some or all of these prior descriptions
and explanations are illegitimate, or else to excogitate new
questions which no one before has thought to ask or been
able to answer.

1   How we explain ourselves

The sort of self-explanations offered by those peculiar

creatures which we are is explanation of conduct in terms
of the agent's reasons for doing what is done, or for
deliberately not doing what is deliberately not done. These
reasons, as we all know, will, in so far as they are the
true reasons, be the wishes, purposes and intentions of
the agent; and they will refer to that same agent's not
necessarily correct beliefs about the situations in which
the actions are performed. It is to this sort of explanation
that, in deference to Max Weber (1864–1920), the label
'verstehen' is applied; 'verstehen' being the German word
for 'understand'. As the motto quotations of the present
chapter indicate, it is, where it is available, "the simplest and
most psychologically satisfying explanation". For indeed,
since people are what we all are, "Man is that which we
all know."

With most phenomena, of course, explanations of this
peculiarly satisfying sort are not available. The fact is that
most phenomena do not happen "because someone wanted it
to happen that way". The progress of the natural sciences and
of cosmological thought has, therefore, required the expulsion of all such anthropomorphic notions from innumerable
areas where neither human agency nor anything like it in fact
occurs. Later, in Chapter 4, we shall be going on to argue that
no one has any claim to be an initiated social scientist until
they have become almost obsessively aware how many of the
consequences of human action, including many consequences
which we are overwhelmingly tempted to put down to design,
were never in fact intended.

(i)

The first presupposition, therefore, of the provision of explanations of this sort is that the behaviour to be explained did indeed
constitute intended action. Action is rated social when it takes
account of the actions of other people. If we remember that
Weber preferred to speak of meaning rather than of motives,
purposes or intentions, then we can fix this point in mind with

a single, short, classical quotation: "Action is social in so far as, by virtue of the subjective meaning attached to it by the acting individual (or individuals), it takes account of the behaviour of others" (Weber 1904, p. 88).

Conduct to be explained in this way has to be, always given the beliefs of the agents about their situations, intelligibly related and appropriate to the claims made in the explanation offered. (Perhaps it will be useful to introduce two dog-Latin terms here: 'explanans' for what is vouchsafed by way of explanation; and 'explanandum' for what it is which is to be explained.)

It is these requirements of intelligibility and appropriateness which alone give purchase to accusations of hypocrisy. For if intentions were like causes, and if – as David Hume (1711–76) so famously maintained – anything could conceivably be the cause of anything, then any intention in any circumstances could conceivably give rise to any kind of conduct. The consequence would be that we could never validly infer that someone's actual conduct proved that their real motives must have been both other, and far less creditable, than those they professed so fervently.

Whereas hypocrites are supposed to be aware of their real motives, those subject to unconscious motivation are not: precisely this is half of what is meant by describing motives as unconscious. (The other half, which perhaps applies only in the primary psychoanalytic context, consists in so extending the notion of a motive that what is not under the agent's control may nevertheless be said to be motivated; albeit unconsciously – Flew 1978, Ch. 8).

When, as nowadays happens frequently, statistical evidence is produced purportedly revealing that some legal system or some recruiting organization discriminates either for or against some subset of a total population, the word 'discrimination' is naturally construed as implying unfairness and impropriety. In consequence there is, whether rightly or wrongly, always dispute: both about whether that evidence is sufficient to prove the case; and about whether the discrimination, if proved, is conscious or unconscious. (Here,

as sometimes later, the words 'set' or 'subset' are employed
in order to disown the unwanted implications carried by
such alternatives as 'class' or 'community'. For, by Cantor's
Axiom for Sets, the sole essential feature of a set is that its
members have at least one common characteristic, any kind
of characteristic.)

(ii)

A second unavoidable limitation upon this sort of explanation
is that it cannot employ any concepts not available to the
agents themselves. Sociologists, anthropologists, and indeed
any other third parties whom anyone cares to mention may,
of course, be able and inclined to subsume particular actions
under their own several preferred concepts; and, in so
doing, they may succeed in indicating some significance in
those actions additional to that which the actions had for
the agents themselves at the time of acting. Those agents,
however, cannot actually have acted for any reasons which
they were not equipped to understand.

The obverse of this observation is that, if they are to achieve
the peculiar understanding which agents are able to have of
their own actions, then the sociologists, anthropologists and
all others have got first to master the concepts employed by
those agents. Only those who have mastered the rules, and
thus the concepts of chess are able to understand what chess
players are doing. Only when he is fluent in the language
of his adopted tribe can the anthropologist be sure that he
understands what the tribespersons know themselves to be
doing, and what their reasons are for doing those things.
Suppose that some Unidentified Flying Object (UFO) were,
for once, actually to identify itself as a spaceship from a
planet in another galaxy, discharging a platoon of Bug-Eyed
Monsters (BEMs). If, however superior their intelligence,
these were too different from us to be able to acquire our
concepts, then, notwithstanding any possible strong powers
to predict our behaviours, they still could not achieve this
special verstehen understanding of our conduct.

It is nevertheless altogether familiar to us all, even to those who have never been exposed to anything deserving the name of science, whether natural or social. So it was entirely fair for Stanislav Andreski, in his astringent and salutary study *Social Sciences as Sorcery*, to use one of the big books of Talcott Parsons (1902–79) as an example of what Andreski ridicules as "Rediscovering America". For, after much fretting over *The Structure of Social Action*, Parsons does rediscover something which everyone else already knew. He finally dignifies his rediscovery with the pretentious label, "the voluntaristic theory of action" (Parsons 1968; and compare Andreski 1972, Ch. 6).

(iii)

A third fundamental point, related to the second, is that agents respond to their predicaments as they themselves believe these to be. They respond, that is to say, to their perceived situations rather than to their actual situations. The latter may be vitally different. Some writers, taking this important point, have gone on to argue that investigators should attend only to perceived and never to actual situations: to do the latter, they say, would be to fall into the new deadly sin of ethnocentrism (Sumner 1940).

Because it requires us to conceal interesting and potentially revealing problems arising from the subsistence of (often glaring) gaps between what people contrive to believe and (what might seem to be the inescapably obvious) facts of their actual situations, this is a serious mistake. Its nature becomes obvious when we consider how often previously puzzling conduct becomes immediately intelligible the moment we realize the difference between the actual situations of certain agents and what those agents themselves believed their situations to be. Why ever did the tank commander lead his squadron in a suicidal attack upon an entrenched battery of anti-tank guns? Because that was not at all how he perceived his situation. Trusting what he had been told by his usually reliable intelligence, he led his squadron into what he believed was a gap in the defences.

The philosopher-anthropologist Ernst Gellner contributes a more sophisticated example. He makes much, and rightly, of two findings from his own fieldwork among the Moroccan Berbers. Igurramen (singular, agurram) are in Morocco highly respected. They perform important functions as arbitrators, and so forth. There is no manifest procedure for selecting igurramen, who are believed to be chosen by God. They are also believed to be: both abundantly, even fecklessly generous; and yet eternally prosperous (B. Wilson 1970, pp. 43–5).

The ethnocentric scientific observer is bound to raise two questions. First, allowing that the ultimate explanation of everything must lie in the inscrutable will of the First Cause, still what are the humbler secondary causes through which God operates in order to make his secret selections publicly effective? Second, since no one could for long be both so generous and so prosperous, how is it that at least those Berbers who are not themselves igurramen manage to maintain two such, in the long run and practically, incompatible beliefs?

(iv)

The fourth fundamental is that there is an enormously large number of kinds of behaviours – including, surely, all those which are peculiarly and distinctively human? – in which the possession of certain concepts is a presupposition of the performance: these concepts are thus integral to performances of these kinds. It is this which makes the by now often quoted methodological manifesto of B. F. Skinner, a leading American behaviourist psychologist, egregiously grotesque: "We can neither assert nor deny discontinuity between the human and subhuman fields so long as we know so little about either. If, nevertheless, the author of a book of this sort is expected to hazard a guess publicly, I may say that the only differences I expect to see revealed between the behaviour of a rat and a man (aside from enormous

differences of complexity) lie in the field of verbal behaviour"
(Skinner 1938, p. 442).

No doubt experiments upon rats must be, somewhere, as
essential as they are convenient. Yet to write 'only' here is
like excusing the omission of the Prince of Denmark on the
ground that he is only one character in *Hamlet*. That it is
possible to concentrate on the behaviour of rats and pigeons
without attending to any verbal behaviour is a clear sign that
experimental psychology, so pursued, is not a human, much
less a social science. The French anthropological writer Lévi-
Strauss, in *Tristes Tropiques*, uttered one lucid, succinct and
true proposition: "Qui dit homme, dit langage, et qui dit
langage dit société" (Lévi-Strauss 1955, p. 421; and compare
Leach 1970).

In deference to Emile Durkheim (1858–1917), another
Frenchman with a German name, consider suicide. To suicide it is necessary: not only to do something which you
expect will result in your own death, and consequently to
die; but also to do it with that intention, and consequently to
die. It is thus possible, appealing to the principle of double
effect, to argue that, when Oates walked out into an Antarctic
blizzard, his sacrificial death was not a suicide. That principle
is characteristic of, but not confined to, Roman Catholic
casuistry. Where some course of action is likely to have
two different effects, one licit or mandatory and the other
illicit, it may be permissible to take that course intending the
one but not the other: for example, to give a terminally ill
patient a heavy dose of morphine to relieve pain knowing
that it might perhaps also prove fatal. Condoms sold from
slot machines in Roman Catholic countries and labelled "For
the prevention of disease only" appeal to the same principle.
(Here and later, readers may find a use for Speake 1934,
A Dictionary of Philosophy, both to learn more about people
mentioned, and to fill vocabulary gaps.)

Again, it may be too much, with La Rochefoucauld, to
claim: "Few men would fall in love if they had not heard
about it." Yet it is the unexaggerated truth to insist that
embarking on or continuing a married life, as opposed to

mating and cohabiting as do the birds, is impossible for creatures not possessed of the notion of a long-term union, and hence incapable of intending any such union. Nor is this truth to be escaped by cynical references to duplicity. For even to pretend to intend, or falsely to promise, such permanent fidelity requires an understanding of what it would be to fulfil that promise.

Besides activities which cannot be understood by others without possessing notions with which the agents explain themselves, and activities in which it is impossible oneself to engage without having the relevant constitutive and directive concepts, there are also, as the Cambridge philosopher Elizabeth Anscombe has indicated, those which cannot be properly understood by an observer altogether unable to perform the activities in question. Her point applies, for example, to mathematics but not to acrobatics.

None of this, however, has any tendency to show that there is something viciously subjective or projective about verstehen explanations. Certainly my knowledge of your reasons for doing what you did is, like all my other knowledge, my knowledge; and that I know facts about you is a fact about me. But this does not make it any the less of an objective fact that you did it, and did it for those reasons; an objective fact, that is, in the sense of a fact altogether independent of any whims or wishes of mine.

(v)

A more elaborate, incorrigibly perverse doctrine of subjectivity and projection is among those taught as sociology of education in the University of London Institute of Education, as well as preached from the radio pulpits of the Open University (Young 1971; and compare Flew 1976, Chs. 2 and 3, and Dawson 1981). These being the two British institutions having the most extensive influence in the teaching of teachers and intending teachers, their miseducation of the educators is properly a matter of public interest.

In what is certainly the most bizarre contribution to a

preposterous set book, Alan Blum, now of York University in Toronto, gives his answer to his own curiously Kantian question: 'How is sociology possible?' It is, he concludes, "easy to see that the methodical character of marriage, war and suicide is only seen, recognized and made possible through the organized practices of sociology. These regularities do not exist 'out there' in [a] pristine form to which sociologists functionally respond, but rather, they acquire their character of regularities and their features as describable objects only through the grace of sociological imputation. Thus, it is not an objectively discernible purely existing external world which accounts for sociology; it is the methods and procedures of sociology which create and sustain that world" (Young 1971, p. 131).

Blum himself appears to think it unnecessary to produce here any warrant for drawing these professionally megalomaniac conclusions. But other evidence suggests that, in so far as they have any basis at all, they are based upon misunderstandings of some of the fundamentals discussed in the present Section 1. None of these, however, provides any good reason for asserting – what is manifestly false – that "the methodical character of marriage, war and suicide is only . . . made possible through the organized practices of sociology." Nor is the fact that certain things can be truly said only of people who possess some relevant concepts a good reason for maintaining that these things cannot even be true of anyone until someone else turns up actually to make the appropriate assertions – that indispensable someone else being, of course, a sociologist equipped with those same essential organizing concepts.

As for Blum's own answer to his Kantian question, it must in truth be an absolute presupposition of the existence of sociology as a science that there are people – or, as Blum prefers to say, "societal members" – capable of doing their own social things, without benefit of sociologists and their imputations. It must be: just as much as it is an absolute presupposition of the existence of the science of the heavens that the stars in their courses exist and revolve in their own right, and are not mere creatures or fictions of the Astronomer-Royal. The truth is flat contrary to what Blum asserts. There has to be, as there is, "an objectively discernible, purely existing external world which accounts for sociology". It cannot be, and it is not, "the methods and procedures of sociology which create and sustain that world". If it were, then that would constitute the decisive reason: both for dismissing its pretensions to be any sort of science; and hence for closing down all schools, departments, and institutes of sociology.

2   Dispossessing such explanations: (i) by reform

There are two quite different ways in which aspiring social scientists may hope to challenge explanations of the familiar kind discussed in Section 1. The first maintains that some sets of such explanations are in fact partly or wholly false. The second urges, much more radically, that in some way all must be inadequate or bogus.

(i)

The first sentence of the Preface to *The German Ideology* reads: "Hitherto men have constantly made up for themselves false conceptions about themselves, about what they are and ought to be" (Marx and Engels 1846, p. 23). Such false notions are forthwith, and very forthrightly, contrasted with the intractabilities of objective truth.

The authors then proceed to develop their own distinctive and potentially fruitful conception of ideology. All ideas, it is said, have material causes: "The production of ideas, of conceptions, of consciousness, is at first directly interwoven with the material activity and the material intercourse of men, the language of real life" (p. 37). But now systematically erroneous notions, usually linked together into some sort of system, are contrasted with correct appreciations of how things actually are. In this understanding ideology is essentially erroneous. A system of ideas is ideological to precisely the extent that it is wrong, and in as much as the error is the work of concealed interests and more or less unconscious motivations: "If in all ideology men and their circumstances appear upside-down as in a *camera obscura*, this phenomenon arises just as much from their historical life-process as the inversion of objects on the retina does from their physical life-process" (p. 32).

When the word 'ideology' is employed in this way the interest is epistemological, concerned with what and how we can know. The opposition is between, on the one hand, falsehood and distortion, and, on the other hand, a clearly focused true picture. Realism requires that we labour to expose false consciousness for what it is: "Whilst in ordinary life every shopkeeper is very well able to distinguish between what somebody professes to be and what he is, our historians . . . take every epoch at its word and believe that everything it says and imagines about itself is true" (p. 64). Such wretched, Brand X, pseudo-historians thus share – in a memorable phrase – *"the illusion of that epoch"* (p. 51).

The word 'ideology' is, however, also employed, from the beginning, in a quite different sense. Especially when the interest is metaphysical, and when Marx and Engels therefore want to affirm the ontological primacy of the material over the ideal, everything in the second of these two great fundamental categories counts as ideological, or as an element in ideology: "Conceiving, thinking, the mental intercourse of men, appear at this stage as the direct efflux of their material behaviour. The same applies to mental production as expressed in the language of politics, laws morality, religion, metaphysics . . ." (p. 37). So in this second sense the term 'ideology' embraces, neutrally and non-committally: not only everything which is ideological in the first interpretation; but also all sound ideas involved in truly reporting the plain facts.

Always when any key term is ambiguous or of otherwise indeterminate meaning it becomes imperative that all those introducing that term begin by indicating which sense or what sense they favour; and equally imperative that they remain constant in their fidelity to that choice. It is, for instance, not acceptable to exploit this ambiguity of the term 'ideological' by simply denouncing some system of beliefs as ideological without first undertaking to show that those particular beliefs are false.

Nevertheless, in many popular works, sound practice would appear to be an exception rather than the rule. Consider, for instance, *Ideology in Social Science: Readings in Critical Social Theory*, one of the paperback collections which were very widely influential in the seventies and which – as part of 'the Long March through the institutions' – continue to have substantial influence in universities, polytechnics and other places of tertiary instruction. Although the Editor eschews any unequivocal ruling, both the fact that 'Critical' is here a code-word for 'Marxist' and the contrast drawn in his first sentence suggest that he is at least starting from the first of the interpretations just now distinguished: "The essays in this collection seek to challenge the prevailing ideologies in the social sciences and to indicate scientific alternatives to these ideologies" (Blackburn 1972, p. 9; and compare Flew 1976).

Then in the second paragraph there is a reference to an "essay by Gareth Stedman Jones entitled 'History: the Poverty of Empiricism' ". In this paragraph we hear tell of ideology "in an entirely different sense". The nearest we get to an explanation of this different sense is, however, in the next sentence but two: "The choice of a particular field of investigation, the choice of a given range of concepts with which to investigate that field, all express assumptions about the nature of society and about what is theoretically significant and what is not." We are thus, within the space of a single short paragraph: both shown how, in the proposed new sense, ideology is for the scientist unavoidable; and assured that this is a sense which still permits us to "counterpose science to ideology" (pp. 9, 9–10 and again 9). In the ordinary exoteric senses of the word such work scarcely merits the diploma self-description 'critical'.

Again, in this and too many similar books, terms such as

'Positivism' and 'Empiricist' – terms ending with the suffixes 'ism' or 'ist' – are employed, or misemployed, in violation of the most basic principles of clear thinking. Take a recent book from what was formerly the most fashionable of 'the Shakespearian Seven' new UK universities of the sixties. Without attempting to explain what, if anything, he himself proposes to mean by the key term this Professor of Sociology considers whether Durkheim and Weber were positivists; speaks of critical theory "in its assault on positivism"; tells us that among "the principal features . . . of recent paradigms" are "an attack on positivism"; and draws attention to Marcuse's contrast between "critical reason" and "positivist sociology" (Bottomore 1984, pp. 3, 20, 26 and 52). Finally, without noticing the self-destructive significance of this belated addition, he adds a note to his first employment of the word: "The question is further complicated by the variety of meanings attached to the term 'positivism' " (p. 10)!

In order, as it were, to clean our intellectual palates, let us treat ourselves to a remark directed most especially at the Frankfurt School – what the remarker wickedly calls "the Frankfurters". For many such people "a 'positivist' is anyone who subjects a favoured theory to the indignity of testing by mere fact" (Gellner 1985, p. 120). The word 'empiricist' too is often misemployed in a similar way.

(ii)

Something must also be said to throw light on the contentions that "Conceiving, thinking, the mental intercourse of men, appear as the direct efflux of their material behaviour"; and that, in terms of two other favourite images, the ideological superstructure is some sort of reflection of the material foundations. Again, and more perplexing, "Legislation, whether political or civil, never does more than proclaim, express in words, the will of economic relations" (Marx 1847, p. 70).

Such contentions recall the thesis of Epiphenomenalism. This, like Occasionalism or Two-way Interactionism, is one of the rival answers to the problem of mind and matter as set by Descartes. In that Cartesian formulation the question is: 'What are the relations between consciousness and stuff?' The Epiphenomenalist maintains that consciousness is always an effect and never a cause. With mind and body it is, it is suggested, as with phosphorescence on water and the water below or – with one mischievous American philosopher – the halo over the saint and the saint beneath. The effects are produced by ongoings in the water – or the saint – but these effects never react back upon their causes (Flew 1964).

Epiphenomenalism, like several similar doctrines, makes a strong, immediate appeal to all who think of ourselves as tough-minded and down-to-earth. For how, after all, could anything so etherial and insubstantial as a moment of consciousness or an idea bring about any effects in the real world of matter in motion? "The general conclusion", according to the classic Preface to the *Critique of Political Economy*, "can be summarized as follows. In the social production of their existence, men inevitably enter into relations . . . The totality of these relations . . . constitutes the economic structure of society, the real foundation on which arises a legal and political superstructure, and to which correspond definite forms of social consciousness . . . It is not the consciousness of men that determines their existence, but their social existence that determines their consciousness" (Marx 1859, pp. 20–1).

The compelling straightforwardness and seeming inevitability of such doctrines disappear just so soon as we begin to probe their content. How bold and how comprehensive are the claims which they are actually making? Or, better – for it is impossible to exaggerate the importance of putting our test questions this way round – what would have had to have happened, or to be happening, or to be going to happen, in order to prove that the doctrine is not, after all, true (Popper 1934, and 1963, Ch. 1)? Certainly, at first blush, an idea or a moment of consciousness must appear too elusive and too etherial to succeed in either effecting or affecting anything. But now, before we can determine the direction of causal relations, we have to identify their terms. And, of course, once that question has been raised, it becomes obvious why our putative entities appeared doomed to ineffective impotence. For thoughts and pains can be identified only by reference to the flesh-and-blood creatures who have them: it simply makes no sense to speak of thoughts or pains subsisting in detachment from any persons to think the ones or suffer the others. The dependence of consciousness upon the organism which it characterizes is thus as total as Epiphenomenalist heart could desire.

In the Introduction to his 'Contribution to the Critique of Hegel's Philosophy of Law' Marx insists that "Material force can only be overthrown by material force . . ." Yet he concedes immediately that "theory itself becomes a material force when it has seized the masses" (Marx 1843, p. 182). It is no less material a force, though weaker, when it is guiding or misguiding a single individual. For persons inspired by even the most elevated ideas and ideals are just as much ordinarily flesh-and-blood human agents as more sordid persons striving merely to maintain or increase their incomes. Once this is appreciated, do we any longer have any sufficient reason for holding that causal transactions between economic foundations and ideological superstructure can go only one way?

That ostensibly bold and strong general hypothesis was, from the beginning, all set to suffer the death by a thousand qualifications. So we should not be surprised to find Engels, in a very late letter to Bloch (21–2 September 1890), conceding that, while of course it remains absolutely and incontestably true, nevertheless it applies not to the appearances but to the substance, not immediately and superficially but ultimately and in the last analysis: "According to the materialist conception of history, the *ultimately* determining element . . . is production and reproduction in real life . . . The economic situation is the basis, but the various elements of the superstructure . . . political, juristic, philosophical theories, religious views and their further development into systems of dogmas, also exercise their influence upon the course of historical struggles and in many cases preponderate in determining their *form*."

Later still Lenin, without for one moment admitting even to himself what he was doing, went on to abandon, first in the practice of his October coup and then in his theoretical justifications of *Our Revolution*, not only the present hypothesis but also the entire materialist conception of history, of which it is an essential part. In this as in so many other ways Stalin went even further in the direction in which Lenin had led (Hook 1975, Ch. 8; and compare Hook 1943 and Conquest 1967, Ch. 1).

Consider, for instance, how it is laid down in the Preface to the *Critique of Political Economy* that "No social order is ever destroyed before all the productive forces for which it is sufficient have been developed, and new superior relations of production never replace older ones before the material conditions for their existence have matured within the framework of the old society" (Marx 1859, p. 21). Then contrast this with Lenin, accepting and indeed underlining the objection that "Russia has not attained the level of development of productive forces that makes socialism possible"; but countering it by asking: "If a definite level of culture is required for the building of socialism . . . why cannot we begin by first creating the prerequisites for that definite level of culture in a revolutionary way, and *then* . . . proceed to overtake the other nations?" (Lenin 1922, p. 837). No reason, perhaps, no reason at all – except that by making your revolution in one of the least advanced capitalist countries and thereafter building socialism you are bound to falsify (to show to be false, that is) the scientific pretensions of your own so-called scientific socialism.

(iii)

"And as in private life one differentiates between what a man thinks and says of himself and what he really is and does, so in historical struggles one must distinguish still more the phrases and fancies of parties from their real organism and their real interests, their conception of themselves from their reality" (Marx 1852, p. 38). Indeed we must. And, furthermore, the categorical imperative of both academic and practical good faith is to exercise the same suspicion – although not, surely, an invincible suspicion? – against every social group and every social institution. Notwithstanding that it is all too often done, it will not do to confine our critical attention to opposing parties and disfavoured institutions. The more sincere we become in our scientific and other stated purposes, the more scrupulous we shall be to recognize and to counter our own inclinations to wishful thinking and self-deception. Not without reason did someone – was it Nietzsche? – describe social study as "the art of mistrust".

In the main Marx and his followers have been interested in what they have perceived as social classes, rather than the actual workings of smaller organizations. Indeed, it has been left largely to people trained in economics, and of an opposite political persuasion, to notice the ideological significance of the fact that people employed in both private firms and public institutions, including those employed at the highest levels, are, just as much as the rest of the human race, apt to strive to maximize their own utilities. A gap thus opens between the official story about the aims of the organization and the true facts of its operation. So that official story necessarily becomes, in the primary and seminal Marxist sense, an ideology.

The, so to speak, official story is that all privately owned corporations have a single-minded commitment to profit maximization. But except in those rare cases in which the pay and perquisites of all employees are very directly linked with the rate of return on capital employed, that story is, to put it very mildly, less than perfectly true. And even in those cases, any individual's share in the profit increase dependent on any particular action or decision may well not outweigh the sum of his or her other, possibly competing, individual utilities. The same is just as true, or even more true, of organizations supposedly dedicated to the fulfilment of some public purpose. The employees will all have – being, along with the rest of us, human – their own private purposes.

The pursuit of these may well conflict with the perceived
public interest in the purpose of the organization. Indeed
the conflicts here are likely to be more important and more
extensive. For it is extremely uncommon, and may often
be impossible, to link the rewards of individual employees
directly, or even at all, with the most economical fulfilment
of such public purposes. (Compare, mischievously but nevertheless realistically, Parkinson 1981 and Lynn and Jay 1988.)

(iv)

The reality of such conflicts, between the so to speak official purposes of organizations and the actual private purposes
of the individuals in those organizations, came out sharp and
cruel in Britain some years ago when all the public sector
labour unions declared their total opposition to proposals
for putting services previously provided directly by local or
national government out to competitive tender. Under the
slogan 'Public service not private profit', they argued that
government could always provide the best and cheapest
services 'because it did not have to make a profit'. Maybe
it could; maybe, maybe. But the union leaders, who were in
a good position to know, made it obvious that they did not
themselves believe that their members in fact were, always or
even most often, providing the best and cheapest possible.
For they became, and remain, committed to opposing any
testing of the question by putting anything out to tender
anywhere. In any such fair and open competition the public
sector alternative is, apparently, bound to lose. The outcome
of the competition would be – in a giveaway phrase – 'the
hole in the dyke'; to be indefinitely expanded by a torrential
surge of privatization.

In the event, after certain of these proposals had been
implemented, the subsequent surge of privatization fell a
long way short of the torrential. Although perhaps tempting
it would nevertheless be mistaken to infer from this that the
implementation of those proposals has been without effect,
and that there can therefore be no case for retaining, and

even reinforcing, the compulsions to put out to tender. For putting out to tender constitutes a threat; a threat to dismiss the direct labour forces if their performance does not at least equal the potential of the private competition. The mistake here, a mistake remarkably common in social thinking, is to assume that threats become effective only in so far as they are actually implemented. This is of course the opposite of the truth, since the whole point of issuing threats precisely is to inhibit the conduct calling for their implementation. Remember what the American Admiral Mahan said about the effectiveness of the threat constituted by British sea-power during the Napoleonic wars: "Those far distant storm-beaten ships, upon which the Grand Army never looked, alone stood between it and the dominion of the world."

(v)

It is unfortunate that in Marx acuteness and a zeal to unmask ideological distortions in the thinking of the class enemy is not paralleled by any anxious awareness of the possibility, indeed the overwhelming likelihood, of similar infections in his own theorizing. This is unfortunate because only by being constantly alert to the dangers of bias, prejudice and individual and collective self-interest can any of us hope to avoid or to correct distortions in our own thinking. Although his prophecies of proletarian revolution and of the wholly happy consequences thereof were based originally upon a high-flying Hegelian philosophical analysis rather than any pedestrian investigations in the Reading Room of the British Museum, Marx appears never to have wondered whether he too might not have succumbed to the temptations of wishful thinking (Marx 1844, and compare Flew 1991b).

Again, very unlike Darwin, to whom Engels would have had us compare him, Marx never committed himself to any full, clearcut and unequivocal statement of what in their correspondence is referred to as "our view", nor to any review of difficulties seen in squaring that view with the facts. So they always found it easy, after an event, to satisfy themselves that "our view" had not been falsified by that occurrence; however little either of them might have anticipated anything of the sort. Nor could Freud have found in the Marx papers anything to match Darwin's private resolution to make an immediate note of any fact seemingly hard to reconcile with his cherished theory (Flew 1984, III, 3). Experience had shown Darwin how easily such intellectual inconveniences will be forgotten!

Here we have to see, to force others to see, and never to allow ourselves or anyone else to fail to remember, that a general obscurity in assertion and, in particular, evasiveness about what would or would not constitute falsifications of assertions made, are clear signs of insincerity in the search for scientific truth. Popper has famously insisted that the proper criterion for distinguishing scientific from non-scientific utterance is falsifiability (Popper 1963, Ch. 1). If we do not know what would have to occur or to have occurred to show that our utterance expressed a false proposition, then we do not know what if anything we proposed in that utterance. Any kind of indeterminateness in meaning is always bound, and often intended, to disable potential critics. Yet to stubborn dissidents preferring their statements to be true criticism cannot but be welcome. To tolerate either unfalsifiability or any other kind of obscurity is, therefore, to reveal an indifference to truth. For anyone deserving to be accredited as any sort of scientist clarity is, as the Marquis de Vauvenargues insisted it was for the philosopher, "a matter of good faith".

(vi)

Such salutary points can be rammed home again with a complementary couple of quotations from two very different great Victorians. The first comes from the biologist T. H. Huxley, via his novelist grandson Aldous: "Be clear though you may be convicted of error. If you are clearly wrong you may run up against a fact sometime and get set right. If you shuffle with your subject and study to use language which will give a loophole of escape either way, there is no hope for you" (quoted in Huxley 1936, p. 63; and compare Orwell 1970, IV, 38 and 45).

The second quotation is from a letter of Marx to Engels, dated 15 August 1857. It should be called in evidence during any discussion of the claim made by Engels that Marx as a social scientist was a match for Darwin in biology: "I took the risk of prognosticating in this way, as I was compelled to substitute for you as a correspondent at the *Tribune* . . . It is possible I may be discredited. But in that case it will still be possible to pull through with a bit of dialectics. It goes without saying that I phrased my forecasts in such a way that I would prove to be right also in the opposite-case" (Flew 1984, III, 3).

3   Dispossessing such explanations: (ii) by revolution

Explanations of actions in terms of desires, beliefs and decisions of the agent may be challenged in two very different ways, one fundamental and the other not. So far we have considered that other; where an explanation of this kind is acceptable, but where the particular specimen previously established is thought to be wrong. But the more fundamental challenge, urging that no such explanation is acceptable at all, comes from behaviourist psychologists and from others under their influence. Thus B. F. Skinner of Harvard, the doyen of them all in the USA, in a popular book under the sinister and threatening title *Beyond Freedom and Dignity*, makes what the dustjacket calls his "definitive statement about man and society". The review in the *New York Times* (22 September 1971) began: "There is just no gainsaying the profound importance of B. F. Skinner's new book . . . If you plan to read only one book this year, this is probably the one you should choose."

(i)

Skinner's most catastrophic misguiding principle is that, to
be scientific, any study of man must eschew all anthropomorphic notions. He begins: "We have used the instruments of
science; we have counted and measured and compared; but
something essential to scientific practice is missing in almost
all current discussions of human behaviour" (Skinner 1971,
p. 7; and compare Flew 1978, Ch. VII). What seems to be
missing is, awkwardly, the absence of certain notions which,
he wants to insist, can have no place in scientific discourse:
"Although physics soon stopped personifying things . . . it
continued for a long time to speak as if they had wills,
impulses, feelings, purposes and other fragmentary attributes
of an indwelling agent . . . All this was eventually abandoned,
and to good effect . . ." Nevertheless, deplorably, what should
be "the behavioural sciences still appeal to comparable internal states . . ." (p. 8). We are, therefore, supposed to regret
that "Almost everyone who is concerned with human affairs
– as political scientist, philosopher, man of letters, economist,
psychologist, linguist, sociologist, theologian, educator, or
psychotherapist – continues to talk about human behaviour
in this prescientific way" (p. 9).

Certainly such discourse is prescientific, in the obvious but
purely temporal sense that it was going on long before there
was anything deserving the diploma description 'science'. But
Skinner is mistaken in implying that it is not merely, in this
innocuous sense, prescientific but also, damagingly, unscientific.
He misconstrues the disowning of anthropomorphic notions
by physicists as being: not a rejection of misapplications
of ideas in themselves entirely proper and indispensable;
but a repudiation of notions, or pseudo-notions, which are
essentially and irredeemably non-scientific.

Skinner puts his first objection to all these everyday explanatory notions in an awkward way: ". . . we do not feel
the things that have been invented to explain behaviour. The
possessed man does not feel the possessing demon and may
even deny that he exists . . . The intelligent man does not feel
his intelligence or the introvert his introversion" (pp. 15–16).

Certainly, if we confine ourselves to these examples, there is something in what Skinner says. But this something does not destroy the obvious truth. The man, for instance, who confesses, 'I am determined to make it with Cyn', very obviously does have, and knows without inference that he has, a will, impulses, feelings, and – definitely – a purpose in life. Yet it is "wills, impulses, feelings, purposes", not the higher-order notions of intelligence and introversion, which Skinner wants to dismiss as prescientific fictions.

In order the better to appreciate what Skinner's first objection really is, we have to turn to certain gurus of social science who have demanded a behaviourist approach. This they have often preferred to label 'positivist' or 'empiricist'. In his *Cours de philosophie positive* Auguste Comte (1798–1857) appears to have been ambivalent. He there wanted to maintain: not only that positive science can admit nothing but behaviour, having no truck with thoughts or desires or anything else supposedly somehow behind and guiding that sole human observable; but also that, because we are ourselves people, we do have what amounts to or is as good as observational experience of such things. They therefore can, after all, be admitted into the solid realm of positive science (Hayek 1978, pp. 321–32).

In *A Scientific Theory of Culture* the anthropologist Bronislaw Malinowski (1884–1942), without equivocation or hesitation, takes his stand as a defining, paradigm-case Behaviourist: thoughts, beliefs, ideas, desires, and so on can be admitted iff "fully defined in terms of overt, observable, physically ascertainable behaviour" (Malinowski 1944, p. 23: 'iff' is the accepted shorthand for 'if and only if').

In *The Rules of Sociological Method* Emile Durkheim is equally emphatic and categorical: "Social phenomena are things and ought to be treated as things . . ."; and "All that is subject to observation has thereby the character of a thing." Ideas, however, "cannot be perceived or known directly, but only through the phenomenal reality expressing them" (Durkheim 1895, pp. 27–8). Again, "Since objects are perceived only through sense perception . . . Science, to be

objective, ought to borrow the material for its initial definitions directly from perceptual data" (p. 43). So, finally, to
be thus scientifically objective the definition of social facts
must "characterize them by elements external enough to be
immediately perceived" (p. 35).

To be able to decide whether "wills, impulses, feelings,
purposes" are "immediately perceived" or in some other
way directly experienced, or whether they are, as has sometimes been asserted, "the phlogiston of the social sciences"
(Lundberg 1963, pp. 53–4), we need to distinguish two radically
different senses of 'experience', and hence two correspondingly
different senses of 'empiricism'.

In the ordinary workaday interpretation of the word, to
claim to have had experience of cows or of political subversion or of anything else is a claim to have had perceptual or
other cognitive dealings with various public realities; realities
wholly independent of the mind of the claimant. In the
second and highly artificial interpretation, an interpretation
much favoured by philosophers since Descartes, verbally
identical claims would not entail the objective existence of
anything. Such a claim would be sufficiently warranted, in
the cows case, by the fact that the claimant had had a
dream or a waking hallucination featuring cows pasturing
in lush meadows. Dreams, however, and hallucinations are
mind-dependent and purely private, in the sense that it is
simply absurd to speak of dreams and hallucinations existing
apart from, and other than as affections of, their subjects
(Flew 1971, Ch. VI, 6).

Given the first or public sense of 'experience', then empiricism becomes the surely unexceptionable contention that all
claims to knowledge of the Universe around us ought to
be somehow based upon, referred back and accountable
to, our actual or possible experience. But if we insist on
construing the word 'experience' in the second or private
sense, then empiricism becomes a most unappealing doctrine. The philosophical constructions of George Berkeley
(1685–1743) and David Hume suggest that the empiricist
in this second understanding will be hard put to vindicate

claims to any knowledge of any mind-independent realities. Yet, having discerned these ruinous implications, on no account must we permit anyone to take them as discrediting empiricism in the scientifically fundamental first sense.

But now, given again that familiar first or public sense of 'experience', we have, surely, every one of us had plenty of experience of "wills, impulses, feelings, purposes", and of all the other items so frequently and so confidently mentioned in our explanations both of our own conduct and of that of other people? None of these, of course, are "material things", those "moderate-sized specimens of dry goods" which are often though falsely believed to be the only objects revealed by "direct perception" and found among our hard "perceptual data" (Austin 1962, p. 8). They are, none the less and undeniably, objects of our everyday experience. As such they are neither to be denied nor ignored by anyone aspiring to develop a science of human beings, as we actually are. Nor, as has been stressed before, is there anything relevantly unobjective or observer-dependent about the facts of people's beliefs, desires, feelings, or what have you. These things are all, if you like, subjective; in the sense of being facts about subjects. But that does not make it any the less a matter of objective fact that some particular subject either wanted this or hated that.

(ii)

Skinner's second objection to prescientific explanations of conduct arises because he wants to ask and to answer questions other than those to which such prescientific explanations are relevant; and because he believes that different explanations must always and necessarily be competing for the same logical space. Thus he writes: "If we ask someone, 'Why did you go to the theatre?', and he says, 'Because I felt like going', we are apt to take this reply as a kind of explanation" (Skinner 1971, pp. 12–13).

We are indeed. For that 'I wanted to go to the theatre', or that 'I am determined to make it with Cyn', may fully explain

conduct previously found puzzling. What these responses will
not do is answer as well the further questions: why I have a
taste, and this particular taste, for the theatre; and why I
find girls, and in particular Cynthia, so powerfully attractive.
But these are the kind of questions which Skinner wants to
press: "It would be much more to the point to know what has
happened when he has gone to the theatre in the past, what
he has heard or read about the play he went to see, and what
other things in his past or present environments induced him
to go . . ." (p. 13).

There are two general lessons to be learnt here. The first
is that explanations are answers to questions, and hence that
explanations answering different questions are not necessarily rivals. The second concerns the suggestion that a truly
scientific explanation of conduct must refer to some sort of
environmental determination.

The first lesson can be taught somewhat frivolously, yet
none the less effectively, with the help of an Andy Capp
comic strip. The tried and suffering Flo is shown, protesting:
"There was twelve light ales in the pantry this mornin' – now
there's only ONE! 'ow d'yer explain THAT?" To which her
incorrigible husband responds, with deadly predictability:
"It was that dark in there, I didn't see it." The cartoonist
Smythe felt no call to spell out the ways in which the
question intended – about the eleven – differed from the
question answered – about the one. Any such superfluous
and heavy-footed spelling out ought to have taken notice
also of the fractionally less obvious truth that the original
challenge was to justify the doubtfully proper rather than
to explain the perplexing. Another, real life, example is
provided by Willie Horton's sociologically uncorrupted and
devastatingly direct answer to the question why he robbed
banks: "Because that is where the money is."

The first moral, therefore, is that there is not just one
single, *the* explanation for anything which we may wish to
have explained. There may instead be as many, not necessarily exclusive, alternative explanations as there are legitimate
explanation-demanding questions to be asked. Before moving

on from the present thesis, notice how it can be set to work to resolve some tough interdisciplinary conflicts.

Commenting on 'Is the Brain a Physical System?', a paper by a physiologically oriented experimental psychologist, a philosopher wrote: "It is a matter of fact, indisputable for all that our knowledge of it is pre-scientific, that much of our behaviour is done because we want to act in the way we do, because we have purposes, motives, wants and intentions, and not because some physiological causal sequence, of which we know nothing, produces some movement such as flinching or starting at a sudden loud noise." To this the experimental psychologist replied: "We can already assign physiological causes to certain wants and actions." He went on to say, "A hypothalamic tumour may turn a woman into a nymphomaniac . . ."; which is – come to think of it – like satyriasis a complaint about which the loudest complaints tend to come from those not themselves directly afflicted (Borger and Cioffi, p. 135; and compare Flew 1973).

More, much more, will have to be said about physically necessitating causes of behaviour. But here and now it is both necessary and sufficient to point out that an explanation of why she did what she did, in terms of her beliefs and desires, is by no means necessarily a rival to an explanation, in physiological terms, of why she happens to be subject to the various desires to which she is subject.

The second lesson to be drawn from Skinner's second objection attaches to his reason for preferring to ask only his own favourite kind of question: "A scientific analysis shifts both the responsibility and the achievement to the environment" (Skinner 1971, p. 25). It is, therefore, according to Skinner, unscientific to claim that anyone ever effected anything. Hence certain unnamed Freudians are rebuked for recklessly "assuring their patients that they are free to choose among different courses of action and are in the long run architects of their own destinies" (pp. 20–1).

Skinner's curious yet common contention is actually inconsistent with the presupposition of universal causality, from which by many it is thought to follow. For, if everything

which has a cause is by that fact disqualified from being in
its turn a cause, then there can be no causal chains. Every
discovery of the cause of what before had seemed to be itself
a cause must be sufficient to show that that original seeming
cause was not, after all, truly a cause. For all true causes must
be themselves uncaused.

Perhaps the main reason why Skinner holds that explanations of human behaviour must be sought always and only in
the environment is that he sees any alternative as involving
the black beast notion of "autonomous man". This he believes
to be the foundation of the to him equally repugnant concepts of human freedom and dignity. Let Skinner explain
himself: "Two features of autonomous man are particularly
troublesome. In the traditional view, a person is free. He is
autonomous in the sense that his behaviour is uncaused. He
can therefore be held responsible for what he does, and justly
punished if he offends" (p. 19).

Two but only two comments can and need to be made at
this stage. The first is that all those who hope to develop
human sciences, and in particular social sciences, should
without preconceptions study people as we actually are. No
one has any business to insist that we cannot be in any way
autonomous, and that every bit of our behaviour must be
inexorably necessitated; just because it would, supposedly,
be so inconvenient and so uncomfortable if we are and if
it were not. The second is that it would be narrow-minded
and gratuitously defeatist to despair of erecting a science, in
the sense of an orderly and growing structure of authentic
knowledge, if ever and wherever we cannot assume such
total necessitation. For both in the life of the laity and in
the writings of historians we encounter innumerable perfectly
satisfactory explanations of human conduct; explanations
provided in terms of the new-named yet in fact immemorially
ancient "voluntaristic theory of action". And it is, after all,
history which is by prescriptive right Queen of the Social
Sciences.

4　Social Parts and Social Wholes

History does *nothing*; it 'does *not* possess immense riches', it 'does *not* fight battles'. It is *men*, real living men, who do all this, who possess things and fight battles. It is not 'history' which uses men as a means of achieving – as if it were an individual person – *its own* ends. History is nothing but the activity of men in pursuit of their ends.

K. Marx and F. Engels, *The Holy Family*, p. 93.

I don't believe in Society. There is no such thing, only individual people, and there are families.

Margaret Thatcher, quoted in *Woman's Own*, 31 October 1987.

Whatever further kinds of questions social scientists may think to ask, and however much extra light answers to these questions may throw upon the institutions and activities studied, explanations of the familiar kind discussed in Chapter 3 will remain always both essential and fundamental. This cannot but be so, since all social collectives are composed of individuals, and can act only through the actions of their components. Whatever is said about any mass movement, organized collectivity, or other supposed social whole, must at some stage be related and in some way reduced to discourse about the doings, beliefs, attitudes and dispositions of its components. Who actually did and thought what; and what led them to act and to think as in fact they did, and not otherwise?

1　Methodological individualism and methodological holism

All this, once it has been sharply stated, should appear

obvious and altogether beyond dispute. Yet it is often forgotten; and sometimes, if only by indirection, denied. Perhaps the extraordinary uproar of indignation and protest which greeted the Prime Ministerial statement quoted above was motivated mainly by a perverse desire to deny even a metaphysical truism when asserted by a person so abominated. But another equally misguided motive may have been methodological. For many have believed that some favoured method is adequately justified only by maintaining a supposedly presupposed metaphysical proposition; a proposition, that is, asserting what sorts of things there *ultimately* are and are not. Thus the prophet of Behaviourism, J. B. Watson (1878–1958), appears to have believed that, if he was to justify his recommendations that psychologists should not introspect but study behaviour, then he had to deny the reality of consciousness. In the present case the preferred method thought to demand a denial of the Prime Ministerial assertion would have been that of betterment through collective rather than individual action (Flew 1989c).

For what comes closer to an outright denial we go to *Education, State and Crisis: A Marxist Perspective*, a prime work by a Lecturer in Sociology at Goldsmiths' College. In the course of disquisitions on the scurvy doings of such hypostatized abstractions as imperialism, racism and monopoly capitalism, the author finds no occasions: either to mention any particular case of someone advantaged or disadvantaged for no other or better reason than the colour of their skin; or to name as much as one single private corporation even alleged to be enjoying a monopoly position. Instead he prefers to write: "It may be useful at this point to indicate how capitalism has grown into a world system of colonial oppression, and how in its economic essence imperialism *is* monopoly capitalism" (Sarup 1982, p. 94). For him, it seems, these are the real and ultimate historical agents; with mere flesh-and-blood human beings their almost never mentioned creatures. He is even prepared outright to denounce "The assumption that the individual is more important than the group or class . . ." (p. 9).

(i)

The previous three paragraphs provide the perspective in which it becomes easy to clarify the issues in dispute: the issues between, on the one hand, Methodological Holism or Methodological Collectivism; and, on the other; Methodological Individualism. There is no need, for instance, for those espousing the latter and repudiating the former: either to deny any sort of reality at all to social wholes; or to maintain that all statements embracing social notions are by logical analysis reducible to statements referring only to single individuals. No such rash commitment is required by the determination to defend the simple truth of the first three paragraphs, and the important consequences to be derived therefrom.

Certainly the Methodological Individualist both can and should concede that, in a way, "The social group is *more* than the mere sum total of its members, and it is *more* than the mere sum total of the merely personal relationships existing at any moment between any of its members." And it is not merely "even conceivable" but a familiar fact "that a group may keep much of its original character even if *all* its original members are replaced by others" (Popper 1957, p. 17). For this is all true of a nation, or of a club, or of a social class.

But these admissions are not in the least inconsistent with the truth that, in the end and at bottom – as Marx put it in a letter to Annenkov – "the social history of men is never anything but the history of their individual development" (28 December 1846). This is the truth because everything done or suffered by the nation, or club, or class can be done or suffered only in the persons of its members; and because, if and when they and their successors are all dead, nothing will remain of that nation, or that club or that class – nothing, that is, save perhaps documents and memories in the possession of others.

(ii)

Again, the Methodological Individualist can afford to

concede the logical irreducibility of social facts and social concepts. And, as Thomas Carlyle (1795–1881) said of the lady who announced her acceptance of the Universe, "Gad, she'd better!" For 'social behaviour' was in Section 1 of the previous chapter, following Weber, defined as behaviour in which the agent "takes account of the behaviour of others". So there can be precious little if any social behaviour which we are able either to describe or to explain without the employment of concepts referring in some way to social institutions.

Take, for example, what two writers on *Rational Economic Man* offered as the nearest possible approach to a brute and atomic economic fact; an unexplained economic fact, that is, and one not susceptible of further analysis. Contending that "All facts are theory-laden and economic facts are 'visible' only to a man with the right economic concepts," they conclude: "Even if 'Raven no. 1 is black' can claim to be theory-free, 'George paid £1 for string' cannot" (Hollis and Nell 1975, pp. 96 and 108). Certainly no one could have access to either of these two facts without first mastering the relevant concepts. But this applies equally to both. Nor does it make the second either more theory-laden or less objective than the first. What is peculiar to that second specimen is its employment of the essentially and irreducibly social notion of money. For what is, in general, money and, in particular, one pound sterling is whatever the relevant social set is prepared to admit and to use as such.

The sort of thing which money is is central to most if not all the studies customarily rated social sciences. These have thus been "called the Appearance sciences – those concerned with the phenomena whose very essence it is that they 'mean' something to participants" (Gellner 1973, p. 152). As John Watkins puts it, pointing the Methodological Individualist moral, "Whereas physical things can exist unperceived, social 'things' like laws, prices, prime ministers and ration-books, are created by personal attitudes. (Remove the attitudes of food officials, shopkeepers, housewives, etc., towards ration-books and they shrivel into bits of cardboard.) But if social objects are formed by individual attitudes, an explanation

of their formation must be an individualistic explanation"
(O'Neill 1973, p. 150; and compare Hayek 1948, Ch. III and
Hayek 1979, Ch. 3).

Such explanation will not and cannot exclude references to
social groups or the use of social concepts. Nor does it have
to be only of the sort which the individuals concerned might
offer for their own actions. But what is imperatively required
is that everyone should recognize, and never forget, that all
social activities, and the operations of all social institutions,
are and cannot but be the actions of individual human beings.
Therefore, whatever else may be added by way of further
explanation in answer to further questions, all those actions
must be explicable, and at least in principle explained, in
terms available to, and understandable by, the agents at the
time of their acting.

(iii)

Consider, for instance the "general and obvious statement"
that "no superior knowledge the observer may possess about
the object, but which is not possessed by the acting person,
can help us in understanding the motives of their actions"
(Hayek 1948, p. 60). To this May Brodbeck responds with a
rhetorical question: ". . . can anyone, at this stage of the
game, really believe that to explain people's actions we need
to know no more than they do, not only about the external
world, but about themselves?" (O'Neill 1973, p. 95).

Suppose now that the announcer who read out the sentence, which in fact signalled the revolt of the four insurgent
generals and the beginning of the 1936–9 Spanish Civil War,
was not himself party to the plot. Then no explanation of
why he performed the speech act of announcing, "There is
a clear sky over Spain", could correctly refer to his intentions
to signal a military coup. For, by the hypothesis, he could
have had no such intention. The historian, however, trying
to piece together his account of how the coup was organized
and launched, does need to know what the announcer at the

time did not; and also how the plotters contrived to get that sentence inserted into his script.

A more sociological and hence more piquant example is provided by Durkheim. Reviewing, in the December 1897 issue of the *Revue Philosophique*, Labriola's *Essays on the Materialist Conception of History*, Durkheim wrote: "I consider extremely fruitful this idea that social life should be explained, not by the notions of those who participate in it, but by more profound causes which are unperceived by consciousness, and I think also that these causes are to be sought mainly in the manner according to which the associated individuals are grouped."

But earlier, in *The Rules of Sociological Method*, when trying to decide whether either or both of two recorded correlations manifested any causal connection, he tackled the task in a different and more Methodologically Individualist way. The correlation between secularization and suicide, rather than that between education and suicide, has to be causal if either is. Why? Because Durkheim cannot think of any psychological process through which the acquisition of secular knowledge could weaken the instinct for self-preservation, whereas the loss of the traditional belief that God punishes suicides by tormenting them for ever is, obviously, the removal of a powerful inhibition (Durkheim 1895, pp. 131ff.).

2   Society as the supposed universal agent

The previous Section 1 dealt with two untenable positions which Methodological Individualists are not required to occupy. What they do have to do – resolutely, systematically and persistently – is to refuse to treat any of the most numerous outcomes of various social arrangements, those outcomes which were not in fact planned and intended, as if they were, what by the hypothesis they are not, the planned and intended consequences of the actions of some super-agent, or of some committee of such super-agents.

(i)

The expression 'the conspiracy theory of society' was introduced more than forty-five years ago, as a label for the
assumption that all outcomes, or at any rate all disagreeable
outcomes, are in fact planned and intended (Popper 1945,
II, pp. 94–5). It has turned out to be a rather unfortunate coinage, commonly misused to warrant unargued and
contemptuous dismissals of evidence for the existence of
conspiracies which may well exist, or even certainly do (Flew
1975, 4.22 and 4.23).

The point which it was originally coined to illuminate is,
nevertheless, hugely important. For all of us and, it sometimes seems, not least those with claims to have enjoyed a
training in, or pretensions to be actually pursuing, social
science, are inclined to detect intention and planning where
no intention or planning is, or was. As a first, piquant though
antique example consider a passage from *The Condition of The
Working Class in England*. Here the revolutionary denounces,
as the calculated consummation of capitalist conspiracy, what
the social scientist cannot but recognize to have been an
unintended consequence of intended action: "To such an
extent has the convenience of the rich been considered in the
planning of Manchester that the plutocrats can travel . . . by
the shortest routes, without even realizing how close they are
to the misery and filth which lie on both sides of the road."

But then, having denounced "this hypocritical town-plan-
ning device", Engels concedes "that, owing to the nature of
their business, shopkeepers inevitably seek premises in main
thoroughfares . . . and . . . the value of land is higher on
or near a main thoroughfare than in the back streets." So
that was how this "hypocritical" result came about, without
direct intention, and in "the very town in which building has
taken place with little or no planning or interference from
the authorities" (Engels 1845, pp. 55–6).

(ii)

A second, more nearly contemporary example was provided

by *New Society*, a weekly which pretended to do for the
social sciences what *New Scientist* still does for the natural.
Commenting on the results of the second UK General Election of 1974 the first leading article in *New Society* began:
" 'Now go back and get on with governing the country' –
this sounds like the main message from the electorate to
their (mainly) reelected MPs" (31 October 1974). It went on,
with its attention concentrated exclusively upon the House of
Commons, to consider two possible dangers: "the oppression
of the majority by a coalition of minorities"; and "the oppression of a bare minority by a bare majority."

But, of course, it is not the case that either British Society in general or those millions of individuals who turned
out and voted constitute a single organism with a perhaps
enigmatic will, which chose a Parliament with a particular
party constitution. In fact every voter voted for one or other
of an always fairly short list of candidates: voters had no
other choice. When we look at these choices, which were
that leader-writer's only evidence for determining the will of
the electorate, we see that it was not a bare majority of the
electorate, but fractionally less than 40 per cent, which put
its individual crosses against the name of the local candidate
of the party which achieved a parliamentary majority.

The surely scandalous fact, concealed by this leader-writer's
mystificatory personification of the British Electorate, is that
the result of that election, as of every other General Election
for the last fifty-six years, has been the oppression of the
majority by a minority. No party since 1935, not even Labour
in 1945, has won an absolute majority of all votes cast; and
there has always been a large proportion even of individual
constituencies in which a majority of voters voted against the
candidate elected. Such are the effects of a monstrously
unfair, unrepresentative and undemocratic electoral system.

But the moral for us now is that what social science is
wanted and needed for is, not to conceal and to mystify,
but to reveal and to clarify, the actual workings of our
social institutions. The business of social science is to reveal
the unintended consequences of intended actions, displaying

them as such. So it is precisely not to hypothesize a many-headed monster called Society or the British Electorate, and then to attribute to that mythical, superhuman beast intentions to produce consequences which were not and, through the actually operative electoral institutions, could not have been, produced intentionally.

(iii)

Among those studying or discussing who ends up holding what capitals and enjoying what incomes, it is the almost universal practice to speak of showing how *Society* distributes *its* wealth and *its* income. But in most of the countries to which such studies and discussions refer there is in fact no such centralized, active and controlled distribution. No super-person and no committee decides what everyone is to have and to hold.

The usual response to this objection when, very rarely, it is heard at all is to try to dismiss it as a mere matter of words. The tactic is to suggest that any proposed alternative is substantially synonymous. Therefore, we are asked to believe, the present objection is on all fours with that of the purist protesting at the introduction of the expression 'societal members' as a jargon substitute for 'people', or preferring 'car' and 'lift' to those terse Americanisms 'automobile' and 'elevator'. But the truth is, rather, that it is that usual response which itself parallels the performance of someone saying that the argument among the jury as to whether their Foreman is to say 'Guilty' or 'Not Guilty' is an argument about a mere matter of words. For there the alternatives are not synonymous but actually incompatible, and their alternative implications make a difference – possibly even a life-or-death difference.

The importance of this misemployment of the active word 'distribution' comes out very clearly when we examine what has perhaps been the most influential work of social philosophy published since World War II. For in what he

miscalls *A Theory of Justice* John Rawls from the beginning
implicitly assumes: both that the distribution of all goods
of every kind is or ought to be an activity consciously and
deliberately performed by central authority; and that all
such goods, whether already produced or in the future to
be produced, are available for such distribution or redistribution free of all prior claims of possession or entitlement.
It remains for him simply, or not so simply, to work out the
principles which ideally ought to guide all such distributions
or redistributions.

Those enormous and unargued assumptions are entrenched
in his very definition (not of 'justice' but) of 'social justice'. This
is, he says, concerned with "the basic structure of society, or
more exactly, the way in which *the major social institutions
distribute fundamental rights and duties and determine the division
of advantages from social cooperation* . . . The justice of a social
scheme depends on how fundamental rights and duties are
assigned" (Rawls 1971, p. 7: italics supplied). As he begins, so
he continues: "For simplicity, assume that the chief primary
goods *at the disposition of society* are rights and liberties, powers
and opportunities, income and wealth . . . All social values –
liberty and opportunity, income and wealth, and the bases
of self respect – *are to be distributed* equally unless an unequal
distribution is to everyone's advantage" (p. 62: italics again
supplied).

This is not the place for any examination of the principles
proposed, although I have myself had some say elsewhere
(Flew 1981, Chs. III and IV). But we do have to emphasize
once more how enormous are the two assumptions to which
Rawls has, apparently all unwitting, helped himself; and how
formidable is the task of justification to which he would
be committed had he not tacitly taken it for granted that
such universal active distributions are everywhere occurring,
accepted, and acceptable. For there are or will be prior
claimants on all the various goods so far produced and in
the future to be produced. So Rawls needs to show that all
these claims ought to be of no account compared with those
of his would-be all-providing state.

It has been argued that this most fundamental objection is met by the attempted derivation of his proposed principles from a hypothetical contract hypothetically made behind a Veil of Ignorance by citizens all themselves hypothetically deindividualized. But, so far from meeting the objection, this proposed response reveals that it has not even been understood. For, waiving all questions about the validity of the putative derivation, the crucial counter to that response is that principles which perhaps would be or would have been adopted under conditions which never have been realized are entirely irrelevant to present questions about the justice or injustice of the claims of actual individuals to what we have honestly acquired and hope in the future to acquire. There is here an enormous unrecognized problem of delegitimation. This has first to be solved if Rawls and his like are to justify their massive unnoticed assumption that all goods, whether already produced or to be produced in future, are available, free of all morally legitimate prior claims, for centrally directed, state-enforced redistribution.

A final, unfriendly comment upon all such redistributive projects comes, perhaps surprisingly, from Otto von Bismarck. It is often forgotten that it was he and not any more recent Socialist or Social-Democratic politician who established the first modern Welfare State. No doubt for reasons of *realpolitik* rather than out of any generalized benevolence, his project was to establish a minimum – a safety net or a welfare floor as the later Conservative phrases had it. It was certainly not universal and total public provision, much less the Radical state-enforced equalization of everybody's condition. Thus he said to the Imperial Reichstag (17 September 1878): "If every man has to have his share allotted to him from above, we arrive at a kind of prison existence where everyone is at the mercy of the warders. And in our modern prisons the warder is at any rate a recognized official, against whom one can lodge a complaint. But who will be the warders in the general socialist prison? There will be no question of lodging complaints against them, they will be the most merciless tyrants ever seen, and the rest will be the slaves of the tyrants" (quoted Schwartzschild 1948, p. 364).

(iv)

To speak of Society distributing wealth and income where there is no active, central distribution is lamentably careless; and can be, as we have just seen, very seriously misleading. But the next pair of cases calls for a much stronger condemnation. For here we have two notions introduced and strenuously propagated in the name of social scientific enlightenment; the notions, that is, of institutionalized violence and institutionalized racism. These new notions suggest, and are surely intended to suggest, that many things which are not in fact the intended results of intended action, on the contrary, in fact are. And, furthermore, these notions are being widely and energetically employed in order to incite the victims of the suggested sinister intentions to react in ways which all would agree to be appropriate if, but only if, their supposed victimization was indeed intended.

As was pointed out earlier in the present Section 2, thus to misrepresent as intended what was not intended is the very reverse of what social scientists should be doing. Yet it constitutes a paradigm case of what one Professor of Sociology quoted in Chapter 2 maintained to be the nature of the subject which he professes. For such institutionalized violence and institutionalized racism do indeed "acquire their character . . . as describable objects only through the grace of sociological imputation."

Consider first structural or institutionalized violence. Violence in the original and proper sense of the word is essentially intentional. A paradigm case of your doing violence to me would be your striking me in a way calculated to cause grievous bodily harm. The reason, furthermore, why people react to injuries caused by violence in ways different from those in which they react to injuries not so caused precisely is that they do, correctly, perceive the injuries caused by violence as intended. This perception is clearly relevant to questions about the relevance of their various reactions since, whereas intenders may possibly be constrained, deterred or punished, neither constraint, not deterrence, nor punishment can be applied without an intending agent.

It is remarkable that in recent years several scholars have contrived to overlook one or both of these defining characteristics: that the injury done is physical; and that it is done intentionally. Thus an academic lawyer, of all people, writes in a BBC publication *The Lawbreakers*: "Why then is violent behaviour perceived as so socially problematic? The answer may seem obvious: because it injures people. However, upon closer examination, such an answer turns out to be inadequate. Other forms of behaviour which are not legally or commonly defined as violence turn out to be much more injurious."

But what is supposed to be the full, true and sociologically sophisticated answer comes from the man who was to become Professor of Sociology in the Open University, writing to assist the Department of Health and Social Security (DHSS) with his social scientific wisdom: ". . . to understand why we fear certain behaviour of young people we must explain how that behaviour comes to be classified as violent behaviour." It seems that it becomes so classified by the fiat of the press or of TV, which "gives it a certain meaning". Events which are, presumably, in themselves unobjectionable are thus made to frighten people. A "moral panic" ensues (quoted Morgan, 1978, Ch. 3).

It is, therefore, not surprising that those subject to such indoctrinated scotoma, capable of this degree of perversity in hypothesis, should be receptive to a concept of institutionalized or structural violence; a concept which permits them to include as the effects of violence every variety of injury and misfortune, including those involving no physical injury, and also including, indeed including especially, injuries and misfortunes not in fact intentionally inflicted. And, even though they may themselves not have noticed either that true violence is essentially intentional or that it is this logical fact which supports the disturbing and affronting overtones of the word, they are nevertheless bound to think, because ingrained speech habits are just as hard to break as any other ingrained habits, that all these things must be, as the effects of violence, intended. Any society, or usually it is only any society not yet fully socialist, thus becomes one in which all the ills to which flesh is heir are inflicted intentionally. It is manifest that such a society can be redeemed, if at all, only by the most total revolutionary transformation.

(v)

The second member of this pair of factitious concepts is that of structural or institutionalized racism. Now racism, in the only proper sense of that properly abusive word, is an essentially intentional as well as an utterly deplorable business. It is a matter of advantaging or disadvantaging people for no other or better reason than they are members of some particular favoured or disfavoured racial set. It is essential to make this particular definition explicit, and to insist upon it. For many people rush to condemn racism and racists without first explaining either what is the kind of behaviour being denounced or why such behaviour is being taken to be morally beyond the pale. Given the definition just proposed the answers to both questions are obvious. The morally obnoxious kind of behaviour is advantaging or disadvantaging people for no other or better reason than that they belong to one particular racial set and not another. And this is self-evidently wrong, because self-evidently unfair and unjust.

Some people prefer to follow some usually unformulated definition making racism partly or even wholly a matter of holding and expressing the allegedly false belief that there are, at least on average, some substantial and sometimes occupationally relevant, hereditarily determined differences between the memberships of some different racial sets. But any definition of the term requiring sincere anti-racists to reject all such suggestions should be put down as altogether unacceptable and obnoxious. For so defining the word makes racism, in the most literal sense, a heresy. Heretics are anathematized not for what they do or fail to do but simply for holding what are alleged to be false beliefs. And if this is what racism is to be, then we are left with no warrant for denouncing the racist as wicked. Of what moral fault are such heretics supposed to be guilty – always, of course, providing that their convictions result from honest, open-minded, truth-directed critical enquiry? (Flew 1976, I 5; and compare Palmer 1986, Ch. 1 and passim.)

The meaning of the key term 'racism' now firmly fixed in mind, the next task is to distinguish two crucially different concepts of institutionalized racism: one legitimate and unproblematic; and the other not. In the legitimate and unproblematic understanding – we might label it 'institutionalized racism' (actual) – institutionalized racism was what you had in South Africa under full Apartheid, or in National Socialist Germany after the proclamation of the Nuremberg decrees. In such cases we can quite properly say that racism was or is institutionalized. For there are various laws and regulations which specifically mandate what therefore cannot but be intentional discrimination on the basis of racial set membership.

In the illegitimate and problematic understanding – let us speak with studied offensiveness of 'institutionalized racism' (factitious) – institutionalized racism is discovered wherever in any occupation, social class, residential area, or whatever else any racial set is not 'represented' in as near as makes no odds the same proportion as in the population as a whole. It is not necessary to show that anyone actually has exercised any racial preference, or that anyone actually has gained or suffered by reason of the mere fact of their racial set membership. On the contrary; it is quite sufficient simply and solely to show that, for whatever reason, some racial set is in fact, relative to the population as a whole, either under-represented in some enviable or over-represented in some unenviable occupation, social class, residential area, or whatever else.

Institutionalized racism (factitious) is thus effectively

defined in terms not of discriminatory intentions but of differential outcomes. One particular formulation – widely employed by LEAs during the eighties to guide and justify policies adopted in the name of anti-racism, and one which a major British official report recently went out of its way to commend – began by talking of "certain routine practices, customs and procedures in our society whose consequence is that black people have poorer jobs, health, housing and life-chances than do the white majority . . . 'Racism' is a shorthand term for this combination . . ." (The word 'black' is previously redefined to embrace all non-whites: in part, presumably, in order to conceal the fact that some racially defined subsets were in many ways doing as well as or better than the white average.)

In this understanding racism is defined specifically in terms of differential consequences rather than discriminating intentions. But for those who insist on employing this concept it is easy and also tempting to make invalid inferences directly from such consequences to such intentions. This is tempting because, as was remarked earlier in connection with the correspondingly factitious notion of institutionalized violence, it is human nature to be much more upset about whatever are seen as evils when these are believed to be or to have been intended. Everyone vigorously committed to opposing something they hold to be evil therefore has an interest in making out that that evil is the intended result of intended action.

So anyone who holds any form of relative disadvantage for any set of people – any 'inequality' – to be evil will have an interest in making out that that relative disadvantage was in fact brought about and is still maintained intentionally. Nowadays the observed relative advantage or relative disadvantage of various racially defined sets is very frequently mistaken to license direct inferences to racist causes for all such offending relativities. The employment of the factitious concept of institutionalized racism encourages such fallacious thinking.

That in turn plays a large part in widespread developments providing practically important illustrations of the way in which intended actions may eventually have consequences opposite to those originally intended. These are developments which cannot but outrage everyone sincerely and clearheadedly opposed to every form of racism. For in several countries laws originally passed and organizations originally formed in order to promote equality of opportunity and combat racism either have already resulted or are tending to result in the actual institutionalization of the very evils which they were supposedly intended to combat.

So far this process has advanced much farther in the USA than in the UK. For instance: there are now frequent reports coming from several of the most highly regarded US universities that the levels of performance on the misnamed Scholastic Aptitude Tests (SATs) which are required for admission vary sharply with the racial set membership of the candidates; much lower than average levels being demanded from black and, consequently, much higher from such notorious high achievers as Chinese or Japanese Americans. (For an international survey of such preferential policies see Sowell 1990. This shows that, however impeccable the original intentions, these policies tend everywhere eventually to promote disharmony and sometimes violent conflict between the sets favoured and consequently disfavoured others.)

Let Section 2 conclude with a choice item from an ever-fattening file. Recently, in his regular column for *The Washington Times* the distinguished (and, as it happens, black) economist Walter Williams referred to the examinations for promotion to the rank of Sergeant in the New York City Police. These have already been revised three times, most recently at a cost of $100,000, to remove any possible racial bias. Yet the pass marks remain racially defined: 75 per cent for whites; 69 per cent for Hispanics; and 65 per cent for blacks. Could any invented illustration be more flagrant than this actual instance of institutionalized racism (actual)?

3   Equality: of opportunity, or of outcome

The crudest form of fallacy is to argue that wherever there
is institutionalized racism (factitious), there the many-headed,
supra-personal monster Society must be guilty of (necessarily
intentional) racist behaviour. Researches into the proportionate under- and over-representation of subsets, and disputes
about the significance of the findings of these researches are,
however, by no means limited to cases where the subsets in
question are defined racially. Once we begin to consider
such researches in general, and without particular limitation,
we soon discover further and somewhat more sophisticated
possibilities of error.

(i)

Suppose someone argues, as so many do, like this. Because
members of some subset of an entire population (the set)
are not represented in some occupation or organization or
whatever in at least roughly the same proportion as in the
set as a whole; therefore there must here have been some
defection from the ideal of equality of opportunity; presumably because members of that subset were either beneficiaries
of favouritism or victims of hostile discrimination.

Once this currently popular form of argument is thus
clearly spelt out, it becomes obvious that it can go through
only on the basis of a very big assumption; the assumption
that, save in respect of whatever may be their defining
characteristics, the members of the subsets in question are
not *on average* in any relevant ways different from members
of the population as a whole (the set). Given that this big
assumption was true – given, that is, that the distribution
of abilities, inclinations, trainings, temperaments, characters,
values, metaphysical beliefs and so on was substantially the
same as between set and subsets – then it would indeed
become reasonable to expect, absent either hostile or favourable discrimination, that there would be at least a roughly

proportionate 'representation' of those subsets everywhere throughout the society as a whole.

Yet to precisely the extent that there is any real point in picking out a particular subset for this treatment – to precisely the extent, that is, that its members see themselves and/or are seen as somehow distinct and different from the set as a whole – that crucial assumption must appear very implausible. Nevertheless in practice it is one for which evidence is very rarely asked, and almost never offered. Just so soon as anyone makes a serious attempt to discover what in any such case the facts actually are, the truth emerges that they are certainly not as they are so widely assumed and expected to be.

By far and away the best and most abundant source is the works of another distinguished American and, as it happens, again black economist, Thomas Sowell. The fact that, up to the time of writing, no copies of any of these works were held by the Library of the Commission for Racial Equality in London suggests that there is in and around that quango what Ernest Bramah's Kai Lung would have called "a well-sustained no-enthusiasm" for the discovery and spread of information indicating that the proper scope for its activities may be much narrower than its employees would wish.

For us perhaps the most useful of Sowell's books is his *Ethnic America: A History* (1981). This studies and compares the track records of all the major sets of immigrants, as distinguished by country of origin. His most relevant finding is innumerable, often very large differences in the rapidity and the nature of the achievements: differences which simply cannot be explained by reference to either hostile or favourable discrimination. For instance: black immigrants from the formerly British Caribbean, who are not visibly different from native-born American blacks, and who have – we may therefore presume – suffered exactly the same amount of hostile discrimination, do very much better. Whereas the average income of native-born American blacks is still well below the average income of all Americans, that of those deriving fairly immediately from the Caribbean is now marginally above that average. The parents of General Colin Powell, for instance, the US Chief of Staff who appeared in every other TV news bulletin throughout the Gulf War, came from Jamaica.

In *Ethnic America*, and in several other books (1975, 1983 and 1987), Sowell presents case after case to show that, and with what effects, the distribution of relevant characteristics in all the most often distinguished subsets can differ, often very widely, from the distribution in the set or subsets with which that particular subset is being compared. Just one or two examples will have to suffice.

First: both achieved fertilities and average ages of marriage differ sharply as between different ethnic sets. This has implications both for the average ages of those sets and for the willingness of their members to embark upon protracted, poorly paid, courses of career preparation. So, because levels of earning are highly correlated with both age and the extensiveness of preparatory training, the extreme differences between the US ethnic set with the highest average income and some of the sets with the lowest is to be explained in large part, though not of course entirely, by a corresponding extreme difference in average ages. American Jews constitute the set with the top earnings, and their average age is over twice that of the lowest earners.

Second: if we are thinking about the often very substantial differences which are found in most if not all countries between the earnings of men and women we have always to allow for marriage and its very different effects on these two sets. For instance: first studies of the earnings of men and women university teachers in the USA suggested gross sex or – as it is now fashionable to say – gender discrimination. But a more sophisticated analysis revealed that, whereas married women did significantly worse than married men, among those who had never married the women did significantly better than the men. These two examples should at least be enough to show that, for anyone wishing to reach correct conclusions about such comparisons, rather than conclusions which are popular or congenially 'user-friendly' there is no substitute for a study of Sowell's writings.

(ii)

Both the unwarranted assumptions discussed in the previous subsection and the consequent equally unwarranted expectations are by now entrenched in the theory and practice of most organizations charged or charging themselves with the tasks of promoting equalities of opportunity and/or combating racist or sexist discrimination. So we should not be surprised to find Lester Thurrow, an economist who was to serve as an economic adviser to Senator McGovern as a Presidential candidate and to other later leaders of the US Democratic Party, in a book entitled *Poverty and Discrimination*, simply defining 'discrimination' as the cause of all actual differences in life-prospects (Thurrow 1969, p. 9).

The same entrenchment of fallacy and falsehood is manifested also in the ambiguous misemployment of the word 'access'. The fact that you are in certainly proves that you were able to get in. *Ab esse ad posse valet consequentia,* as the Scholastics loved to say: the argument from actuality to possibility is valid. But the fact that you are not in does not prove that you could not have got in; much less that you were 'denied access'.

A suitable textbook example of these faults, found in the report of a major sociological survey, is provided by Raymond Boudon, who previously wrote the Penguin Books guide to *The Logic of Sociological Explanation*. His own later study of *Education, Opportunity and Social Inequality* is introduced in the USA by Seymour Martin Lipset as the work of "France's leading sociological theoretician and methodologist"; who, fittingly, "holds the chair at Paris once occupied by Durkheim" (Boudon 1974, pp. vi and vii). On the first page of his own Preface Boudon defines 'inequality of educational *opportunity* (IEO)' as "differences in the level of educational *attainment* according to social background". From this definition he immediately infers that "a society is characterized by a certain amount of IEO if, for instance, the probability of going to college is smaller for a worker's son than for a lawyer's son" (1974, p. xi: emphasis added). Next 'inequality of social opportunity (ISO)' is defined similarly. The parallel immediate consequence is that "a society is characterized by a certain amount of ISO if the probability of reaching a high social status is smaller for the former child than for the latter" (p. xi).

Boudon thus from the beginning collapses not just one but two crucial distinctions. For he is not only confounding outcome with opportunity. He is also failing to distinguish: on the one hand, the question whether contestants were treated fairly – whether, that is, they were all accorded the chance to compete on equal terms; and, on the other hand, the question of who, even given such ideally fair competitive conditions, was in fact most likely to win. The actual chances (probabilities) of success will be equal for all contestants only if and where those contestants all happen to be in all relevant respects equally well endowed and equally well disposed.

It is, sadly, as unsurprising as it is significant that Alan Little, chosen to review Boudon's book for *New Society*, completely missed these points. Having faithfully quoted both of Boudon's disastrous definitions, Little ended almost on his knees before such "originality in approach, a mixture of creative imagination and intellectual vigour, a continual juxtaposition of logic and fact, statistical sophistication, theoretical acumen and wide reading" (23 May 1974).

The significance of the whole incident is underlined by the further fact that it was not a sociologist, but rather the experimental psychologist H. J. Eysenck, who two weeks later intervened in the correspondence columns to remark: "Boudon constructs a whole model of education and social opportunity . . . very much as if every child . . . were an identical twin to every other child" (6 June 1974). Had Eysenck been willing to incur still greater unpopularity among professing social scientists, he might have added a mention of an extreme environmentalist ruling made in the *Encyclopaedia of the Social Sciences* at a time when the customer could have any colour he liked just so long as black was his beautiful: ". . . at birth human infants, regardless of heredity, are as equal as Fords" (quoted in Hayek 1978, p. 290).

5   Making Visible the Invisible Hands

> But it is only for the sake of profit that any man
> employs a capital in the support of industry. ... As
> every individual, therefore, endeavours as much as he
> can ... to employ his capital ... that its produce may
> be of the greatest value; every individual necessarily
> labours to render the annual revenue of the society as
> great as he can. He generally, indeed, neither intends
> to promote the public interest, nor knows how much he
> is promoting it. ... By directing ... industry in such
> a manner as its produce may be of the greatest value,
> he intends only his own gain, and he is, in this as in
> many other cases, led by an invisible hand to promote
> an end which was no part of his intentions. Nor is it
> always the worse for the society that it was no part of
> it. By pursuing his own interest he frequently promotes
> that of the society more effectually than when he really
> intends to promote it.
>
> Adam Smith, *An Inquiry into the Nature and*
> *Causes of the Wealth of Nations,* IV (ii).

This motto passage must be in all *The Wealth of Nations* the
one to which reference is most often made. It can well bear
all, indeed rather more than all, the attention which it does
in fact get. For very few even of those who have actually read
it seem to become seized of its full significance. I myself met
it first nearly forty-five years ago, as an undergraduate in
the University of Oxford. It was cited then in a popular
series of lectures given by G. D. H. Cole, the then Chichele
Professor of Political and Social Theory. Like most of us in
his audience, Cole could see nothing more here than the
occasion for a swift passing sneer. This was, after all, merely
a piece of apologetics for those obviously outmoded and altogether indefensible arrangements called by Cole laissez-faire

capitalism; the arrangements which Smith himself knew only as "the natural system of perfect liberty and justice", or "the obvious and simple system of natural liberty" (A. Smith, IV (vii) 2 and IV (ix)). To such principled secularists as Cole this particular defence was made the more repugnant by what we misinterpreted as the suggestion that these ongoings are benevolently guided by the Invisible Hand of an All-wise Providence.

Certainly Cole and the rest of us were right to see in this passage some defence of pluralistic and competitive capitalism. For it does indeed offer, for that and against monopoly socialist alternatives, an argument far more power-ful than anything which Cole was able to recognize; or, I will now add, to meet. But where we were utterly wrong was in suspecting Smith of making some sort of anti-scientific appeal to supernatural intervention. On the contrary: this text is a landmark in the history of the growth of the social sciences. For – almost a century before Darwin's *Origin* – Smith was uncovering a mechanism by which something strongly suggesting design might, indeed must, come about quite spontaneously and without direction.

Like so much else in Smith, the argument here begins from an uncynical yet coolly realistic appreciation of our human nature. Any political economy for this world must treat people as we are, not as we might become, yet will not. As George Stigler said in a volume of bicentennial essays: "*The Wealth of Nations* is a stupendous palace erected on the granite of self-interest" (Skinner and Wilson 1976, p. 237). It is indeed; Scottish granite, and erected also on Scottish self-reliance: "It is not from the benevolence of the butcher, the brewer or the baker that we expect our dinner, but from their regard to their own interest. We address ourselves, not to their humanity but to their self-love, and never talk to them of our own necessities but of their advantages. Nobody but a beggar chooses to depend chiefly upon the benevolence of his fellow-citizens" (A. Smith 1776, I, ii).

Put in marginally more modern terms, the nub of Smith's argument is that the most productive, the most wealth-creating, the most economically efficient investment decisions are likely to be made by persons who have some large and direct personal interest in achieving the most satisfactory combination of the maximum security of, and the maximum return on, the capital employed. Of course there is no guarantee that all such persons will get all their decisions right. Even those who do turn out usually to have spotted winners will sometimes pick losers. It is indeed precisely because things are so difficult, and so apt to come unstuck, that anyone concerned to increase the wealth of nations has such an excellent reason for wanting to have the crucial initiatives made, the crucial initiatives taken, always and only by directly and appropriately interested parties.

Also, where and in so far as people are – as Smith nicely has it – "investing their own capitals", the unsuccessful will, to the extent that they have made bad investments, necessarily be deprived of opportunity to make further costly mistakes; while the successful will, by a parallel necessity, be enabled to proceed to further and hopefully greater successes. Smith himself appears not to have seized this additional point about feedback, although it must be of the last importance in any consideration of alternative ways of providing for the taking of economic initiatives.

1   Smith and the other Scottish Founding Fathers

So far we have been giving general consideration to Smith's argument that a free capital market, with all the individual owners of capital seeking the best possible return on any investment made, must tend to maximize the gross national product. It is time to concentrate upon one particular sentence: ". . . he intends only his own gain and he is, in this as in many other cases, led by an invisible hand to promote an end which was no part of his intentions". It is on his attention, "in this as in many other cases", to such unintended consequences of intended action that Smith's claim to have been one of the Founding Fathers of the social sciences must rest.

(i)

To understand that claim is to realize how totally wrong it must be to construe Smith's invisible hand as an instrument of supernatural direction. To do this would be as preposterous as to interpret Darwin's natural selection as being really supernatural selection. For Smith's invisible hand is no more a hand directed by a rational owner than Darwin's natural selection by supernatural intelligence. As was suggested earlier, both Smith and Darwin were showing how something which one might be very tempted to put down to design could and indeed must come about: in the one case without direction, in that direction; and in the other without any direction at all. By uncovering the mechanisms operative in the two cases they both made supernatural intervention superfluous as an explanation.

Adam Smith's invisible hand is not a hand, any more than Darwin's natural selection is selection. Or, putting the point in a somewhat more forced and technical way, 'invisible' and 'natural' are in these two cases just as much alienans adjectives as are 'imaginary' or 'positive' in the expressions 'imaginary apples' or 'positive freedom'. Alienans adjectives – this technical expression is part of our Scholastic inheritance – do not pick out a sub-class of that wider class to which their noun refers. Instead they indicate that it is not a sub-sort of that sort which is to be discussed. Imaginary apples are not, like Golden Delicious, a variety of apples; while positive freedom is not freedom at all, but being able but also required to act in whatever ways are approved by those commending certain courses of action as constituting exercises of positive freedom (Flew 1989a, Ch. 4).

(ii)

Nor, continuing, would it be fair to accuse Smith, as he so often is accused, of assuming or asserting that the unintended results of the operations of all such social mechanisms are always, if only in the long run, Providentially happy. (In the long run, as Lord Keynes famously remarked, we are all dead.)

The most elegant refutation of this charge against Smith can be drawn from his treatment of the division of labour. Certainly, he writes, this "is not originally the effect of any human wisdom, which foresees and intends the general opulence to which it gives occasion. It is the necessary though very slow and gradual consequence of a certain propensity in human nature which has in view no such extensive utility: the propensity to truck, barter, and exchange one thing with another" (A. Smith 1776, I, ii). But Smith himself goes on to describe and lament the dehumanizing consequences of the more extreme developments of this occasion of opulence. It is precisely these purple passages which find a place in *Capital*, colourfully adorning this part of the author's polemic (Marx 1867, I, pp. 362 and 459–60). It should nevertheless be noted, partly because it so infrequently is, that Marx himself has precious little to say about how socialism as centralized ownership and control is supposed to be going to achieve abundance without both the division of labour and, hence, the ills necessarily consequent thereon.

Another example of a social mechanism producing results not merely other than but even flat contrary to both the intentions and the best interests of the participants is 'The Tragedy of the Commons' (Hardin 1977). Where, without restrictions of private property, access to some resource is common to several, those sharing that access will all, and quite rationally, be inclined to make the most use they can of that resource. It will, therefore, tend to be wastefully and rapidly exhausted or destroyed; a result universally unintended and unwanted. In our contemporary world one appalling token of this type is the ruin of the Sahel. There, as the then UN Secretary-General Kurt Waldheim warned, "the encroachment of the desert threatens to wipe four or five African countries from the map". Certainly other causes have exacerbated the problem. But the basic trouble is that on unenclosed land no one has an individual interest in doing what stops, or not doing what starts, desertification (Burton

1978, pp. 69–91). Notoriously, as philosophers and others ought to have learnt first from the critique of Plato's *Republic* in Aristotle's *Politics*, everyone's business tends to be no one's. By contrast, as one of Smith's own younger contemporaries used to say: "Give a man the secure possession of a bleak rock and he will turn it into a garden: given him a nine years lease on a garden, and he will convert it into a desert." (That younger contemporary was Arthur Young, the first great agricultural journalist.)

(iii)

Nor was it only Smith who, "in this as in many other cases", was systematically developing this sort of approach to social phenomena. He was in fact one of a small group, a main part of "the Edinburgh Enlightenment". This group also included, among others, the sometime Chaplain to the Black Watch and later Edinburgh professor Adam Ferguson, William Robertson, and – slightly older and starting to publish much earlier – David Hume.

It is to the point here to recall that Hume presented his own first published work not as an essay in conceptual analysis but as *A Treatise of Human Nature*; "an attempt to introduce the experimental Method of Reasoning into Moral Subjects". The word 'moral' in this subtitle is roughly equivalent to 'human'; as in the fossil phrase 'moral sciences', preserved in its ancient meaning by the University of Cambridge until well into the second half of the present century. The word 'experimental', as Hume's Introduction eventually makes clear, should have been replaced by 'experiential'. His list here of his major recent predecessors excludes Berkeley, but, most significantly, includes Bernard de Mandeville (1670–1733). This Anglo-Dutch doctor with a French name published in 1723 the final and fullest version of *The Fable of the Bees, or Private Vices, Public Benefits*. This mischievously provocative yet profoundly unfrivolous work is increasingly recognized as another landmark in the history of the development of the social sciences. (Anyone who appreciates Mandeville will get

similar pleasure and profit from Walter Block's equally mischievous yet perhaps even more seriously purposed *Defending
the Undefendable*.)

Hume's characteristic contentions, even where he is dealing
with what is in the narrowest sense most strictly philosophical,
clear the way for the open-minded discovery of causes which
are altogether unlike their effects: "If we reason apriori",
he argues in *An Enquiry concerning Human Understanding*,
"anything may appear able to produce anything" (Hume
1748, p. 64); whereas the contrary assumption "is the bane
of all reasoning and free inquiry" (p. 26). Indeed it is; and,
above all, this is true in the areas of social science and
social policy. For, especially but not only when partisan
passions are running high, we are all tempted to argue from
(sometimes falsely) attributed intentions to actual outcomes;
without labouring to investigate whether what has in fact
resulted falls short of, exceeds, or simply differs from what
those attributed intentions might have led us to expect. The
burden of Hume's great negative thesis about causality is,
in our present context, that the unintended consequences
of intended actions may be altogether surprising, and are
certainly not to be determined apriori. ('Apriori' – which,
since it has been a landed immigrant for over a quarter of a
millennium, I insist on rendering as a single unitalicized word
– means without or prior to investigation.)

One astonishing example of such unsound argument from
intention to effect should alert us all. It has, as was remarked
in Chapter 2, long been customary for successive Ministers
of Education of both main parties in Britain to boast that
they and their parties have increased the amounts spent per
pupil head and the total numbers of teachers employed,
have 'improved' the teacher/pupil ratios, and so on. They
then infer: because the intention has been to ensure that
pupils learn more, and better; therefore the educational
results must have been as near as makes no matter precisely
proportionate to the educationally intended expenditure.

In spokespersons for the teachers' unions this argument,
and the unwarranted assumptions upon which it is based, are,

no doubt, unsurprising. But it should be shocking to find a Minister, who before becoming a Member of Parliament had been a Fellow and Tutor in Economics, arguing in calm and considered print: ". . . expenditure on education rose from 4.8 per cent of GNP in 1964 to 6.1 per cent in 1970. As a result, all classes of the community enjoyed significantly more education than before" (Crosland 1976, p. 20).

The second proposition thus appears to be being asserted here as an immediate inference from the first. Certainly only one further reason is offered to sustain that conclusion: "The huge expansion in the supply of teachers produced a steady reduction in the pupil/teacher ratio." That such a reduction, and the corresponding increase in the teacher/pupil ratio, is bound to produce educational improvement, all other things being equal, is another of those common assumptions for which adequate evidence is rarely asked and almost never offered. Even if it is correct, we still need to know the answer to the question with which the Irish poet W. B. Yeats greeted the news that he had won the Nobel Prize for Literature: "How much? How much?" For without answering that further question we cannot rationally decide how to allocate available resources so as to achieve the best possible results: more, or still more on this; or more, or still more, on that?

To return to Hume. His undogmatic and openminded approach became characteristic of all the leading members of "the Edinburgh Enlightenment". Robertson, for instance, in a long methodological note to the Proofs and Illustrations of his *History of Scotland,* first published in 1759, compares the institutions and customs of the Germans, as seen by Caesar and Tacitus, with those of the North American Indians, as studied by Father Charlevoix and Monsieur Lafitour. It is a remarkable insistence upon fundamental uniformity underlying enormous variety: "A philosopher", Robertson concludes, "will satisfy himself with observing, that the characters of nations depend on the state of society in which they live, and on the political institutions established among them; and that the human mind, whenever it is placed in the same situation, will in ages the most distant and in countries the most remote, assume the same form, and be distinguished by the same manners" (Robertson 1890, I, p. 372).

Later, in his *History of America*, first published in 1777, one year after *The Wealth of Nations*, Robertson unwittingly staked a claim to have anticipated Marx in formulating what came to be called (not A but) *The* Materialist Conception of History: "In every inquiry concerning the operations of men when united together in society, the first object of attention should be their mode of subsistence. Accordingly, as that varies, their laws and policy must be different (II, p. 104. Since Marx certainly knew the works of Robertson and Ferguson as well as Smith, Marx could have been borrowing).

(iv)

In the same eighteenth century, but with no other connection with these Edinburgh social scientists, we find John Wesley analysing an unwelcome yet apparently inevitable development in the movement which he founded: "I fear, wherever riches have increased, the essence of religion has decreased in the same proportion. Therefore I do not see how it is possible, in the nature of things, for any revival of true religion to continue long. For religion must necessarily produce both industry and frugality, and these cannot but produce riches. But as riches increase, so will pride, anger and love of the world in all its branches. How then is it possible that Methodism, a religion of the heart, though it flourishes now as a green bay tree, should continue in this state? For the Methodists in every place grow diligent and frugal; consequently they increase in goods. Hence they proportionately increase in pride, in anger, in the desire of the flesh, the desire of the eyes, and the pride of life. So, although the form of religion remains, the spirit is swiftly vanishing away" (Runciman 1978, p. 165: a British colleague drew Weber's attention to this passage, which Weber quotes in his famous article on 'The Protestant Ethic and the "Spirit" of Capitalism').

2 *Intended actions and unintended consequences*

What in the first place Smith is pointing to in our motto
paragraph is a mechanism by which a certain sort of intended
action produces unintended consequences. And, even if not
the whole, it is certainly a main part of the truth about the
social sciences that "They are concerned with man's actions,
and their aim is to explain the unintended or undesigned
results of the actions of many men" (Hayek 1978, p. 41). A
second point to emphasize is that what Smith and the others
were offering was evolutionary as opposed to creationist.

A sophisticated capital market is not put together over-
night, to open on a statutorily determined Vesting Day;
and the division of labour "is not originally the effect of
any human wisdom. . . . It is the necessary consequence
of a certain propensity in human nature. . . ." Nine years
earlier Adam Ferguson had made the same point quite
generally: "Mankind in following the present sense of their
minds, in striving to remove inconveniences, or to gain
apparent and contiguous advantages, arrive at ends which
even their imagination could not anticipate. . . . Every step
and every movement of the multitude, even in what are
called enlightened ages, are made with equal blindness to
the future; and nations stumble upon establishments, which
are indeed the result of human action but not the execution
of human design" (Ferguson 1767, pp. 122–3).

(i)

The same seminal passage at once proceeds to enforce the
point that – at any rate in default of sufficient independent
evidence of their particular existence – there is no longer
any call to postulate great creative culture heroes to explain
the origin of such "establishments". For, "If we listen to
the testimony of modern history, and to that of the most
authentic parts of the ancient; if we attend to the practice of
nations in every quarter of the world, and in every condition,
whether that of the barbarian or the polished, we shall

find very little reason to retract this assertion. . . . We are therefore to receive, with caution, the traditionary histories of ancient legislators, and founders of states. Their names have long been celebrated; their supposed plans have been admired; and what were probably the consequences of an early situation is, in every instance, considered as an effect of design. . . . If men, during ages of extensive reflection, and employed in the search of improvement, are wedded to their institutions, and, labouring under many inconveniences, cannot break loose from the trammels of custom; what shall we suppose their humour to have been in the times of Romulus and Lycurgus?" (p. 123).

Durkheim once said in this connection, in his lectures on *Montesquieu and Rousseau, Precursors of Sociology,* that the myth of the inspired and revolutionary legislator had, more than anything else, been the hindrance to the development of his subject. Notice too that there are parallel, indeed still more forceful objections to the hypothesizing of creation not by an individual but by a collective. Already in the *Treatise* Hume had deployed many of these objections to dispose of suggestions that the actual origins of all governments must have been in historical contracts: "philosophers may, if they please, extend their reasoning to the suppos'd *state of nature*; provided that they allow it to be a mere philosophical fiction which never had, and never cou'd have any reality" (Hume 1739–40, p. 493). Later Hume speaks in precisely parallel terms about the legend of historical social contracts made to end that "*state of nature*" (Ibid. III, ii, 8). Since the justificatory employment of one of these "mere historical fictions" has been revived by Rawls, it is well to emphasize that in this at least Rawls is operating with Hume's consent).

(ii)

Hume's insight is that not only government but also other fundamental social institutions neither in fact arose nor could have arisen through a contract from a pre-social state of nature; if only because promising itself already essentially presupposes the social institution of language.

Hume's own solution to this problem of actual origins is subtle, hard-headed, and profound; notwithstanding that some of the terms in which he states that solution must, unfortunately, suggest the sociologically unsophisticated crudities which he himself is striving to reject. Where his less enlightened opponents tell tales referring back to deliberate foresight and contractual agreement, Hume argues that the fundamental social institutions could not have originated from this sort of planning. What *is* possible is that recognitions of common interest will lead to the regulation of conduct in ways which are not, and often could not be derived from prior contracts: "Two men, who pull the oars of a boat, do it by an agreement or convention tho' they have never given promises to each other. Nor is the rule concerning the stability of possession the less deriv'd from human conventions, that it arises gradually, and acquired force by a slow progression. . . . In like manner are languages gradually establish'd by human conventions without any promise. In like manner do gold and silver become the common measures of exchange. . . ." (Ibid. p. 490).

To philosophers, from Socrates to Austin, that penultimate illustration should be the most impressive of all. To think that the natural languages, formations whose richness and subtleties it is so hard even faithfully to delineate, not merely may but must be in the main evolved, and not planned, by-products of the actions and interactions of people who were themselves, whether individually or collectively, incapable of designing anything of comparable complexity. In what language, after all, would the Select Committee charged with the task of designing the first natural language have conducted its deliberations?

For Socrates the illustration should have been impressive because it refers to the source of what has come to be called the Socratic Paradox. Those who are completely competent in their employment of particular words can be utterly incompetent to spell out the perhaps extremely complex principles upon which these words become correctly applicable. Typically, in the early and more authentically Socratic dialogues,

Plato's Socrates cross-examines some prime exemplar of a particular virtue, in order to reveal his inability to produce an acceptable definition of the relevant word. In the *Laches*, for instance, the paradox is that the hero Laches simply "does not know what courage is".

Anyone not yet sufficiently impressed by the richness and subtlety of the vocabularies of natural languages, as well as all those who have learnt everything they think they know about 'Linguistic Philosophy' immediately or ultimately from Gellner's *Words and Things*, should treat themselves to a study of that witty masterpiece 'A Plea for Excuses' (in Austin 1961). From that they will learn: both the richness of the relevant vocabulary in colloquial English; and that – contrary to what has so often been polemically alleged – Austin himself always insisted that even these abundant and too often unexploited resources may sometimes need supplementation or correction.

It is no wonder that, in considering the magnificent structures of the more highly developed natural languages, Ferguson becomes lyrical: "This amazing fabric . . . which, when raised to its height, appears so much above what could be ascribed to any simultaneous effort of the most sublime and comprehensive abilities." Indeed, he goes on, "The speculative mind is apt to look back with amazement from the height it has gained; as a traveller might do, who, rising insensibly on the slope of a hill, should come to look from a precipice of almost unfathomable depth, to the summit of which he could scarcely believe himself to have ascended without supernatural aid" (Ferguson 1792, I, p. 43).

The eccentric and studiously old-fashioned Lord Monboddo, who surely knew as much about linguistics as any of his contemporaries, but who was not so fully seized of the evolutionary possibilities, takes up Ferguson's hint of some supernatural aid. He "can hardly believe but that in the first discovery of so artificial a method of communication, men had supernatural assistance". So he is "much inclined to listen to what Egyptians tell us of a God, as they call him, that is an

intelligence superior to man, having first told them the use
of language" (Burnet 1774, IV, p. 484).

(iii)

The third main point which needs to be made about these
insights into social mechanisms consists in underlining a
distinction which seems not to have been developed either
by any of these Scottish Founding Fathers themselves or by
their most sympathetic modern interpreter, F. A. Hayek. In
a posthumous masterpiece published a year or so later than
The Wealth of Nations, Hume recognized that something which
had not been designed either by one individual or even by
a committee might nevertheless be the ultimate product of
innumerable more-or-less intelligent initiatives. In Part V of
the *Dialogues concerning Natural Religion* Philo is scripted to
say: "If we survey a ship, what an exalted idea we must
form of the ingenuity of the carpenter, who framed so
complicated, useful and beautiful a machine? And what
surprise must we entertain, when we find him a stupid
mechanic, who imitated others, and copied an art, which,
through a long succession of ages, after multiplied trials,
mistakes, corrections, deliberations, and controversies, had
been gradually improving?" (Hume 1779, p. 167).

The distinction needed is: between, on the one hand,
social mechanisms producing results unintended by, and
even contrary to the wishes of, those whose actions constitute
the operations of these mechanisms; and, on the other hand,
the generation of what may suggest brilliant individual or
collective design through the not intentionally and collectively
coordinated initiatives and responses of various persons or
groups of persons, most of whom cannot have been directly
acquainted with one another.

It is often said – by people who have, apparently, forgotten
the King James Bible – that no great work of art ever
emerged from a series of committee meetings. Yet it is,
surely, true to say that at least some of the greatest – the *Iliad*
and the *Odyssey,* for instance – were the ultimate achievements

of successive generations, with many individual bards making their several anonymous contributions piecemeal. Certainly the natural languages themselves must be products of still continuing processes of this kind. It has been well said that the history of every language is a history of corruptions; in the sense that every change must involve some deviation from what was previously established as correct usage. Presumably it was ever so. Presumably the whole growth of language has, from the beginning, been a series of unplanned lapses and intended initiatives; some of which have, through the effluxion of time, become accepted usages. This was indeed one of Darwin's models for his account of evolution by natural selection in biology (Flew 1984, III, 2 (iii)).

The contemplation of either of the two kinds of phenomena just distinguished should teach us how fallacious it is to argue that, if something is the product or result of conscious human agency, then it must always be in practice possible radically to redesign and reshape that product or that result in such a way that it shall the better accommodate the wishes of the persons concerned. It may be, or then again it may not. Every case needs to be examined separately, and argued on its individual and particular merits.

Descartes was, therefore, quite simply wrong when in Part 2 of the *Discourse on the Method* he made his characteristic claim that there is, typically, "less perfection in works composed of several portions, and carried out by the hands of various masters." So too, and consequently, is the entire tradition of 'constructivist rationalism' – epitomized "by the innocent sounding formula that, since man has himself created the institutions of society and civilization, he must be able to alter them at will so as to satisfy his desires or wishes" (Hayek 1978, p. 3). This tradition resonates to the cry of that early French socialist Etienne Cabet: "Nothing is impossible for a government which really wills the good of its people." But nowhere and by no Providence is it guaranteed that good intentions will produce all and only their intended good effects. To the disappointed it should nevertheless be some consolation to contemplate the other side of the coin. For intentions less than perfectly disinterested and universally benevolent are perhaps the more common; and these too, in this Universe, are equally liable to produce consequences additional and even contrary to those intended.

3 Social functions and social needs

Closely associated with the idea of social mechanisms are the notions of social functions and social structures. To say that this is a function of that is to say that this is something, presumably and typically something useful, which results from the availability and operation of that; and which, all other things being equal, would not come about if that were removed or its operation prevented. The function for instance, of the heart, is to circulate the blood; and this is indisputably useful to the organism since without a properly functioning heart it will die.

(i)

The choice of this familiar biological illustration should remind us that, especially when we are discussing human affairs and human institutions, it is always tempting to argue that anything said to have and to fulfil a function must therefore: both have been originally designed to fulfil that function; and now be deliberately maintained precisely and only for that purpose. But, of course, the argument is not valid: neither of these conclusions follows. Those succumbing to the temptation to argue in this way will also be inclined to think that to have established that a social institution does in fact fulfil such and such a function is at one and the same time to have explained: both how that institution first came into existence; and how and why it continues. It was, they will assume, first created by people who had and who saw that they had some interests here; and it is maintained still by persons having, perceiving and pursuing those interests. They may furthermore assume, if they are gripped by Methodological Essentialism, that that institution essentially has been, is now, and ever will be nothing but an instrument for fulfilling its consciously intended purpose; whatever that may be.

It was again Sir Karl Popper who first distinguished and labelled the Methodologicl Essentialist approach (Popper 1945, I, pp. 32, 109 and 220–1; and II, pp. 5ff. and 291–2; also Popper 1957, Ch. I Section 10). The tradition ultimately derives, by way of Aristotle, Hegel and Marx, from Plato's Theory of Forms (or Ideas, or Essences). These etherial, time-less, unchanging Platonic Ideas, laid up in a heaven accessible only to the pure vision of the intellect, are together supposed to constitute the immaterial infrastructure of our everyday world of common sense and common experience. All such banausic, changing, merely sensible, material realities are in truth – Plato would have us concede – unrealities. Hence, the Methodological Essentialist argues, the truly scientific student of social institutions must seek to discover their essential natures. Thus the essence of the state, once discovered, will be both what the state originally was and what it is bound to remain. No doubt it could be destroyed; it might (or it might not!) simply 'wither away'; but what cannot happen is any progressive transformation into something substantially different. The *locus classicus* for Methodological Essentialism is *The Origin of the Family, Private Property and the State* (Engels 1884; and compare Engels 1878 and Lenin 1917).

To say that some approach or some method is unsound, or that some form of argument is invalid, is not of course to hold that all the findings or conclusions thus derived or deduced must be false (Flew 1975, Ch. 1). Some may even, on other grounds, be known to be true. In *The Republic,* for example, Plato takes it that the social function of beliefs about both the gods and a future life is to assist in sustaining good order and discipline. It is reminiscent of the legendary 1948 Italian election poster where, under a picture of a wavering voter in the privacy of the polling booth, the caption read: "Stalin can't see you. But God can. Vote Christian Democrat!"

It was in order that this function might be more adequately fulfilled in his allegedly ideal state that Plato recommended a literary purge: the home life of the Olympians, as recorded by Homer and other literary authorities, was so unlike that of Plato's golden Guardians, or, for that matter, that expected of their subjects! But his mother's cousin Critias, later leader of the notoriously murderous Thirty Tyrants, expressed in verse the conjecture that religious doctrines had been originally invented and introduced by some anonymous culture hero: "And lawlessness turned into law and order" (Popper 1945, I, p. 142: Fragment 25 in Diels). While there is no good reason to believe that the conjecture of Critias is correct, we do have abundant evidence of the exploitation of religious beliefs for purposes of political control in the Ancient World (Farrington 1965); and in more recent times too.

This same fallacy is often mediated through the notion of need. If the fulfilment of some function can be seen as answering to a need in some social set, then, it is invalidly inferred, this discovery of the function and of the corresponding need is at the same time a discovery of two explanations: it explains who originally created the institution which has that function, and for what end; and it explains who are those who are sustaining it, and why. But the argument is no more valid in this elaborated form. For there are several possible slips between a need and its satisfaction. First, the persons whose need it is may not recognize that they have this need: while each one of us may be the best expert on our own wants, someone else may be in a position to insist that what we really need is something which we would very much not want to have (Flew 1981, Ch. V). Second, even when we do accept the need and want it to be satisfied we may decide that, in our present circumstances, as we see them, other things are more important to us than trying to satisfy that particular need. Third, we may not see what it is that we ourselves could do in order to satisfy that need: there may not even be any courses of action open to us which would in fact do the trick.

Once these various points about functions and needs have been clearly stated, and once the fallacious form of argument involving these two notions has been starkly displayed, it all begins to look too obvious to have been worth doing. Yet obviousness, of course, really is, what so many other things are nowadays falsely said to be, essentially relative: what is obvious to us now might not have been obvious to us or to anyone else at another time, or in another place. Failure to take account of what are now to us obvious considerations has greased the slipways for launching many a grotesquely unseaworthy assertion.

(ii)

Consider, for example *The Culture of Inequality*, a book described in its Foreword and by rave reviewers as a "milestone study" by "a skilled, judicious social scientist", presenting a "brilliantly reasoned argument", in a "daring attempt to unravel the ideological knots". The thesis of the author is: "Because of its peculiar history American society has given rise to a . . . culture of inequality", such that "many Americans make of their commonplace successes praiseworthy achievements by viewing disadvantage as the just desert for insufficient effort . . ."; and hence that "the maintenance of poverty is . . . a function of the collective need to sustain a visible population of pariahs . . ." (Lewis 1980, pp. 87–8 and 184).

He takes it for granted, presumably on the strength of unsound arguments of the kinds previously exposed, that to point to a supposed need, which some institution would satisfy, just is to show both why and how that institution is maintained. Consistently with his chief contention he too, like so many others, prefers to speak of deprivation or of low pay rather than of poverty or of low earnings. This is a difference which makes a difference. For the preferred terms suggest: not only that the people in question are intended victims; but also that there is little or nothing of a non-political kind which they could do, or be helped to do, in order to raise themselves. On the opposite side, the author sees a collective of those who "invest in the perpetuation of an under-class of objectionables" (p. 28). Yet he never even tries to tell us what the individual members of this supposed collective are from day to day actually doing or not doing with intent to satisfy their supposed collective need.

Whatever, if anything, they have in truth been and are so doing, certainly they have not succeeded in preventing the Congress from continuing to vote enormous funds for various programmes originally launched as elements in President Johnson's War on Poverty. In the year of *The Culture of Inequality* Milton and Rose Friedman published calculations purporting to show that, "If these funds were all going to the poor, there would be no poor left – they would be among the comfortably well-off at least" (1980, p. 108). Appearing four years later Charles Murray's *Losing Ground: American Social Policy 1950–1980* was perhaps the most practically important piece of social scientific research of the entire decade. It showed that, in reaching their conclusion, the Friedmans forgot a fundamental of analytical economics. The Law of Supply and Demand states that increasing demand tends to generate increasing supply.

If, for instance, you insist that all mothers without discrimination must at the taxpayers' expense be provided with an apartment and a minimum income, then – deplorably yet necessarily – you diminish both the incentives to responsible paternity and the disincentives to unmarried motherhood. This inconvenient yet ineluctable principle Murray generalizes into "*The Law of Unintended Rewards*. Any social transfer increases the net value of being in the condition that prompted the transfer" (Ibid., p. 212).

Murray also gave us there good reason to fear that we shall find ourselves acting in accordance with two other less demonstrably true principles: "*The Law of Imperfect Selection*. Any objective rule that defines eligibility for a social transfer program will irrationally exclude some persons"; and "*The Law of Net Harm*. The less likely it is that unwanted behavior will change voluntarily, the more likely it is that a program to induce change will cause net harm" (Ibid., pp. 211 and 216. For further discussion of the significance of these US findings, and for an enquiry into possible parallels in the UK, see Murray 1988 and Murray and others 1990).

(iii)

A second example, immeasurably more important on a world scale, shows the invalid argument moving in the opposite direction: from the disappearance of the (original) function to the disappearance of the institution. In a chapter of *Anti-Dühring* later to form part of *Socialism: Utopian and Scientific*, perhaps the most widely read of all Marxist works, and in a passage quoted and expounded by Lenin in *State and Revolution*, Engels wrote: "Former society, moving in class antagonisms, had need of the state, that is, an organization of the exploiting class . . . for the forcible holding down of the exploited class. . . ." But, come the Revolution, "*The proletariat seizes the state power, and transforms the means of production into state property*. . . . The interference of the state power in social relations becomes superfluous in one sphere after another and then ceases of itself. . . . The state is not 'abolished', *it withers away*" (Engels 1878, pp. 308 and 309, quoted Lenin 1917, p. 15; and compare Kautsky 1918).

There is no doubt but that the proposed transformation of the means of production into state property is, by definition, socialism. But, if anything ever has been utopian rather than scientific, it is the assertion that organizations with monopolies on military and police power are bound, once they are fulfilling no functions useful to outsiders, to *wither away*. It would be easy, yet it is scarcely necessary, to bring forward long lists of organizations and institutions much less powerful, and therefore much less attractive to their own members, which seem all set to survive indefinitely, notwithstanding that they are doing no good and some harm to the rest of us.

It is, however, more constructive to point out that in Marx and Engels this cherished conclusion about the withering away of the state is not based solely upon invalid arguments about social functions and social needs. It is sustained also by their more fundamental but surely false doctrine of the priority of economics; a doctrine which is part if not the whole of The Materialist Conception of History. Consider, for instance, two characteristic claims from the *Communist Manifesto*: first, that "The executive of the modern state is merely a committee for managing the common affairs of the whole bourgeoisie . . ."; and, second, that "Political power, properly so called, is merely the organized power of one class for oppressing the other" (Marx and Engels 1848, pp. 82 and 105).

But now, when we are told that those who seem to be the rulers, the men of power, really are the independently powerless creatures of various outside interests, then we have to demand, not only as social scientists but also as practical people, accounts of the effective checks and pressures by which those external collectivities contrive always to keep these merely seeming rulers subordinate to their own actual control.

Had Marx and Engels ever tried to provide such detailed, Methodological Individualist accounts, then they could scarcely have failed to discover that it is not by any means true that the immediate exercisers of military and political power are always and everywhere the subservient creatures of outside class interests. No doubt cabinets in Britain, from the Glorious Revolution until the great Reform Bill, were devoted to the welfare of – indeed they very largely consisted in members of – the landowning class. But elsewhere, and in other periods, it is all too easy to find examples of civilian rulers or military commanders pursuing ends of their own, ends quite independent of and even flat contrary to any interests attributable to economic classes outside the state machine. After all – to put things at what is at the same time not only the simplest but also the most fundamental level – it is only in so far as, and to the extent that, there are men with guns, able and willing to maintain and defend property rights, that rich people can possess that access to political power, which, allegedly, riches always offer. Those major industrialists, for instance, who financed the rise of Hitler's

National Socialists, soon discovered, once he was secure in office, that they were the suppliants now.

This Marxist failure – indeed, more truly, this Marxist refusal – to investigate actual and possible social mechanisms through which rulers may be made accountable to those whom they rule has, among the faithful, continued to this day; and this despite the ever-accumulating evidence of how totally parties of the new Leninist type can exercise autonomous and arbitrary rule over a whole society – not least over the class of which they profess to be the devotedly representative leading cadres. It was reluctance to recognize and accept falsifications of the misguiding doctrine of the priority of economics which induced Marx to abandon studies of *Oriental Despotism* (Wittfogel 1981; and compare Seligman 1907).

4   Structures and functions: (i) Functionalism

It was in *Argonauts of the Western Pacific*, a 1922 report on his fieldwork in Melanesia, that Bronislaw Malinowski formulated the doctrine in its first and most extreme form: "The functional view insists . . . upon the principle that in every type of civilization, every custom, material object, idea and belief fulfils some vital function, has some task to accomplish, represents an indispensable part within a working whole." This doctrine was extremely influential, not only on the work of such other anthropologists as A. R. Radcliffe-Brown and E. E. Evans-Pritchard, but also on sociologists such as Talcott Parsons (who studied with Malinowski in 1924) and R. K. Merton. But it was, almost from the beginning, strongly attacked. It has since been "virtually criticized to death" (Pratt 1978, pp. 117ff. and compare Jarvie 1973).

(i)

The first point for us to stress is that Functionalism takes very seriously the analogy so often drawn between human societies and individual organisms. Just as (most) organs serve some function useful to the organism, so, it is asserted, every social institution "fulfils some vital functions, has some task to accomplish, represents an indispensable part within a working whole." Again, just as organisms are integrated, with their several organs mutually adapted for cooperation, so the Functionalist will look for ways in which the various apparently disparate institutions of any particular society are integrated, and adapted one to another. Again, they will discern the phenomena of homeostasis not only in organisms but also in societies: just as organisms have mechanisms for maintaining internal equilibrium through changing external conditions so too, they will insist, do societies.

(ii)

The second and subsequent point is that Functionalism would be better presented: not as a rashly universal doctrine about what is always in fact there to be found; but rather as an heuristic maxim, telling us what it is always worth looking for, even if in the end we shall have to concede that it is sometimes not there. Indeed careful contemplation even of the biological model teaches caution. For, surely, we have all been told that the vermiform appendix is a vestigial organ, which no longer performs any function useful to the human organism? And human societies are in any case not often under the strong selective pressures of a state of nature.

(iii)

The third thing to notice is more complicated but no less important. It is that the analogy between societies and organisms breaks down in several often crucial respects. For a start, organisms are composed of cells, all of which will die fairly soon after the death of the whole. But the individuals or families composing a human society are capable of surviving separately or as members of another society. So, as the anthropologist Edmund Leach has wittily remarked, when a culture dies out or a society decomposes it may mean no more than that "Cowboys and Indians have learned to drive Cadillacs"; a development to be regretted, perhaps, but not in anyone's book a fate worse than death.

(iv)

Fourth, because societies unlike organisms are composed of individual human beings, it is entirely possible that some institution which meets some need and has some function for some set of members of some society, and which may even yield some general collective benefit, simultaneously and necessarily imposes severe costs upon some other set. Again, some institutions, perhaps even those same institutions, may be essential to the preservation of a particular society in approximately its present form without being by any means essential to the preservation of any society at all. All this would seem to be true of, for instance, human sacrifice among the Aztecs at the time of the Spanish conquest, suttee among traditional Hindus in nineteenth-century India, and female circumcision among the Kikuyu of contemporary Kenya.

Functionalism has frequently turned out to be a very conservative doctrine, at least with regard to the institutions of the sort of peoples studied by anthropologists. (Many believing and practising Functionalists have been incongruously reluctant to apply their doctrine to their own societies, and to draw equally conservative conclusions there; or, as the case may be, here.) Repudiating whatever they saw as ethnocentric, and therefore believing themselves to be committed to maintaining the absolute wrongness of trying to impose our alien and always relative or subjective valuations, such Functionalists have proved ready to support the conservation of many practices which in their hearts they knew ought not to be conserved. Yet none of this is to deny: either the heuristic value of Functionalism, in leading researchers to ask and answer questions about the functions of those institutions which do happen to have functions; or the more practical value in application of pointing out, either likely but unwelcome knock-on consequences of abolishing some particular and especially obnoxious practice, or possible alternative institutions for fulfilling necessary or desirable functions at lower cost. (For one altogether delightful example of the latter, see Grimble 1952 on how cricket was itself transformed when introduced to replace more lethal inter-village contests in his islands.)

5   Structures and functions: (ii) Structuralism

"A spectre is haunting the intellectual scene – structuralism, or better, *le structuralisme*. It is important, it is fashionable, but what the devil is it?" (Gellner 1973, p. 150). The temptation is to call a halt on reaching the third interrogative response offered to this excusably exasperated question: "Is it just the latest Left Bank fashion, filling a gap left by the exhaustion of Existentialism?" (p. 150). For that seems to be just about it. Nor is enthusiasm stirred in reading a judgement by a most sympathetic interpreter of the Modern Master of Structuralism, Lévi-Strauss: "The outstanding characteristic of his writing . . . is that it is difficult to understand; his sociological theories combine baffling complexity with overwhelming erudition" (Leach 1970, p. 8). Yet one or two things can perhaps usefully be said.

(i)

One expositor invokes as his motto the claim: "Science would be superfluous if there were no difference between the appearance of things and their essence." In saying this Marx was going to suggest that under socialism – where, it is alleged, social relations will always be exactly what they appear to be – there will be no room for social science (G. A. Cohen 1972). But a Structuralist will want to contrast underlying and surface structures, rather as Robert Merton in the first chapter of *Social Theory and Social Structure* contrasted

'Manifest and Latent Functions'. Both the Structuralist and the Functionalist will, naturally, be more eager to discover the underlying and the latent than to record the surface and the manifest: the former is more of an achievement, and more like science.

These underlying and surface social structures also seem to have something in common with the underlying and surface structures of Linguistics. For the elements from which the structures are formed are in both cases typical objects of what have been described as "the Appearance sciences – those concerned with phenomena whose very essence is that they 'mean' something to participants" (Gellner 1973, p. 152).

So far, perhaps, so good. Nevertheless we should begin to feel uneasy when we are told that social structures composed of such seemingly insubstantial elements do something so apparently physical as *generate* the surface social phenomena. What is the cash value of all this in terms of "societal members" – real flesh-and-blood people – doing this and suffering that? It cannot be emphasized too often or too heavily that a social structure is no more capable of producing real effects, without the involvement of people, than is a social movement, or a social class, or any other social force.

That such emphatic reiteration is necessary can be brought out best by referring yet again to Marx and Engels. For both produced most eloquent statements of the fundamental thesis of what would today be called Methodological Individualism. Yet both, especially in their more prophetic moods, remained apt to appeal to social forces operating somehow behind and beyond, rather than in and through, their component individuals. Under the continuing influence of Hegel (1770–1831), albeit a Hegel whom they had long since stood back upon material feet, they were unable to accept, always and consistently, that the subject of the social sciences must be the intended and unintended consequences of intended, individual, human actions. Instead they both hankered after materialist analogues of the activities of the Hegelian Cunning of Reason, directing people to achieve collective ends other than and independent of whatever

their own individual purposes might happen to be. These
were postulated as transcendent and offstage prods, rather
than immanent and onstage transactions.

It is significant that this comes out most clearly in the
retrospective review, *Ludwig Feuerbach and the End of Classical German Philosophy*. Engels there contrasts pre-human
biological evolution with "the history of human society". In
the latter "the actors are all endowed with consciousness, are
men acting with deliberation or passion, working towards
definite goals; nothing happens without a conscious purpose,
without an intended aim". Nevertheless, Engels insists, "the
course of history" is governed by necessitating laws: "where
on the surface accident holds sway, there actually it is always
governed by inner, hidden laws. . ."

"Men make their own history", the following paragraph
begins, boldly. Yet there is a but: "But, on the other hand,
we have seen that the many individual wills active in history
for the most part produce results quite other than those
intended – often quite the opposite . . ." So far so good.
The moral which Engels draws, however, is not that the
social scientist needs to study the mechanisms through which
particular intentions produce alien and even contrary results.
In his view the proper objects of investigation are hidden,
transcendent causes, rather than anything immanent in the
activities themselves. So for Engels "the further question
arises: What driving forces . . . stand behind these motives?
What are the historical causes which transform themselves
into these motives in the brains of the actors?" (Engels 1888,
pp. 58–9).

Soon it emerges that history is not, after all, really made
by innumerable individual men acting and interacting. The
ultimate historical causes are instead largely unconscious and
collective: "it is a question of investigating the driving powers
which – consciously or unconsciously – lie behind the motives
of men in their historical actions, and which constitute the
real ultimate driving forces in history". These are, of course,
"classes" (1888, p. 60). Where the metaphysical idealist Hegel
had discerned direction by the invisible and cunning hand of

presumably conscious Reason, the still Hegelian materialist Engels now sees individual men as the for the most part unwitting creatures of direction and control exercised by the necessarily unconscious collective intentions of hypostatized classes.

(ii)

Quite apart from discussions of Structuralism, much is said nowadays about social structures and, in particular, power structures. It is, therefore, worth making two simple conceptual points: one about the meaning of 'power'; and the other about an ambiguity of 'structure'.

Roughly speaking: to say that one person is exercising power over another is to say that the first person is getting the second to do or to undergo something which the first wants the second to do or to undergo, but which the second would not himself or herself independently wish to do or to undergo; while to say that the first person possesses power, but is not exercising it, is to say that he or she could exercise it if he or she chose. It is, surely, beyond dispute that the definitions sketched in the previous sentence are, if not perfectly polished, then at any rate substantially faithful to the ordinary meaning of the word 'power' as applied to persons.

There is, however, good reason to spell out this ordinary meaning here. For some social scientists have presented and adopted very different definitions: apparently without realizing how drastically they were innovating; and, hence, without providing any justification for introducing a new and inevitably confusing technical sense for a familiar colloquial term.

In the *International Encyclopaedia of the Social Sciences*, for instance, Robert Dahl asserts that 'C has power over R' means that 'C's behaviour causes R's behaviour'. Confining our attention, as is presumably intended, to the cases in which both C and R are persons the immediate objection is that this gets us off on the wrong foot by confounding possessing with exercising power. Dahl's definition would also require us to say that C was exercising power over R if, by his abominable rudeness, C caused R to punch him on the nose.

Again, many contemporary political scientists apparently want to define 'power' in such a way that to exercise power over someone necessarily involves some sacrifice of that subordinate person's interests. This perverse redefinition has been soundly criticized for making the term partly evaluative rather than purely descriptive (Lukes 1974). But the truly overwhelming objection is that it would make all exercises of power which were allowed to be in the interests of the persons over whom the power was exercised not exercises of power at all. A truly benevolent despot must thus become a conceptual rather than a practical impossibility.

The necessary distinction is between two senses of 'order', and hence two senses of 'structure'. Here the Greeks really did have not a word but two words. One of these, 'kosmos', from which we derive our 'cosmic' and 'cosmology', describes an order or a structure which exists or forms itself independent of any human will directed to its formation or maintenance. The other sort of order or structure is that produced and maintained by deliberate and purposive human ordering and control. This the Greeks called a taxis (pronounced to rhyme with praxis), and, significantly, this was also their word for a military formation.

6 Natural or Human Science, Necessity or Choice?

> ... all animals, according to the known laws by which they are produced, must have a capacity of increasing in a geometrical progression ... Elevated as man is above all other animals by his intellectual faculties, it is not to be supposed that the physical laws to which he is subjected should be essentially different from those which are observed to prevail in other parts of animated nature.
>
> Thomas Robert Malthus, *A Summary View of the Principle of Population*, pp. 123 and 121–2.

> A struggle for existence inevitably follows from the high rate at which all organic beings tend to increase ... This is the doctrine of Malthus applied with manifold force to the whole animal and vegetable kingdom; for in this case there can be no artificial increase of food and no prudential restraint from marriage.
>
> Charles Darwin, *The Origin of Species*, pp. 116–17.

Thomas Robert Malthus (1766–1834) published a long, pole-mical pamphlet on *The Principle of Population* in 1798. Both this *First Essay* and his later two-volume treatise, now known as the *Second Essay*, were in the first half of the nineteenth century enormously influential. After declining in the interval this influence has been felt again since World War II, not so much directly as by contra-suggestion. For Marx and Engels abominated "Parson Malthus". In consequence their followers, even when in power, have been reluctant to admit and to tackle problems of overpopulation. Had the Chinese Communists been ready to recognize the nature and serious-ness of these problems from the beginning of their rule, then the Chinese people might have been spared some of the most drastic measures to which, their rulers now argue, there is no (longer) any more tolerable alternative.

Our present concern with Malthus is, however, different. It is with a conceptual scheme modelled on classical mechanics. By examining that scheme, and the amendments necessary to take account of the realities of choice, we shall bring out how an acceptance of this reality, and an appreciation of its implications, is fundamental and essential to the progress of any human science. One main implication is that there neither are nor can be any laws of nature necessitating human action. This conclusion raises the question of what weaker and more restricted sorts of regularity and predictability social scientists may reasonably hope to discover. It also carries the corollary that it must be wholly misguided: either to insist that any human science has to assume that all human behaviour is determined by an absolute environmental necessitation; or to accept that the actual findings of such sciences are already showing that this is indeed the case.

1   A conceptual scheme for population studies

Malthus, like Comte, was soundly grounded in physics and applied mathematics. But Comte, after performing brilliantly in his first years at the Ecole Polytechnique was, just before his final examinations, sent down for ringleading insubordination. By contrast Malthus, who was "remarked in college for talking of what actually exists in nature or may be put to real practical use", concluded his undergraduate career with the achievement of first class honours in the schools.

In taking classical mechanics as his model for social theorizing Malthus put himself into a long and distinguished tradition, extending back at least as far as the Hume of the *Treatise*, and on well into the nineteenth century, and after. There is a comprehensive account of this hardy perennial aspiration to become "the Newton of the moral sciences" in the Chapter 1 of Halévy's study of *The Growth of Philosophical Radicalism*. Malthus himself, even in his first polemical pamphlet, goes out of his way to express his admiration for "the grand and consistent theory" and "the immortal mind" of Newton. Much more to the point, the theoretical scheme which guided and structured all his work on human populations does bear a very close resemblance to that of classical mechanics; which is perhaps rather more than can truthfully be said of the products of many other "bold attempts" to construct a physics of some sort of human action.

(i)

The basic theoretical scheme of Malthus is, except for one practically important innovation in the *Second Essay* and after, always presented as being, with only the most minor refinements, substantially the same. But for us it is crucial to bring out that neither Malthus nor his critics came anywhere near appreciating the full theoretical significance of that one practically important innovation. He just slipped it in, and they accepted it, as a fortunate second thought; happily enabling him "to soften some of the harshest conclusions of the *First Essay*", while leaving the rest of the theoretical framework unaffected.

The foundation of the whole structure, the very Principle of Population, is perhaps best stated in our motto passage from the *Summary View;* which was a separately published version of an article for the *Encyclopaedia Britannica.* The key clause is: ". . . all animals, according to the known laws by which they are produced, must have the capacity of increasing in a geometrical progression".

The next stage, again the same in every successive treatment, is: first to assert that "population, *when unchecked,* increases in geometrical progression . . ." (italics supplied); and then to argue that "the means of subsistence, under circumstances the most favourable to human industry, could not possibly be made to increase faster than in an arithmetical ratio". It is from a comparison between these misleadingly precise, yet by the same token powerfully persuasive, supposed ratios that Malthus then proceeds to derive his first conclusion. This does indeed become more cautious with the passage of the years. In the final *Summary View* he claims to have proved only that "it follows necessarily that the average rate of the *actual* increase of population over the greatest part of the globe . . . must be totally of a different character from the rate at which it would increase, if *unchecked*" (Malthus 1824, p. 242; emphasis added).

Having to his own satisfaction thus established that powerful checks must always or almost always be operating to offset the mighty power of population: "The great question, which remains to be considered, is the manner in which this constant and necessary check on population practically operates." But, of course, like almost every social scientist, Malthus always had, in addition to this speculative and academic interest in how things are, a practical concern with how they ought to be. This duality of interest led him to mix two entirely different systems of classification.

The neutral one divides all recognized possibilities into positive and preventive: "foresight of the difficulties attending the rearing of a family acts as a preventive check; and the actual distress of some of the lower classes, by which they are disabled from giving the proper food and attention to their children, acts as a positive check". But then in addition to this neutral system there is another, which is from the first offered as comprising exhaustive though surely not in every context exclusive categories. This cuts right across the neutral system. It is itself not neutral but belligerent. Thus he concludes in the *First Essay*: "In short it is difficult to conceive any check to population which does not come under the description of some species of misery or vice."

In his Preface to the *Second Essay,* however, Malthus announces the admission of a third category: ". . . another check to population which does not come under the head of either vice or misery; . . . I have endeavoured to soften some of the harshest conclusions of the *First Essay*" (italics and a capital supplied). This member of the trinity is Moral Restraint, very narrowly defined as one of "the preventive checks, the restraint *from* marriage which is not followed by irregular gratifications" (italics supplied). With this one vitally important modification, the old claim to exhaustiveness is repeated: "the checks which repress the superior power of population . . . are all resolvable into moral restraint, vice and misery" (Malthus 1802, I, p. 240).

To complete his theoretical structure Malthus makes the point that the values of the various possible checks do not vary entirely independently: "The sum of all the positive and preventive checks, taken together, forms undoubtedly the immediate cause which represses population . . . we can certainly draw no safe conclusion from the contemplation of two or three of these checks taken by themselves because it so frequently happens that the excess of one check is balanced by the defect of some other" (Ibid., I, p. 256).

Although his general statements about the relations between the various checks considered as variables are usually, like this one, curiously weak, his particular arguments again and again depend on the subsistence of far stronger connections. Thus in the *First Essay* he remarks that the failure of Richard Price, after supposing that all the checks other than famine were removed, to draw "the obvious and necessary inference that an unchecked population would increase beyond comparison faster than the earth, by the best directed exertions of man, could produce food for its support" was "as astonishing, as if he had resisted the conclusion of one of the plainest propositions of Euclid." Again, in the *Second Essay*, Malthus quotes with approval the remark of a Jesuit missionary: "if famine did not, from time to time, thin the immense number of inhabitants which China contains, it would be impossible for her to live in peace". Most significant of all, the whole force of the argument for Moral Restraint lies in the contention that this check might be substituted for those others which Malthus classed as species of Vice or Misery.

(ii)

The second stage itself involves two steps: first, to underline the similarities; and then to indicate how Malthus was led astray by his natural scientific model.

In both schemes the master question is in form negative: "The natural tendency to increase is everywhere so great that it will generally be easy to account for the height at which the population is found in any country. The more difficult, as well as the more interesting, part of the inquiry is, to trace the immediate causes which stop its further progress. . . . What becomes of this mighty power . . . what are the kinds of restraint, and the forms of premature death, which keep the population down to the level of the means of subsistence?" Earlier in this same *Second Essay* Malthus had quoted the question which Captain Cook asked of New Holland in his *First Voyage*, "By what means are the inhabitants of this country reduced to such a number as it can subsist?"; remarking that, "applied generally", it may "lead to the elucidation of some of the most obscure, yet important, points in the history of human society. I cannot so clearly and concisely describe the precise aim of the first part of the present work as by saying that it is an endeavour to answer this question so applied" (Ibid. II, p. 240).

Newton might have spoken in parallel terms. For, as stated in Book I of the *Principia*, the First Law of Motion runs: "Every body continues in its state of rest or of uniform motion in a right line *unless it is compelled to change that state by forces pressed upon it*" (italics supplied). Since in actual fact all bodies are in motion relative to some other bodies, and since this motion never continues for long in a right line, the questions arise: Why do bodies *not* continue in a state of rest or of uniform motion in a right line, what forces operate to prevent this, and how?

Again, in the *1817 Appendix* Malthus defends his talk of a natural tendency, which in fact is always to a greater or lesser extent checked by counteracting forces, by appealing to the practice of "the natural philosopher . . . observing the different velocities and ranges of projectiles passing through resisting media of different densities". He complains that he cannot "see why the moral and political philosopher should proceed upon principles so totally opposite" (Malthus 1817, II, p. 405).

We must have the more sympathy with his complaint when we see how he was treated by one once well regarded modern critic: "The invalidity of Malthus' ratios could never have escaped detection if he had stated the real series of increase and hence deduced all that it implied" (K. Smith 1951, p. 234). One might as well argue the invalidity of the First Law of Motion on the ground that real bodies do not for long continue in a state of rest or of uniform motion. For Malthus laying down his Principle of Population perfectly parallels Newton laying down his First Law of Motion. Both were propounding ideal limiting cases, and then going on to ask why it is that that ideal is never in fact realized. This exercise generates the heuristically fertile notions: in the one case of checks; and in the other of impressed forces.

The same method has been followed by others; usually, no doubt, without realizing that Newton and Malthus were among their predecessors. Above all Weber made much of the notion of ideal types. These had for him a primary classificatory purpose: authorities were classified as legal, traditional or charismatic; and economic systems as – among other possibilities – handicraft, city economy, capitalism, or socialism. Ideal types also served to generate questions: in what ways, and why, does this or that particular instance fall short of the ideal? It is important to recognize that the ideals here are purely theoretical, not practically prescriptive: there can be ideal types of social forms which all would agree to be unadmirable.

Nevertheless, this said, everyone needs to be alert to the fact that some famous ideal types or theoretical limiting cases have been for some at the same time ideals which ought to be realized in practice. It is, for instance, many years now since the logician father of the economist Maynard Keynes observed in a treatise on *The Scope and Method of Political Economy* that, perhaps especially in England, there had been a tendency to accept the conceptual ideals of laissez-faire theory as moral norms (J. N. Keynes 1904, pp. 50–1).

Today there is, even more certainly, a tendency to see the theoretical limiting case of ideal social equality as, simultaneously, the prescriptive imperative. Courses are advertised and taught on the assumption that any kind of social inequality is self-evidently bad, and hence that the task of social science is to show, both how such inequalities arise, and how they might be abolished. This fallacious inference is, presumably, often mediated by the unthinking false identification of justice with equality. But would anyone admit as just a system insisting on treating the innocent in exactly the same way as the guilty? The truth, as a moment's thought reveals, is that rules of justice, like all rules, require us to treat in the same way not all cases but only all relevantly like cases (Flew 1981, Chs. I–IV; and compare Flew 1989, Part II). We therefore have here a welcome target of opportunity for a poet-scholar's reproach: "Three minutes thought would suffice to find this out: but thought is irksome; and three minutes is a long time" (Housman 1931, p. xi).

So much for similarities; we have next to notice a crucial dissimilarity. This lies in the difference between the power of a human population to multiply if "left to exert itself with perfect freedom"; and the kind of natural power described by the First Law of Motion. It is a difference of which Malthus began to take account when he admitted the possibility of Moral Restraint. But this admission demands theoretical adjustments much more drastic and pervasive than he ever recognized to be required.

It is essential to distinguish two senses of the word 'power'. In one, the only sense in which the word can be applied to inanimate objects and to most of animate nature, a power simply is a disposition to behave in such and such a way, given that such and such preconditions are satisfied. Thus we might say that the bomb ('the nuclear device') dropped at Nagasaki possessed an explosive power equivalent to that of so many tons of TNT, or that full-weight nylon climbing rope has a breaking strain of (a power to hold up to) 4,500 pounds. Let us, for future ready reference, label this 'power' (physical). In another sense, the sense in which the word is typically applied to people, and perhaps to people only, a power is an ability at will either to do or to abstain from doing whatever it may be. Let this be 'power' (personal). Notice too, and resolve systematically to adopt, the good practice of giving easily remembered names to senses distinguished. The example to follow is that of the colloquial distinction between 'funny' (ha ha) and 'funny' (peculiar) – eschewing the esoteric and obfuscating self-indulgence of those too indolent to offer anything but eminently forgettable numbers and letters.

More, much more, has to be said about what is presupposed and implied by asserting that someone possesses "an ability at will either to do or to abstain". But first we have to distinguish two senses of the word 'tendency'. This distinction was well made in 1832 by Archbishop Whately in the ninth of his *Lectures on Political Economy*. In one sense a tendency to produce something is a cause which, operating unimpeded, would produce it; in the other to speak of a tendency to produce something is to imply that that result is in fact likely to occur.

Malthus, misled perhaps by his favourite physical paradigm, seems to have slipped without distinction: from the first interpretation, which comes easily to the theoretical natural scientist, to the second, which belongs rather to the discussion of practical and human affairs. It is as if one were to argue that, because the First Law of Motion is, in the first sense, a law of tendency, it must therefore follow that it is probable or certain that everything, in the second sense, tends to remain at rest or to move uniformly, in a right line. In a similar way, especially but not only in the *First Essay*, Malthus was inclined to construe the multiplicative power of human populations as a natural force rather than as, what it is, a power (personal).

It is these confusions which mainly determine the gloomy conclusions actually drawn in the *First Essay*. For if the Principle of Population really were a power (physical), then this presumably would imply what we may in mischievous flattery christen Parkinson's Law of Population – the doctrine that always and everywhere human populations must press hard up against whatever resources can be made available for their support. It was this doctrine which Malthus employed to shatter all utopian dreams of universal egalitarian abundance.

It must, surely, have been precisely and only because Malthus was throughout this *First Essay* construing his Principle of Population on a Newtonian model, and in a way which made it imply population Parkinsonism, that he became unable to recognize any possibilities of voluntary control, any possibilities of individual or collective policies for the inhibition of this mighty and menacing power of multiplication. Certainly it has to be seen as a fact crying out for explanation that so able and so concerned a writer should for so long have failed to recognize the possibility in this area of any form of Moral Restraint. For Malthus was never committed to any general doctrine of hard determinism, requiring him to deny the possibility of choice in this and all other particular cases. On the contrary: even in the *First Essay* itself he has a bit to say about the avoidable wrongness of choosing vicious rather than virtuous alternatives.

Once the fundamental distinctions have been made, and their implications understood, the true practical moral emerges. It is still, more than ever, both hugely important and extensively uncongenial. William Nassau Senior, another of the classical economists, summed up the agreement achieved in his own controversy with Malthus in this way: ". . . no plan for social improvement can be complete, unless it embraces the means both of increasing production, and of preventing population making a proportionate advance."

2   The inescapable reality of choice

The practical importance of that undeniably sound yet perennially neglected moral, especially for the peoples of the poorest countries, would be hard to exaggerate. But our present concern is with what must be, in the first instance, a more theoretical implication. Whereas in studying natural selection Darwin could, as he saw, afford to discount choice (Darwin 1859, pp. 116–17), choice is something of which every social scientist should be forever mindful. For we are all members of a kind of creatures who can, and cannot but, make choices. Choice is essentially involved in every human action, since all agents as such must in some sense be able to do other than they do do. So it is not possible for the behaviours of agents actually acting to be inexorably necessitated. Consequently a book such as this cannot pretend to be complete without a full frontal assault on the question of what agency involves and implies.

(i)

Perhaps the best way to bring out, both what is meant by "an ability at will either to do or to abstain", and that we are all of us throughout our waking hours possessed of more or less wide ranges of such abilities, is with the help of Book II, Chapter xxi, 'Of Power' in *An Essay concerning Human Understanding*. John Locke (1632–1704) writes in its Section 5: "This at least I think evident, that we find in ourselves a *Power* to begin or forbear, continue or end, several actions of our minds, and motions of our Bodies. . . . This *Power* . . . thus to order the consideration of any *Idea,* or the forbearing to consider it; or to prefer the motion of any part of the body to its rest, and *vice versa* in any particular instance, is that which we call the *Will*" (Locke 1690, p. 236).

Locke's explanation continues in Section 7, marred only by the fact that he sees himself as spelling out what is meant by 'a free agent' rather than, more simply and more fundamentally, by 'an agent'. The three Latin words refer to St Vitus's dance: ". . . everyone, I think, finds . . . a power to begin or forbear, continue or put an end to several actions in himself . . . We have instances enough, and often more than enough, in our own bodies. A Man's Heart beats, and the Blood circulates, which 'tis not in his Power . . . to stop; and therefore in respect of these motions, where rest depends not on his choice . . . he is not a *free Agent*. Convulsive Motions agitate his legs, so that though he wills it never so much, he cannot . . . stop their motion (as in that odd disease called *chorea Sancti Viti*), but he is perpetually dancing: he is . . . under as much Necessity of moving, as a Stone that falls or a Tennis-ball struck with a Racket" (p. 237).

Now, let us call all those bodily movements which can be either initiated or quashed at will movings, and those which cannot motions. Obviously there are plenty of marginal cases. But so long as there also are, as there are, plenty – indeed far, far more – which fall unequivocally on one side or the other, we have stubbornly to refuse to be prevented from making a distinction of enormous practical importance by any such diversionary reference to marginal cases.

This particular stubborn refusal is a token of a more general type. For most of those distinctions which are of the greatest human interest refer to differences of degree; in the sense that the two opposed extremes are linked by a spectrum of actual or possible closely resembling cases, such that it is not possible to draw any clearcut and non-arbitrary dividing line at any point in the middle zone of the spectrum. This applies not only to actions as opposed to necessitated behaviours but also to the distinctions between riches and poverty, age and youth, sanity and insanity, a free society and one in which everything which is not forbidden is compulsory, and so on. So it manifestly will not do: either to dismiss all such differences of degree as *mere* differences of degree; or to profess to be unable to discern any decisive differences save where clearcut and non-arbitrary lines can be drawn (Flew 1975, 7.13–7.24).

(ii)

If, having thus seized the high ground, we remain inflexibly resolved to hold it, we are positioned to see off any and every necessitarian counter-attack. For, once 'action' has been ostensively defined in terms of movings, there remains no possibility whatsoever of denying: either that all of us often are agents; or that, when we are, we must be able to do other than we do. ('Ostensive definition' is definition by reference to actual examples satisfying the requirements of the definition.)

The most doctrinally infatuated necessitarian theoreticians

can scarcely hope to bring themselves to deny that some of everyone's bodily movements are movings rather than motions; and, this given, there is no room for doubt but that with respect to these movings, and in the most fundamental sense, ostensively defined precisely and only by reference to such movings, they can do other than they do do.

Locke is in this chapter indicating a way of defining a long string of closely associated notions: 'choice'; 'action'; 'agent'; 'an ability at will either to do or to abstain'; 'could do otherwise than they do do'; and so on. But he is at the same time also indicating how to define 'physical necessity'. (The implicit contrast with 'logical necessity' will be explained in Chapter 8, below.)

By thus showing that (the members of) these opposing (sets of) notions both can and indeed have to be defined ostensively, Locke demonstrates that we do all have experience both of this sort of necessity and of choice. It is, therefore, just not on to maintain that everything in the Universe, including the senses (directions) of all human actions, is subject to ineluctable physical necessitation.

Against this philosophically sophisticated yet totally direct appeal to experience, other philosophers would argue that it is always conceivable that we are mistaken about what is or is not in fact subject to our wills; that some of us in the past have been afflicted by sudden paralyses, and all unwitting we may be now; or that any of us may suddenly have acquired powers of psychokinesis. Certainly this is all conceivable: we are none of us either infallible or all-knowing. But the great mistake is to assume that knowledge presupposes infallibility; that, where we may conceivably be mistaken, there it is impossible for us ever to know. The truth is that actually to know we need only to be in a position to know, and to be claiming to know, something which is in fact true. If it really were the case that, where it remains conceivable that we might be mistaken, there we could never truly know; then we could, as fallible human beings, never know anything – not even that we could never know anything (Flew 1989b, Chs. VIII, Sections 1–4 and IX).

Anyone doubting whether it is correct to claim that these notions can be defined only by ostension must be challenged to provide alternative explications not referring to our experience of necessity and choice. These two ideas, although opposed, are connected and almost complementary. For how could creatures living in a world of total physical necessitation find any intelligible contrast against which to understand that actually, by the hypothesis, all-pervasive feature? And how is it that we in our different world acquire the idea of making things happen, of making this physically necessary and that physically impossible, if it is not by acting in one way while being all the time aware of the possibility of not so acting?

The concept of the contrary-to-fact, of what would have happened had some condition been satisfied which in fact was not, is essentially involved in that of this causing that to happen. Wherever such causal propositions are asserted, some contrary-to-fact propositions are entailed. If I say that the cause of the explosion was my pressing down the plunger, then I imply that, all other things being equal, had I not pressed down the plunger, the explosion would not have occurred. But then again, how could this key notion of contrary-to-fact alternatives be acquired by any creatures which were not, in the sense just now explained, agents?

(iii)

Having said this much about causation it is worth adding, as it were between parentheses, two further points. The first is that it is, though often tempting, false to say that historians and other social scientists can have no truck with what might have been. To the extent that they have anything to say about causes, and are not mere annalists, they cannot but say things which carry implications about what might have been but was not. John Grigg's *1943: The Victory that Never Was* was thus unfortunate in its reviewers. A. J. P. Taylor in *The Observer* wrote: "It is hard enough to find out what happened, without dreaming what might have happened." In the *Chicago Sun-Times* David Kahn spoke of such dreaming as, while "one of the most fascinating of intellectual pastimes", nevertheless, "probably the most fruitless undertaking in historiography". Weber knew better (Runciman 1978, pp. 117ff.).

The second further point about causation concerns only the causes which will, in Section 3 immediately below, be distinguished as causes (physical). Such causes (physically) necessitate the occurrence of their effects, while it is (physically) impossible to produce the total cause without thereby producing its effect. It is only and precisely because these ideas of necessity and impossibility are indeed essential elements in what is meant by 'cause' (physical) that we become licensed to draw inferences: from causal propositions asserting that events of this sort (physically) cause events of that sort; to the truth of such contrary-to-fact, or counterfactual conditional propositions as that, if an event of the first sort had occurred on such and such an occasion in the past – which we know that in fact it did not – then an event of the second sort would have followed as a causal consequence. We know that it would have done because (we presume that) we know that, given an event of that first sort, it is (physically) necessary that an event of the second sort should follow and (physically) impossible that it should not. Propositions asserting that some natural law obtains similarly embrace the ideas of (physical) necessity and (physical) impossibility, and likewise license the drawing of counterfactual conditional conclusions. Causal propositions (physical) and natural law propositions together constitute the category nomological ('nomos' being the Greek for law).

(iv)

The points made in the previous paragraph need to be laboured. For, following Hume, many philosophers have tried to reduce both these two kinds of nomological propositions to mere statements of universal but unconnected and 'just as it happens to be the case' regularities. (It is "following Hume" since Hume famously denied the legitimacy of any conceptions of physical necessity and physical impossibility.)

One of the great attractions of such manoeuvres is that they facilitate the adoption of a Compatibilist position: if there really was no such thing as physical necessity then unnecessitated choice would not be incompatible with an universal nomological determinism. But the truth is: that the ideas of physical necessity and physical impossibility are essential elements in the meaning of nomological propositions; that it is only and precisely this which licenses inferences to counterfactual conditionals; and that it is the legitimacy of such inferences which is the accepted criterion for distinguishing nomologicals from the other sort of universal unrestricted propositions – "mere statements of universal, as it just happens to be the case regularities".

To get a better hold on the nerve of this distinction consider the example of the Two Ideal Clocks. This illustration was introduced by the Flemish Occasionalist, philosopher Arnold Geulincx (1625–69). He invented it precisely and only in order to bring out that and why such statements of mere 'just as it happens' regularities cannot be equivalent to authentic nomologicals.

Imagine two ideal clocks, equipped with mechanically independent, perpetual-motion movements; and suppose that no one ever is going to interfere with either movement. Then we shall certainly have, in the tellings of given o'clocks by one clock and the other, perfect series of regular accompaniments. Or – suppose we choose to stipulate that one starts a split second fast on the other – we shall have perfect series of regular successions. Nevertheless no one will want to say: either that a law of nature links these two regularly related series of events; or that members of the earlier cause members of the later. This is, surely, because we all recognize that there are no practically unbreakable connections here. No one could bring about or prevent changes in the readings of one clock by tampering with the readings of the other. Connoisseurs of paradox in the history of ideas may now relish the reflection that the account given by Hume of what causation involves, indeed of all that it can involve, fits perfectly to what everyone has always been ready to admit to be a paradigm case of regularity *without causal connection* (Flew 1986, Ch. 5; and compare Ch. 8).

3   Freedom, compulsion and physical necessity

We noticed at the beginning of the previous section that Locke saw himself as explicating the meaning of 'a free agent' rather than of 'an agent'. This was a mistake. It is a perennially persistent mistake, which has led to the traditional misrepresentation of the philosophical problems arising in this area. These are thus wrongly described as problems about freewill or the freedom of the will rather than about agency and choice (Flew and Vesey 1987). Before we can go on to see just what the admission of these realities does imply for social science, we have to correct both this fundamental misconception and various consequent or otherwise connected errors.

(i)

The first necessary step is to appreciate that, in ordinary untechnical English usage, action of one's own freewill is contrasted: neither with physically necessitated nor with merely predictable behaviour; but with action subject to coercion or compulsion – these typically consisting in pressure from other human beings. Both persons who act of their own freewill and persons who act under compulsion act. So, in the more fundamental sense, definable in terms of the distinction between movings and motions, they could have done other than they did. Their behaviours, therefore, are not in either sense to be categorized with the spasmodic and involuntary tics, jerks, quivers, tremblings, flutters and twitches which are conventionally but misleadingly labelled 'reflex actions' or 'compulsive actions'. All these are, presumably, what no true action can be, physically necessitated.

So when we say of someone who did in this most ordinary sense act under compulsion that, as things were, they had no choice, or that, considering all the circumstances, they could not have acted otherwise than they did, these common and easily charitable expressions need to be construed with caution. If they really did act, albeit under compulsion, then it cannot be true: either that they literally had no choice at all; or that, in the more fundamental sense, they could not have done otherwise. The point, rather, is: not that they had no alternative at all, but that they had no tolerable alternative; and not that, in that more fundamental sense, they could not have done otherwise, but that, although of course they could, it was in every way unreasonable to expect that they either would or should. The case, for instance, of the recalcitrant businessman, receiving from *The Godfather* "an offer which he cannot refuse", is vitally different from that of the errant mafioso, who is without warning gunned down from behind. The former is an agent, however reluctant. But the latter, in that very moment of sudden death, ceases to be.

This whole batch of idioms really is quite extraordinarily misleading. We have no business to be surprised that so many even of the wise and good have been, and are, misled. For the clear implication of the previous two paragraphs is that, when we say, in the ordinary everyday sense, that someone had no choice at all, or that they could not have done other than they did, we are not saying that, in the most fundamental sense, they did not have any choice, or that they could not have done other than they did. On the contrary: we are presupposing that they did and that they could.

"Here I stand. I can no other. So help me God." So spoke Martin Luther before the Diet of Worms. To misinterpret this as evidence for a necessitarian determinism, as both Freud himself and his official biographer were inclined to do, is to require that we read Luther as at the same time both explaining and excusing what appeared to be, yet was not, an act of defiance; upon the memorably implausible grounds that he had been suddenly afflicted with a paralysis rendering him physically incapable of retreat! (See Flew 1978, VIII–IX.)

(ii)

In this case, as in many others where expressions like 'could have done otherwise' are employed in their secondary sense, what is in question is not only the (impartial) explanation of conduct but also its (partial) justification. So it becomes worth distinguishing two senses in what is often a key word, 'expect'. Mr Worldly Wiseman will not always (descriptive) expect people to do what he may quite consistently (prescriptive) expect them to do (Flew 1975, 5.9 and 6.11). In his famous signal before the Battle of Trafalgar – "England expects every man to do his duty" – Nelson was, surely, playing on this ambiguity? Since he was undoubtedly the darling hero of the whole fleet he must, by issuing that signal, have increased, at least marginally, the chances both that its prediction would be fulfilled and that its prescription would be obeyed. It remains for us only to insist – against the denials of, among others, many sociologists of education (Young 1971, Ch. 5) – that, in so far as we are agents, we are not the completely helpless creatures of our environments. Nelson's signal had its desired effect, in so far as it did, because he was respected and even loved. But I myself reacted to my teacher's uttered prediction of my certain failure in French in such a way that this in fact caused me not to fail but (only just) to succeed. (Maybe he even – descriptively – expected that it would!)

(iii)

In saying, in the penultimate sentence of the previous paragraph, that "my teacher's uttered prediction . . . caused me not to fail but (only just) to succeed", I am of course asserting that I made that particular speech act my reason for launching an all-out effort. This provides occasion for distinguishing two fundamentally different senses of the word 'cause'. When we are talking about the causes of some purely physical event – an eclipse of the Sun, say – then we employ the word 'cause' in a sense implying both physical necessity and physical impossibility: what happened was physically necessary; and anything else was, in the circumstances, physically impossible.

Yet this is precisely not the case with the other sense of 'cause', the sense in which we speak of the causes of human actions. If, for instance, I give you good cause to celebrate I do not thereby make it inevitable that you will celebrate. To adapt a famous phrase from Gottfried Leibniz (1646–1716), causes of this second, personal sort incline but do not necessitate. So it remains entirely up to you whether or not you choose to celebrate.

It is best to borrow terms to mark this crucial distinction between two senses of 'cause' from Hume. For although, denying physical necessity, he could not make the distinction quite as we have done, his choice of labels does nevertheless point to a fundamental difference between the moral or social and the natural sciences. In his essay 'Of National Characters' Hume wrote: "By *moral* causes, I mean all circumstances, which are fitted to work on the mind as motives or reasons. . . . By *physical* causes I mean those qualities of the air and climate, which are supposed to work insensibly on the temper, by altering the tone and habit of the body. . ." (p. 198).

Given these two fundamentally different senses of the word 'cause' it becomes clear that we now need, if only within the human sphere, to distinguish two correspondingly different senses of 'determinism'. To be committed to the doctrine that absolutely everything that happens including all human behaviour, is completely determined by physical causes must be, surely, to be committed to a strong doctrine of the ultimate inevitability of everything.

But determination by moral causes has to be another matter altogether. It was in fact just such a non-necessitating determinism which Freud labelled 'psychic', although he then at once went wrong by assuming that this psychic determinism was nothing but the psychological particular case of a universal determinism of physical causes. No one would suggest that psychic determinism applies to anything except those elements in human behaviour (and possibly some brute behaviour) which are actions; while anyone recognizing and adopting this fundamental distinction between kinds of cause has to conclude that psychic determinism is incompatible with, rather than a particular case of, the universal determinism of physical causes (Flew 1978, Chs. 8–9).

By failing to make these crucial distinctions, first between two senses of 'cause' and then between two corresponding senses of 'determinism', many are misled into construing all explanations of conduct in terms of any kind of cause as providing support for a doctrine of physically necessitating determinism. Thus it seemed to the author of one excellent review of criminological studies that "if causal theories explain why a criminal acts as he does, they also explain why he *must* act as he does. . ." (J. Q. Wilson 1977, p. 58). Again, and notwithstanding that she is consistently clear in her insistence that environmental factors which have been found to encourage nevertheless do not at all necessitate delinquent behaviour, the authoress of the exciting research recorded in *Utopia on Trial* has been attacked for preaching an environmental determinism of the very kind which she would most emphatically deny (A. Coleman 1985). Presumably her Radical critics are discomfited by the revelation of possibilities for extensive yet remarkably cheap reform! (See Section 4 of Chapter 7, below.)

7 Natural Laws of Human Action?

> When a society has discovered the natural law that
> determines its own movement, even then it can neither
> overleap the natural phases of its evolution, nor shuffle
> them out of the world by a stroke of a pen. But
> this much it can do: it can shorten and lessen the
> birth-pangs.
>
> Karl Marx, Preface to *Capital*.

> Communism is at the end of all the roads in the world:
> we shall bury you.
>
> Nikita Khrushchev, Chairman of the USSR
> Council of Ministers, in an address to a
> diplomatic reception in Washington, DC,
> during September 1959.

In his extremely influential George Macaulay Trevelyan
lectures on *What is History?* E. H. Carr proposed to define
'determinism' – he hoped "uncontroversially – as the belief
that everything that happens has a cause or causes, and could
not have happened differently unless something in the cause
or causes had also been different" (Carr 1961, p. 87). This
might indeed have been allowed to pass as uncontroversial
if only he had gone on to distinguish two senses of 'cause' –
physical and moral – and two corresponding senses of 'determinism' – necessitating and non-necessitating. But Carr, who
had not made these crucial distinctions, nevertheless insisted
that determinism – in what was thus naturally taken to be
a necessitarian understanding – is a presupposition both of
critical history and of all other rational inquiry. It was on this
ground that he ridiculed Popper's *Open Society* and Berlin's
Historical Inevitability for daring to challenge what appears
to be the obvious implication of the thesis of universal
causal determinism, so understood: namely, the absolute
inevitability of everything. Yet Carr remained too good a

historian comfortably and consistently to accept that implication. Instead he tried to have things both ways (Flew 1978,
Ch. III, 4).

1   The refutation of historicism

The Dedication of Popper's *The Poverty of Historicism* reads:
"In memory of the countless men and women of all creeds or
nations or races who fell victims to the fascist and communist
belief in Inexorable Laws of Historical Destiny." The one
expression of such a belief cited in the text forms the first
motto to the present chapter. It is sufficient to show that the
historicism against which Popper was polemicizing consists in
a belief in natural laws of historical development. The statement quoted as the second motto expressed Khrushchev's
conviction that a particular law of this kind does in fact
obtain. (All his speeches during this US tour were promptly
published under the perhaps somewhat incongruous title *Live
in Peace and Friendship*!) Popper's own official definition of
'historicism' is totally different: "It will be enough if I say here
that I mean by 'historicism' an approach to the social sciences
which assumes that *historical prediction* is their principal aim,
and which assumes that this aim is attainable by discovering
the 'rhythms' or the 'patterns', the 'laws' or the 'trends' that
underlie the evolution of history" (Popper 1957, p. 3).

(i)

The articles from which *The Poverty of Historicism* was
developed were originally turned down by *Mind*, and first
published some years later in *Economica*. G. E. Moore, the
then Editor of *Mind*, presumably refused to accept them
until and unless this and other similarly gross faults were
remedied. 'Gross', surely, is not too strong a word? For
Popper was proposing to introduce a fresh sense for an
already somewhat overworked word. It behoved him to
supply an accurate and unequivocal account of the meaning
which he wanted it to be given.

Instead he first brings in and gives heavy emphasis to the irrelevant idea of *"historical prediction"*. This is irrelevant, because many commentators have succeeded in making, and in deploying tolerably good reasons for making, correct predictions, without pretending to derive these from putative natural laws of historical development. Here, as elsewhere in discussions of choice, it is a mistake to focus on predictability as such. For what, if anything, precludes choice is not the possibility of predicting the senses of choices yet to be made, but the possibilities of prediction on the basis of knowledge that movements in those senses will be physically necessitated. No one, for instance, should think that the possibility of predicting my future voting behaviour on the basis of my known political convictions is a reason for fearing that I shall not be able, in the more fundamental sense, to do other than vote as predicted.

It is, again, irrelevant, or worse, to bring in rhythms, patterns and trends, as if these were on all fours with the vastly stronger notion of laws of nature. Since it is hard to see how there could be any intelligible and illuminating historical writing if we had to abandon all these weaker notions too, Popper's wretched definition gives purchase to charges of obscurantism from hostile and (according to Popper's actual usage) historicist critics. Perhaps it is in hopes of forestalling these charges that Popper proceeds to present what he holds to be "a really fundamental similarity between the natural and the social . . ." This putative "fundamental similarity" arises, he thinks, thanks to "the existence of sociological laws or hypotheses which are analogous to the laws or hypotheses of the natural sciences" (p. 62).

By thus insisting on the subsistence of natural laws determining human action Popper deprives himself of the most direct and decisive refutation of historicism. For, if there is a conceptual incompatibility between action and necessitating determination, then there can be no such laws: hence it must be even less possible to have an especially grandiose sort determining macroscopic historical development. Again, it is only because we take it for granted that the senses of our choices are not inexorably necessitated by descriptive laws of nature that there can be point and purpose in prescribing that people ought to act in these ways and not those: there is, that is to say, a parallel conceptual incompatibility between descriptive and prescriptive laws.

There are hints of such a more decisive refutation both in Popper's earlier and in his later works. Thus in *The Open Society* it is claimed that "it is necessary to recognize as one of the principles of any unprejudiced view of politics that everything is possible in human affairs" (II, p. 197); while one of the three volumes of what has been nicknamed his *Concluding Scientific Postscript* is entitled, boldly, *The Open Universe: An Argument for Indeterminism*.

What is in fact offered in *The Poverty of Historicism* is an argument for the inherent unpredictability of future scientific advances: "The course of human history is strongly influenced by the growth of human knowledge"; but "We cannot predict, by rational or scientific methods, the future growth of our scientific knowledge. (This assertion can be logically proved . . .)" (Popper, 1957, pp. ix–x). This logical proof is best grasped by quoting Humphrey Lyttleton's reply to an interviewer asking him where jazz was going: "If I knew it would be there already." Popper's logical proof may be sufficient, though it is not quite as strong as at first it seems. For what is of historical importance is, in the main, not theoretical advances but technological applications. And we may well be able to predict that something will become technically possible, without first solving all the problems which will have to be solved in order to make it so.

(ii)

Popper attempts to dispose of the suggestion that there are no sociological laws in a characteristically forthright and straightforward way: "I will now give a number of examples" (1957, p. 62). But he makes his self-imposed task more formidable by stressing, quite rightly, that a proposition expressing a law of nature must carry entailments of physical necessity and physical impossibility. Thus he says, on the previous page: "As I have shown elsewhere, every natural law can be expressed by asserting that *such and such a thing cannot happen*; that is to say, by a sentence in the form of the proverb: 'You can't carry water in a sieve'" (p. 61).

The reason why so many otherwise alert and well-girded writers have failed to see any problem about laws of nature in the social sciences, and have thought that an introduction to the philosophy of the social sciences could be completed without coming to terms with any questions about choice, is that they have accepted Humian analyses both of (physical) causation and of laws, of nature. These, as we saw in Chapter 6, reduce such causation and such laws to mere regularities of accompaniment or succession, denying that we have any knowledge of practical necessity or practical impossibility.

If these regularity analyses were correct, then there would perhaps be no problems here. Certainly, if they were right, then no one could suggest that there might be a conceptual incompatibility between action, on the one hand, and laws or nature of (physical) causation, on the other. Certainly too, if physical necessity is not necessity but only unconnected and unnecessitated regularity of succession, then the "reconciling project" of Hume's first *Enquiry* goes through at the trot: total 'necessity' and liberty or choice become fully compatible (Hume 1748, VIII; and compare Flew 1986, VII). It is, surely, only upon these Humian assumptions that so many philosophers have been able to be, what I myself once was, Compatibilist. (Compatibilists maintain that there is, after all, no incompatibility between universal necessitating determination and the realities of choice; while Incompatibilists, unsurprisingly, contradict that contention.)

The most persuasive of the several supposed specimens deployed by Popper is: "You cannot have full employment without inflation." No doubt it is true that wherever you do have full employment you will also find some measure of wage-push inflation; and that there are no measures, or at any rate no tolerable measures, which government can take which will completely neutralize this inflationary pressure.

There is, however, no call to argue about this in the immediate present context. For if Popper had really laid his hands upon a true law of nature determining social actions, then the practical necessities and practical impossibilities entailed by that law would have to constrain all the agents concerned. It is not enough that such necessities should apply only to those in and around governments, and then only to governments inhibited by some scruples against, or some constraints upon, the totalitarian full employment of an overwhelming state power. The necessities of a genuine law of nature would have to apply equally to all, including all those outside government whose several individual determinations to do the best they can for themselves sum up to the pressure for wage-push inflation. And, however strong and well-grounded our confidence that they – that we – will never in fact suppress our unrelenting drive to better the condition of ourselves and our families, we do nevertheless all know equally well that, in the more fundamental sense already explained, we could.

"You cannot have full employment without inflation" is Popper's most promising candidate for the position of a true sociological law of action. It is, as we have just seen, not nearly good enough. Some of the others are so terrible that it is hard to understand how Popper ever brought himself to enter them. Take, for instance, "You cannot introduce agricultural tariffs and at the same time reduce the cost of living" (p. 62). Of course you can; always supposing that you are – perhaps in your capacity as a Minister in the cabinet of Saudi Arabia or as yourself the Sultan of Brunei – you are so fortunate as to possess the means for effecting some more than corresponding reductions in the prices of some other items in the cost of living index.

If we are now told that this wretched candidate has to be assessed as if it had contained an all other-things-being-equal clause, then we must come back hard with the reply that this makes the claim true but only at the cost of making it tautological. Certainly it is true – all too true– that any increase in the price of any item in a cost of living index will result, all other prices remaining the same, in an overall increase in that index. But if a candidate is to be accepted as a law of nature it has to be not tautological but substantial. This is why the economists' often mentioned yet rarely stated Law of Supply and Demand does not constitute a true law of nature. For, if it is to be true that increased demand tends to generate increased supply, then this demand has to be qualified as effective. It is not enough that there should be people wanting something, but unable or unwilling to pay for it. Demand is effective only in as much as the demanders are able and willing to provide potential suppliers with some sufficient motivating reason to fill that demand.

Or again, take another of Popper's examples: "You cannot introduce a political reform without strengthening the opposing forces, to a degree roughly in ratio to the scope of the reform" (p. 62). This one is simply not true. Nor is there here any parallel possibility of withdrawal beckoning into the sanctuary of tautology. For there are plenty of reforms which, once implemented, win the more or less grudging acceptance of those previously opposed. There are also reforms which create interests making reversal politically difficult if not impossible. Consider, for instance, any measures anywhere for substantial extensions of the franchise, such as the long and bitterly contested great Reform Bill of 1832, or, more recently but again in the UK, the selling off at bargain prices by successive Thatcher administrations to their sitting tenants of a million or more previously publicly owned housing units – an exercise said to have constituted the biggest transfer of property into individual hands since the dissolution of the monasteries by King Henry VIII in 1536–9!

All the other examples presented by Popper can be collapsed in the same way. Either, that is, they are just false; or they make insufficiently universal claims about physical necessities; or, in order to be made true, they have to be so amended and so qualified that they become tautological. His own suspicions ought to have been aroused – at latest – when he found that he was having to construct candidates out of his own head, and that there were no ready-named specimens pushing themselves forward. For why is it that textbooks of

sociology index no references to Comte's Law or to Spencer's
Law; paralleling those to Boyle's Law, to Ohm's Law and all
the others which we can find in any textbook of physics?
(Such suggested exceptions as Gresham's Law, Parkinson's
Law, and Michel's Iron Law of Oligarchy – exceptions rarely
if ever mentioned in textbooks – can all be collapsed by the
methods just now demonstratively employed.)

The moral for us to draw is that proposed already. The
reason why Popper can neither find any established and
accepted sociological laws in the textbooks, nor excogitate
presentable substitutes on his own account, simply is that
there neither are nor could be any laws of nature necessarily determining action; and that this fundamental truth,
together with the inexpugnable reality of action, constitutes
the surest bases for the decisive disposal of historicism, in
Popper's understanding of that term. For if there are not
and cannot be any laws of nature which determine and
necessitate the senses of the actions of individual human
beings, then, surely and *a fortiori*, there cannot be any natural
laws of historical development?

(iii)

The particular putative law of historical development which
Popper had centrally in his sights, and upon which Khrushchev
too was grounding his obituary prediction, is, of course, the
one which Marx claimed to have discovered. In words quoted
from *Capital* and from the *Communist Manifesto* in Chapter
1, when "The death knell of private property sounds", the
"expropriators are expropriated." Why? Because "the bourgeoisie . . . produces . . . its own gravediggers. Its fall and the
victory of the proletariat are equally inevitable."

To this assertion, as to all assertions of historical inevitability, the immediate response should be a question: "Inevitable
by whom?" For in human affairs there are all manner of
developments which could be or could have been prevented
not by their patients but by their agents. Consider the example which leapt to mind at the time of writing. There was

in 1990 nothing which the Kuwaitis could have done to halt the Iraqi invading forces. But that fact provides no warrant for saying that those forces and their commanders could not have refrained from launching and pressing the aggression. If, however, what is being asserted actually is a law of nature then the development determined and necessitated by that law must be inevitable by absolutely anybody and everybody, without any exceptions at all.

The natural first response to the apparent discovery of such a law on the part of those who would welcome the developments predicted is enormous encouragement. The statement made by one Russian Populist on first reading *Capital* was to become representative of many: "The knowledge that we feeble individuals were backed by a mighty historical process filled one with ecstasy and established such a firm foundation for the individual's activities that, it seemed, all the hardships of the struggle could be overcome" (Quoted, Wesson 1976, p. 46).

But then, if the outcome truly is inevitable why bother with the struggle? Why suffer what are now apparently unnecessary hardships or make supposedly superfluous sacrifices? Labours to promote the inevitable must be redundant; struggles to prevent it futile. Marx gave his answer to this objection in the first of the motto quotations for the present chapter: supporters can at least, and at best, "shorten and lessen the birthpangs"; which birthpangs opponents must correspondingly be able only at most, and at worst, to lengthen and intensify. The weight to be accorded to this response must depend both upon the extent of the shortening or lengthening and upon the nature of the longer term consequences of either, on the one hand, shortening or lengthening or, on the other hand, lessening or intensifying the birthpangs. But, just so soon as we cash Marx's obstetric metaphor into more discussably literal terms, further questions must arise about *The Role of the Individual in History* (Plekhanov 1898).

One sort of answer is developed by Tolstoy in *War and Peace*: people in high positions are not important, only the

spontaneously moving masses matter. The alternative, taken
in what has been accepted as the classic statement by G. V.
Plekhanov, always recognized by all factions as the Father
of Russian Marxism, is equally implausible. It is to say
that, although particular individuals do make some differences, they never make substantial and lasting differences
to anything that matters: general trends, tendencies and
movements are all-important. Sidney Hook provided the
most elegant and compelling refutation of these and all
other attempts to deny the world-historical importance of
the presence of particular people in particular positions at
particular critical moments. For *The Hero in History* deploys
abundant evidence to show that, at every critical moment
in the development of Bolshevism – from the first splitting
of the RSDP, via the April Theses to the forcible seizure
of power in the October coup, and then on throughout
the subsequent struggles to retain and extend that power –
Lenin's presence and Lenin's activities were indispensable.

2   The socialist project: (i) promise and practice

The development promised, or threatened, by Marx's supposed law of nature is triumphant proletarian revolutions
and, in very short order, the consequent establishment of
socialism. The general nature of that project as originally
understood is made perfectly clear in both the two most
widely circulated Marxist documents: the *Communist Manifesto*; and *Socialism: Utopian and Scientific*. The former, though
drafted by Marx, was published as the joint work of Marx
and Engels. The latter is a substantial pamphlet excerpted
from *Herr Eugen Dühring's Revolution in Science (Anti-Dühring)*.
Although both pamphlet and book were published in the
name of Engels alone, every chapter in draft had been read
to and approved by Marx. So both the *Communist Manifesto*
and *Socialism: Utopian and Scientific* constitute considered and
authoritative representations of what in their correspondence

both collaborators used to characterize as "our view" or "our theory".

The later work explains that its foundations are "two great discoveries, the materialist conception of history, and the revelation of the secret of capitalist production"; both of which putative discoveries Engels then asserts that "we owe to Marx. With these discoveries Socialism became a science" (Engels 1880, p. 44). Socialism is here understood to involve essentially the collective ownership of "all the means of production, distribution and exchange".*

According to this "materialist conception of history" there comes a time when *The proletariat seizes political power and turns the means of production into State property*" (Engels 1880, p. 75). "With this ... the social anarchy of production gives place to a social regulation of production upon a definite plan, according to the needs of the community ..." (p. 74). "The expansive force of the means of production bursts the bonds that the capitalist mode of production had imposed upon them. Their deliverance from these bonds is the one precondition for an unbroken, constantly accelerated development of the productive forces, and therewith for a practically unlimited increase of production itself" (p. 80).

It was the fulfilment of this promise of "practically unlimited" abundance which would, it was believed, make possible the transition from Socialism to Communism. According to *A Critique of the Gotha Programme* (Marx 1875) the distinction between these two stages of social development ought to be grounded upon their different principles of distribution. In the former and earlier, once due provision has been made for various other imperative calls on the public purse, the

---

*Those last words are quoted from the original Clause IV of the Constitution of the British Labour Party, and used to be printed as the Statement of Aims on every membership card. It was in this understanding that that party fought and won the 1945 General Election on a Manifesto – *Let us Face the Future* – proclaiming itself to be "a socialist party, and proud of it"; which intended, when elected, to nationalize – for a start, and in its first term – the industries providing railway, bus and air transport and producing and distributing gas, electricity, coal and steel.

principle should be: "From each according to their abilities, to each according to their work." In the latter and later it could and should be: "From each according to their abilities, to each according to their needs." Few seem to have noticed the no doubt unintended suggestions of austerity and authoritarianism implicit in this second formula. Necessities, notoriously, are antithetical to luxuries; and, while we are all the best experts on our own wants, others may be entitled to insist that what we really need is something quite different, and probably most unwelcome (Flew 1981, Ch. V).

Later both Lenin and Stalin were to contend that it was the enormous increase in productivity, promised consequent upon the bursting of the bonds with which 'late capitalism' allegedly constrains the forces of production, which both guarantees and justifies the triumph of socialism. Thus in 1919 in 'The Great Initiative' Lenin claimed that, "In the final instance, labour productivity is the most important, decisive circumstance for the history of the new social order. Capitalism has created labour productivity which was unknown under feudalism. Capitalism can be vanquished, and will finally be vanquished, through a new, much higher productivity, created by socialism." (See Vol. XXIX in the *Collected Works*.)

Two decades later Stalin, as usual following studiously in the steps of both Marx and Lenin, during a speech introducing the first Five Year Plan, insisted that "Not abstract justice but socially necessary labour time justifies socialism." Later still, at the Twenty Second Congress of the Communist Party of the Soviet Union in 1961, Khrushchev as General Secretary announced a new party programme, promising that, thanks to the uninhibited and assured growth in productivity, the Soviet people would have achieved Communism "in the main" by 1980; when they would be enjoying "the highest living standard in the world".

It has not happened. And since General Secretary Gorbachev opened the era of glasnost – but especially since the East European revolutions of 1989 – there is scarcely anyone anywhere any longer prepared to deny: either that the only "practically

unlimited increase in production" in the Soviet-type economies (STEs) has been of armaments and of pollutants; or
that the populations suffering under such social systems
have become – to put it very mildly – at least relatively
impoverished. See, for instance, Eberstadt 1988; and, for
an increasing wealth of further information about the STEs,
any of the publications of the Centre for Research into Communist Economies (CRCE) – an offshoot of the Institute of
Economic Affairs in London.

3 The socialist project: (ii) what went wrong

When predictions based upon a theory have been thus
decisively falsified scientific curiosity, and indeed scientific
integrity, require us to seek out the errors and deficiencies
which misled the theorists to commit themselves to such
false predictions. For until the mistakes have been identified we cannot hope to learn from them.

(i)

In the first place, as the Austrians Ludwig von Mises and F.
A. von Hayek demonstrated in the great Calculation Debate
of the twenties and early thirties, without the institution of
several property – without, that is, the institution of property
possessed by several different owners – without that, and the
consequent possibility of prices determined by the interplay
of relative scarcity and effective demand, rational economic
calculation is impossible. This is the main reason why in
every STE it has taken at least twice as much energy and
raw material to produce a given unit of output as in the
countries of the European Economic Community (EEC) and
the European Free Trade Associaiton (EFTA). For a review
of that Calculation Debate see Hoff 1988.

The most reliable as well as the most impressive comparisons of EEC and STE performance are, as might be expected,

coming from now reunited Germany. It is, for instance, from studies done there that we can learn: that the average returns on capital employed in the whilom German Democratic [sic] Republic were wretched compared with those in the original German Federal Republic; and that the former was emitting more than four times as much sulphur dioxide per head as the latter – and that at less than half the living standards. And so on.

(ii)

Second, whereas Engels claimed that it was through Marx's revealing of "the secret of capitalist production" that "Socialism became a science", the truths are: that that secret had already been revealed during the previous century by Adam Smith – in the vivid and memorable paragraph quoted as the motto of Chapter 5, above; but that its significance appears never to have been adequately appreciated by Marx.

What is crucial for the promotion of economic growth are the decisions where and when to invest and where and when to disinvest. Before the event, however, there is precious little if any certainty to be found in the making of such decisions – especially perhaps with those where the payoff for getting it right is greatest. So if the decisions actually made here are to be maximally wealth-creating and minimally wealth-destroying, then surely it becomes prudent to ensure that those who make these decisions are subject to the incentives and disincentives appropriate to the achievement of these objectives; and still more prudent to ensure that those making decisions which turn out to have been right (or wrong) are consequently enabled to make (or prevented from making) bigger (or any) investment decisions in the future? But, as we saw at the beginning of Chapter 5, precisely this is what is achieved when the people making these decisions are either "investing their own capitals" or serving as directly responsible agents investing capitals for others.

There is abundant illustrative material from the experience of the UK in the sixties and seventies. (See G. and P. Polanyi

1976, Redwood 1980, and Pryke 1981; and, on several more particular decisions, compare Broadway 1976, Jones 1977, Bruce-Gardyne 1978, and Burton 1979.) In that period, under administrations of both main political colours, a substantial proportion of all investment decisions were made by, or somehow emerged from the interactions of, various persons and groups not having, and often required not to have, any individual stake in the achieving of the maximum, or indeed any, return on capital employed. Again and again these investments of 'public money' were made in places and projects in which no one in their senses would have risked their own. Indeed, in many cases this was one of the main reasons actually given for putting up 'public money'!

(iii)

In view of the oft-repeated Marxist claims to have transformed the socialist project into a science the third failure is perhaps the most remarkable. For this pretended social science manifests what some will be inclined to see as a traditionally Teutonic refusal to recognize any sort of social order but that of command and obedience; that is to say – in terms of the distinction made at the end of Chapter 5 – any kosmos as opposed to a taxis. The economic order of a market is, paradigmatically, a kosmos; while that of a command economy is, equally paradigmatically, a taxis. But Engels, wilfully blind to this possibility, persistently describes competition between capitalist suppliers or would-be suppliers as being or resulting in "the anarchy of production".

"The present anarchy of production", Engels insists, in which "economic relations are developed without uniform regulation must give way to the organization of production." Under socialism "Production will not be directed by isolated enterprisers independent of each other and ignorant of the people's needs; this task will be entrusted to a specific social institution. A central committee of administration, being able to review a broad field of social economy from a higher vantage point, will regulate in a manner useful to the whole of society, will transfer the means of production into hands appropriate to this purpose, and will be specially concerned to maintain a constant harmony between production and demand" (Quoted Wolfe 1967, pp. 256–7).

The propounders of a project for what they were pleased to call *scientific* socialism thus refused to recognize the realities of the market order, in which this constant harmony actually is maintained. It is in fact maintained, not by a total centralization of all relevant information (something which Hayek has surely shown to be impossible), but by price signals, which transmit the necessary information to all those concerned, while at the same time providing incentives to employ that information in an economically rational way. Could one ever find a parallel in a market economy for what was being reported in the Western press as occurring in the USSR at the time of writing – a miners' strike provoked by the fact that soap, for which they were able and willing to pay, was not available in any local store?

The socialist project for replacing markets and the price mechanism – social institutions which evolved naturally as the unintended results of intended actions – by deliberately established central committees issuing specific directions to all is *The Fatal Conceit* (Hayek 1988) of constructivistic rationalism. It is the innocent sounding yet massively misguiding notion that, "since man has himself created the institutions of society and civilization, he must also be able to alter them at will so as to satisfy his desires or wishes" (Ch. 5, 2, (iii), above).

In one brilliant study of various social mechanisms, both fortunate and unfortunate, the economist-author suggested that we draw from comparisons with "the way ant colonies work" a moral opposite to the one that is usual: "no ant designed the system. Each ant has certain things that it does, in coordinated association with other ants, but there is nobody minding the whole store" (Schelling 1978, p. 21; and compare Lavoie 1985). But the number and complexity of the operations coordinated without any conscious intention or planning in an ant colony is as nothing to the number and complexity of the individual decisions, and the number and complexity of the for the most part unforeseen and therefore unintended longer range consequences of those decisions, which are more or less effectively coordinated in a modern market economy.

(iv)

Of course this system does sometimes break down. No human arrangements ever are perfect, or ever will be. Sometimes the products paid for are not delivered; sometimes the sizes we want are not in stock; sometimes possible investments which would be profitable are simply not made; and so on. But if we think first of the tens of millions of people making billions of choices among the alternatives perceived to be open to them, and of how well their actual decisions are in practice integrated and coordinated without benefit of commands from any central committee, and if next we remind ourselves of some of the cases of government failure most familiar to us, then it must become very difficult to believe that even ideal committees could do a better job than actual markets. And, anyway, where in the real world could we find that ideal committee?

The practical problems of managing a fully socialist economy, and the dangers of the concentration of power needed for such management, were deliberately and systematically ignored by Marx. He always, as he put it, refused "to write cookbooks for the future". So the only model for such management available to Lenin was that of the war economy of Imperial Germany. It was this which, in an article on 'Socialism' written at about the same time as the Bolsheviks were seizing power, Weber argued could not be applied in peacetime (in Runciman 1978, pp. 251–62).

The refusal of Marx and his leading followers to face these practical problems of the future for which they hoped and struggled was politically prudent. For their concern was to organize and unite an opposition. But the only thing about which all the members of such a movement are necessarily agreed precisely is their opposition. So there must be a danger that any discussion of what is to be done once their opponent has been overthrown will reveal and accentuate disruptive disagreements. This persistent, politically prudent refusal constitutes yet another example of Marx the politician systematically sacrificing the concerns proper to the social scientist. To describe as Scientific Socialism a project which, while undoubtedly socialist, stubbornly eschews all examination of the practicalities of the system which it is intended to realize is paradoxical to the point of perversity.

4   What can and cannot be discovered

There is no call to be distressed by the outcome of Chapter 6 and of the previous sections of the present Chapter 7. For there remains abundant room for the discovery of any number of true and sometimes interesting and important sociological propositions of all the forms there distinguished from nomologicals. But in the light of all that previous discussion we do become able to see that many of what are retailed as the fruits of social scientific enlightenment neither are nor could be truths; and that some of the proposed objects of inquiry neither are nor could be there to be found. The common cause of all these troubles is the refusal to recognize, and to take appropriate account of, the realities of choice. The reason why these popular propositions neither are nor could be true, and these sought-after objects neither are nor could be there to be found, is that their truth, or their existence, presupposes, what is manifestly false, that we are not creatures which make, and which cannot but make, choices.

(i)

The logical fact that, in so far as people are agents, their actions cannot be completely necessitated, does not by any means rule out all possibility of making true assertions about the physical necessities circumscribing social action; whether this is only social action in certain restricted contexts, or all social action always and everywhere. Nor does it foreclose on the possibility of inferring, from such and such statements about their character and circumstances, that, it follows necessarily, so and so did act or will act thus and thus. (Retrodictions and predictions of this form do not assert physical necessities: the necessity qualifying 'it follows' is, as we shall see in Chapter 8, of quite another kind.)

One example of the realization of the former possibility is provided by Popper's "You cannot have full employment without inflation"; if suitably supplemented by an account of the far less than universal reference of the 'you'. Another promising vein is that of propositions about the possibly unintended consequences which must be produced by various patterns of social action. Here the necessities, since they are not determining the actions themselves, might be completely universal: they would obtain, that is, wherever and whenever social actions were performed forming these specified patterns; and this universality is not prejudiced by the fact that the same patterns are not in fact found in all times and places. It is curious that sponsors of laws of nature in the social sciences have not been more eager to present candidates of this most promising kind.

Nor is there any shortage of true premises of the second sort, yielding similarly true predictive and retrodictive conclusions. What, however, arguments of this form cannot provide is covering law explanations of conduct of the type standard in the natural sciences. This will distress all, but maybe only, those committed to contending that there must be no fundamental differences between the natural and the social sciences. Covering law explanations explain by showing that and how the truth of the explanandum can be deduced from the truth of the conjunction of one or more nomologicals with statements of the circumstances. Explanations of conduct cannot be of this type since, as has been insisted ad nauseam and beyond, there cannot be laws of nature determining particular courses of action. (For further

discussion, with particular reference to historiography, see
Gardiner 1952 and Dray 1957).

(ii)

Some historical writers, by reason of their commitments
to what they saw as the presuppositions of any genuinely
scientific history, have been misled to believe that their own
researches have warranted unwarrantably strong nomological conclusions. The distinguished Victorian, H. T. Buckle,
for instance, in a much quoted passage from the first chapter
of his *History of Civilization in England*, commended the belief
"that every event is linked to its antecedent by an inevitable
connection, that [every] such antecedent is connected with
a preceding fact; and that thus the whole world forms a
necessary chain, in which indeed every man may play his
part, but can by no means determine what that part shall
be" (Buckle 1903, I, p. 9).

Later, after citing some remarkable year-to-year regularities
in vital statistics, he continues: "In a given state of society, a
certain number of persons must put an end to their own life.
This is the general law; and the special question of who shall
commit the crime depends of course upon special laws . . ."
Nevertheless, "the power of the larger law is so irresistible, that
neither the love of life nor the fear of another world can avail
anything towards even checking its operation" (p. 28).

(iii)

In his Preface to the third German edition of *The Eighteenth Brumaire of Louis Bonaparte* another Victorian – rarely
described as such and even more rarely, though with equal
truth, described as a sometime shareholder/manager in a
mini-multinational – commended his friend the author for
composing "a concise, epigrammatic exposition that laid
bare the whole course of French history since the February
days . . . [and] reduced the miracle of December 2 to *a
natural, necessary result*". It is greatly to the credit of that

recently deceased friend, and highly significant, that, in his own Preface to the second edition, the only claim made was much more modest: "I . . . demonstrate how the class struggle in France created circumstances and relationships that *made it possible* for a grotesque mediocrity to play a hero's part" (Marx 1852, pp. 8 and 6: italics removed and supplied).

(iv)

Earlier we quoted the author of *Thinking about Crime* as arguing that "if causal theories explain why a criminal acts as he does, they also explain why he *must* act as he does" (J. Q. Wilson 1977, p. 58). This argument is valid if the word 'cause' is being employed not in its moral but in its physical sense. But that is not a distinction made either by Wilson or by the many other writers whose work he is reviewing. So, while they are apt, on finding moral causes of criminal behaviour, invalidly to infer that they have thereby shown that and why these criminals *must* act as they do, Wilson, for all his stubborn common sense and conservative concern for the victims, fails to put his finger on the fallacy.

Wilson also fails in much the same way in his dealings with the sort of criminologist for whom "the individual who is confronted with a choice among kinds of opportunities does not *choose*, he 'learns deviant values' from the 'social structure of the slum'" (p. 63). This refusal to recognize that people make choices, that we are none of us the totally helpless creatures of our environments, that different people, or even the same people at different times, may respond in different ways to the same environments, Wilson apparently sees as a perverse individual eccentricity. Perverse it most certainly is, since the facts which criminologists of this sort are refusing to recognize are within the common everyday experience of us all. Yet it is not a mere minority aberration.

No doubt the historians and the economists are for the most part immune: in any case they tend neither to think of themselves nor to be thought of as social scientists. But among the sociologists, the social policy researchers and their

like, as well as among those boasting of having acquired some
social science background in the course of their professional
training, such refusals are not found solely as the oddities
of licensed eccentrics. Instead they are largely unnoticed
features of a whole climate of opinion. Skinner, as we saw
in Section 3 of Chapter 3, puts forward a bold and explicit
formulation of these refusals, insisting that they must be
the presuppositions of any human science. But for what
sometimes seems to be the great majority, both of practising
social scientists and of those who have merely suffered some
instruction in the social sciences, they are, rather, rarely if
ever formulated, continually misguiding, deep background
assumptions.

(v)

Again, consider the following report of a conversation between two modern mothers: "One mentioned how, on a visit
to her child's school, a particular seven-year-old appeared
to be in the process of dismantling the classroom while the
teacher stood passively by. 'Can't you stop him?' asked the
mother. 'He comes from a broken home', the teacher fatal-
istically replied. 'Well,' said the mother, 'he can bloody well
learn, can't he?'" (Morgan 1978, p. 57).

No doubt that fatalistic teacher had been told, either during
some Sociology of Education course at college, and/or by some
social worker who had also got it from some similar source,
that there is, as indeed there is, a high positive correlation
between broken homes and bad behaviour and low achievement at school. But even if this were allowed to be enough
to warrant the conclusion that a particular misbehaving
seven-year-old from a broken home is misbehaving because
he comes from such a wretched home, it does not even
begin to show that he could not, given firm discipline and
good teaching, become one of those who, all handicaps
notwithstanding, perform up to the top level of their native
abilities. Such sociological correlations only seem to warrant

fatalistic conclusions when people fail to make and to insist upon crucial distinctions: between physical and moral causes; between the more and the less fundamental senses of 'can no other'; between the prescriptive and the descriptive meanings of 'expect'; and so on.

The most that such correlations show is that it is very likely that people from homes of such and such a sort – rich or poor, close-knit or broken, bookish or bookless, working-class or whatever else – will in fact act in this or that way. They cannot show that they will not be acting at all, but behaving instead under an absolute necessitation. In fact the correlations, even when they are both significant and positive, are always a lot less than perfect; that is to say, one to one.

So when someone claims, on the basis of the actual or alleged subsistence of such a correlation, that such and such a condition is the, or a, cause of this or that sort of behaviour, they should always be challenged to tell us why the minority behaves differently – if indeed it actually is a minority and not an untroublesome, silent and hence unnoticed majority. Such questions are especially to the point, and perhaps most often unasked, when the behaviour under discussion is in some way deplorable, and the practical reason for seeking its causes lies in the hope of discovering cures. Why do not ALL the members of such and such a set become delinquents? And how might the non-delinquent minority – or majority – be increased?

(vi)

As we began to appreciate in Chapter 4, the refusal to recognize that people make and cannot but make choices, and that people who are in most ways similar may choose in different senses, infects almost all the most frequently cited work on racial, sexual or educational equality. For to infer inequalities of opportunity directly from observed inequalities of outcome, as so many so commonly do, is to assume that inclinations and abilities – to say nothing of qualities like determination, and persistence with ventures once undertaken – are found in substantially the same distributions in all the various sets which are being compared. It is this same false assumption which misguides all those – and today their name is legion – who insist that there cannot but be racist or sexist discrimination wherever the sexes and the races are not in every subset distributed in the same way as in the whole set of the population.

There is in fact an enormous amount of usually neglected evidence, drawn from many countries and many cultures, showing how big these differences of inclination and of actual choice can be. For instance: thanks to various forms of what is called positive discrimination – a commended euphemism for those racist discriminations approved and required in the name of 'anti-racism' – many racially Chinese Malaysian nationals have to study abroad. Nevertheless, "although there are approximately equal numbers of Chinese and Malays in Malaysian colleges and universities, the Chinese out-number the Malays by more than eight-to-one in the sciences and fifteen-to-one in engineering" (Sowell 1983, p. 139). Again: "Back before World War I, a study in New York City showed that German and Jewish school children graduated from high school at a rate more than a hundred times that for Irish or Italian children" (p. 38). Now that really was for the Irish and Italians an achievement in under-achievement! Nor, in view of the later rises of both the Irish-Americans and the Italian-Americans, is it plausible to try to diminish this negative achievement by postulating any genetically determined inferiorities.

An even more striking example of this besetting occupational reluctance to admit the importance of choice, and of the differences between the senses of choices made, is provided by the monumental study reported in *Inequality: A Reassessment of the Effect of Family and Schooling in America*. This is most remarkable among sociological works for its willingness to admit, at least as between individuals, large genetically determined differences in abilities. Yet, in examining factors favouring financial success, the researchers collapse into one residual miscellany, called "varieties of luck and on-the-job competence", all those various human differences which they either cannot measure or have not tried to measure (Jencks and others 1973, p. 8). Into this discounted category of unmeasured unequalizables are flung all disregarded differences in respect of inclination and choice; to say nothing of those regarding the supposedly officerlike qualities of drive, initiative, energy, resource, enterprise, creative imagination, and – you name it.

(vii)

Economists, by contrast, are professionally concerned with choices between alternative employments of scarce means; and perhaps also inclined to believe that, at least typically, people make their choices in the senses which – on the basis of the information available to them – appear most likely best to serve their several individual ends. Given these commonsense convictions, economists are further inclined to believe that the Royal Road to reducing the amount of any kind of disfavoured behaviour must be to decrease its perceived rewards and/or to increase its perceived costs.

It would be hard to find any assumptions more alien to most sociologically oriented criminologists. They often believe that social scientists have discovered that no potential criminal is ever deterred (Rockwell 1974, p. 51). Apart from the general occupational disbelief in the reality of choice, this particular 'discovery' seems to depend on two quite inadequately supportive particular facts: that the death penalty does not seem to deter murders within the family; and that present prisoners, who are the persons most accessible to criminological investigation, were not deterred from committing the offences which landed them in prison. (Curiously, our 'discoverers' never reflect how they can themselves be deterred from parking illegally by a credible threat to tow away and impound all illegally parked cars!)

It is, therefore, not surprising that, when the American Enterprise Institute organized an incursion of economists into criminological preserves, the results were intellectually

exhilarating; sufficient to restore anyone's faith in the possibilities of wholly realistic and doctrinally unblinkered social
science. (See Rottenberg 1973: not only for several further
references to silly statements about the ineffectiveness of all
deterrents; but also for calculations showing that, given the
present condition of the American criminal justice system, a
criminal career is for many the course of supreme economic
rationality.)

4   Radicalism: the bigotry and the prejudice

One kind of works presented as contributions to the social
sciences deserves a whole section to itself. Since these are
works dedicated to the promotion of the revolutionary socialist project in some more or less Marxist understanding, such
a section constitutes an appropriate conclusion to the present
chapter. Throughout the sixties and the seventies and on
into at least the early eighties works in this genre have been
advertised in every successive list from nearly all the major,
most prestigious publishers. Yet reviewers have rarely treated
such stuff with the harshness it deserves, and scarcely anyone
has ever challenged the academic and political good faith of
the authors. Almost never, that is to say, has there been
any public raising and pressing of doubts as to whether the
authors of these Radical books are sincerely pursuing truth,
or whether their actual political objectives are those humane
concerns to which they themselves pretend to be devoted.

(i)

Perhaps the first person to put such charges into print was
my former colleague, the late Paul Halmos – a lifelong,
'revisionist' Social Democrat, driven from his native Hungary
by the Communists. In Halmos 1974 and 1976 he questioned
the commitment both to sincere sociological enquiry and to
human welfare of those who, often arrogating to themselves
the label 'Critical' (in practice a codeword for 'Radical' or

'Marxist'), were reviewing the perceived failures of the British welfare state and their putative causes, while remaining studiously silent about corresponding phenomena, or the lack of them, in the USSR and other countries of the Socialist Bloc. Similar charges were more fully developed and more widely applied in Gould 1977. Gould was in consequence much abused by those whom the cap of accusation fitted. He was even summoned before the Executive of the British Sociological Association. It seems that they wished: not to determine whether he could prove his charges; but to reproach him for daring to criticize fellow professionals – who were, apparently, to be presumed or even assumed innocent whether or not they had been proved guilty!.

Correctly to appreciate the burden of these accusations we need to develop a contrast between present and earlier generations. Up till World War II and for a decade or two thereafter there was in Britain, as in most similar countries, only one significant organization of the extreme left, the Communist Party (Muscovite). When then members or fellow-travellers of that party maintained that some actual or alleged evil was due to capitalism, they normally accepted the responsibility of labouring to show that in the USSR, under socialism, it either had already disappeared or at least was disappearing. When too they advocated Marxist-Leninist policies as the only answer, they also accepted the corresponding responsibility, to show that the implementation of these policies was in fact delivering the goods, exactly as promised. Whether they did or could succeed in showing what they had to show, is, of course, another story. Here the crucial point is that, to the credit of their sincerity, both academic and political, they tried.

The effluxion of time has, however, made it enormously more difficult to defend the actual results of the recommended revolutionary transformations; while simultaneously giving birth to many other correspondingly converted societies. Perhaps it is for these very reasons that today the usual form is to concentrate exclusively upon 'Western', or 'capitalist', or 'late capitalist' societies; to say or to suggest that everything picked out for condemnation is peculiar to such societies, a product of their distinctive and damnable social system; but then stubbornly to eschew all relevant questions about contemporary socialist societies – or, as is often said, under pressure and for no sufficient reason given, contemporary 'so-called socialist societies'.

This, surely, is intolerable. Most certainly it would not and will not be tolerated by anyone genuinely wanting to know: either whether the causal hypotheses asserted are true; or whether the remedies proposed for the ills identified have been or will be effective.

(ii)

In the present context the opposite of Radical is Reformist. The nature of this antithesis comes out very clearly in a statement from a collection of essays significantly entitled *Counter Course: A Handbook for Course Criticism*: "Applied social science assumes the prevailing ideology of 'piecemeal social engineering'. Racialism, poverty, labour 'unrest' or underdevelopment are not seen as the expressions of basic social contradictions but as problems which can be solved by appropriate reforms" (Pateman 1972, p. 26). The Radical is thus to be defined here as a person who believes that all these evils can be remedied, but only through the 'wholesale Utopian social engineering' of a revolutionary socialist transformation.

Just so soon as the meaning of these two antithetical terms is understood, it should become obvious that a heavy, double burden of proof rests on Radicals. They must justify a pair of assumptions which it would be over-generous to characterize as no more than just egregiously implausible: both that what Radicals call bourgeois societies cannot be reformed piecemeal; and that their own proposed and preferred wholesale, Utopian revolutionary socialist alternative would constitute the panacea. It will not do, notwithstanding that this is what has been and is frequently done, simply to describe and dismiss the contrary Reformist assumptions as an ideology. For, as we saw in Section 2 of Chapter 3, to justify such a dismissal of a set of ideas it is first necessary – and in the present case, surely, impossible – to show that they are mistaken.

Indeed that first response to the Radicals' pretended revelation of the supposedly concealed, contrary assumptions of the Reformists is far too weak. For it is the far-fetched factitious assumptions of the Radicals themselves which really demand justification; justification which is in fact attempted only in the original, unrevised Marxism of the *Communist Manifesto* and *Capital*. For it was precisely and only the theorizing of that 'big book' which was supposed to provide, in the shape of an historicist law of historical development, the talisman to transform what previously deserved to be dismissed as unrealistic Utopian dreams into the solidly based predictions of Scientific Socialism.

And it was the decisive falsification, by the reforming achievements of the second half of the nineteenth century, of the first of the two defining Radical assumptions which produced within the professedly Marxist German Social-Democrat Party the Revisionist movement of Edward Bernstein (Kolakowski 1978, I, Ch. IV).

We have already seen, in Section 2 of Chapter 1 and later, something of Marx's practice of misrepresentation, and of evading or ignoring the most powerful objections. During his lifetime the most formidable of these arose out of the new marginalist and subjectivist insights in economics, first published during the eighteen seventies. There is no evidence of Marx taking any notice, either in public or in private, notwithstanding that these insights obviously could be developed and deployed to demolish something which for Marx was crucial; namely, the Labour Theory of Value. (Famously, in Bohm-Bawerk 1895 they were so employed.)

The Radicals of today follow, in this and other respects, in the steps of their master. Louis Althusser, for instance, in *For Marx* and *Reading Capital*, praises that theory and, without hesitation or reserve, asserts it. So what has he to say about, and in response to, Bohm-Bawerk and the rest of the critical literature? Absolutely nothing. (For much more

about Althusser, and about the parallel performances of all
too numerous others, see Scruton 1985, Ch. 9 and passim.)
There is a word for such stubborn, insistent, persistent
reaffirmations of the rationally unjustified and rationally
unjustifiable. That word, which we must not hesitate to apply
to such secular religious faith, is 'bigotry'.

(iii)

Consider, for example, a pair of books by a Lecturer in Sociology at Goldsmiths' College; books which confess to being
based upon lectures given there to intending schoolteachers.
Both too were selected by a Professor of Education from
another university for inclusion in a series of 'Education
Books', all of which we can expect to see available in the
libraries of most if not all UK institutions for the training of
schoolteachers. One of these books, we are told, was compiled
from the teachings of "a compulsory course in multiracial
education"; teachings which the author's pupils presumably
have been and are required first to swallow and then upon
occasion to regurgitate – under penalty of disqualification for
employment as teachers in UK maintained schools.

In Sarup 1982 various elements of the Marxist magisterium
are presented as jewels of gospel truth. There is no attempt
at critical appraisal, no deployment of supporting evidence,
and no reference whatsoever to any intellectually formidable
objections. In a chapter entitled, characteristically, 'Race,
Imperialism and Education' we are just told that "Lenin's
pamphlet *Imperialism, the Highest Stage of Capitalism* is one of
the most significant and insightful writings of this century.
Though written in 1916, it is amazingly contemporary – and
therefore relevant" (p. 94).

Certainly we may well allow that Lenin's *Imperialism* is
relevant to contemporary affairs. For, whether rightly or
wrongly, innumerable people do accept its contentions as
correct. To sustain the claim to insight, however, it is not
enough to present a summary of those contentions while
absolutely refusing to entertain any whisper of dissent. But

if Sarup has his way none of his pupils will ever know: either
that Lenin's 'Smorgasbord Statistics' have become a textbook
example of unsound social scientific method (Sowell 1985,
pp. 211–12); or that works such as Bauer 1976 and 1981 have
revealed the enormous harm done to so many of the peoples
of the Third World by drawing ruinous practical morals from
Lenin's misguiding doctrines.

Sarup 1986 defines 'racism': not, as in Chapter 4 we argued
should be done, as a matter of unjustly advantaging or
disadvantaging individuals; but in terms of "the domination
of one social group identified as a 'race' over another social
group identified as a 'race'" (p. 7). He thus further encourages himself to do things which he would no doubt have been
eager enough to do without any encouragement at all. At one
place or another he makes – indeed by his Marxist bigotry he
makes himself make – all the mistakes usual in discussing
overrepresentations and underrepresentations. Wherever he
perceives any racial set as under - or overrepresented relative
to its proportion of the population as a whole, Sarup immediately infers and denounces racially discriminatory intention.
"One of the best known cases of discrimination", he requires
us to believe, "is the fact that most black children are put
in the lowest streams and are overrepresented in special
schools" (Sarup 1982, p. 105).

We have already said in earlier chapters enough to show
that and why this immediate inference is invalid. But it is
worthwhile to make two further points by the way. First, if
anywhere it so happens that a disproportionate number of
black children do actually need some special sort of educational help, then both their teachers and all the authorities
concerned – if they are to escape an unleashing of the furies
of such 'anti-racists' – will have to conspire to deny that help
to some of those children. (For evidence that in the USA
such denials have already occurred, and for these reasons,
compare Flew 1976, pp. 74–6).

Second, if with Sarup we abuse the word 'black' to embrace
everyone who is not white, then what he here asserts to be
a fact is simply not a fact. For in 1987 the Inner London

Education Authority (ILEA) published statistics of the O-level and CSE examination results for the years 1985 and 1986. These showed that the only racially defined sets of pupils performing even worse than the whites were the Afro-Caribbeans and the Bangladeshis. The blacks from Africa, the Indians and the Pakistanis all did better; the Indians and the Pakistanis very, very much better.

(iv)

A piquant, paradigm case of Radical prejudice, and of its costs to practical reform, is provided by David Donnison as Director of the Centre for Environmental Studies. He would at that time, I think, unlike most of the others employed in that Centre, still have claimed to be himself a Reformist rather than a Radical. Nevertheless in his Foreword to *From Birth to Seven*, a report on the National Child Development Study (Davie and others, 1972), Donnison wrote: "The patterns glimpsed . . . are so deeply embedded in this country's economic and social structure that they cannot be greatly changed by anything short of equally far-reaching changes in that structure."

In a manner which is in fact altogether typical of educational sociologists, the authors themselves remark: "Poor housing is often mentioned as one of the contributory causes of school failure" (p. xvi); and they then proceed to quote the here rather Radical R. M. Titmuss, maintaining that it is impossible to do much good in the schools "while millions of children live in slums without baths, decent lavatories, leisure facilities, room to explore and space to dream" (p. 54). So committed are they to these pessimistic preconceptions that, without for one moment allowing themselves to reflect on educational achievement in any of the places or periods in which all but the most tiny minorities have suffered housing worse than the most deplorable in contemporary Britain, they proceed to calculate how much retardation in reading age is to be put down to overcrowding and how much to the lack of basic amenities.*

Our Radical researchers contrived, such is the power of prejudice, not to grasp the refutatory significance of certain items in their own tables of data. Had their Titmussian assumptions been correct, then, presumably, areas with a lot of overcrowding would also have to have a deal of poor reading. So what do we find, when we take our own critical look at their data? Far and away the worst region in the United Kingdom for overcrowding is Scotland, where 39 per cent of children live in conditions rated 'overcrowded'. In none of the other regions distinguished did the figure go above 20 per cent, and four were below 10 per cent.

Now what about the percentages of those accounted 'good readers' and 'poor readers'? Still without apparently noticing its relevance, they give the decisive answer: "In reading attainment the most striking feature to emerge from the results (Fig. 34) is that the proportion of good readers (Southgate reading test score 29–30) in Scotland is markedly higher than in any other region of Britain. The difference is even more marked for poor readers (score 0–20). For example, for every eighteen poor readers in Scotland there were, proportionately, twenty-nine poor readers in England and thirty in Wales" (pp. 107–8).†

It was, in the present case, bad enough that all concerned should have allowed themselves by their shared prejudices to be misguided to produce manifestly unsound results. What

---

*Had they been writing today their Radical prejudices would have required that they ignore also evidence such as that of Chew 1990. This reports the strikingly superior achievement in tests of English spelling of Zulu fifth-formers in South Africa as compared with pupils at a Sixth Form College somewhere in England. The Zulu children were of course operating in a second language, and came from on average much poorer families living in much worse housing. Incidentally – a point for all those assuming that increases in the teacher/pupil ratio constitute or necessarily result in educational improvement – these Zulu children, like children in high-achieving Japan, were being taught in classes of forty or more.

†*From Birth to Seven* has not been the only report on the NCDS in which well-publicized conclusions have not in fact been sustained by the data deployed in their support (Cox and Marks, 1980 and 1982).

was, however, much worse was their consequent failure to put and to press the question how we are to account for the apparent superiority, at least for the teaching of reading, of the Scottish schools. For, if only we could discover the correct answer, it could, presumably, be put to use helping teachers and pupils to do better in England and Wales. (I confess, not very shamefacedly, that I get rather angry when I hear such people pretending to be 'critical social scientists'; and still more when they preen themselves on their 'caring', 'compassionate' superiority to their allegedly 'callous' and 'heartless' political opponents.)

8 Matters of Fact and Relations of Ideas

All the objects of human reason or enquiry may naturally be divided into two kinds, to wit, *Relations of Ideas*, and *Matters of Fact*. Of the first kind are the sciences of Geometry, Algebra and Arithmetic; and, in short, every affirmation which is either intuitively or demonstratively certain. *That the square of the hypotenuse is equal to the square of the two sides*, is a proposition which expresses the relation between these two figures. *That three times five is equal to the half of thirty*, expresses a relation between these numbers. Propositions of this kind are discoverable by the mere operation of thought, without dependence on what is anywhere existent in the universe . . .

Matters of fact, which are the second objects of human reason, are not ascertained in the same manner; nor is our evidence of their truth, however, great, of like nature with the foregoing. The contrary of every matter of fact is still possible; because it can never imply a contradiction, and is conceived by the mind with the same facility and distinctness, as if ever so comfortable to reality. *That the sun will not rise tomorrow* is no less intelligible a proposition, and implies no more contradiction than the affirmation, *that it will rise*.

David Hume, *An Enquiry concerning Human
Understanding, see IV, pt i, pp. 25–6.*

The challenge presented in the motto passage above is known as Hume's Fork. It is a merit of this nickname that it suggests, correctly, that Hume is engaged in forceful inquiry. He is not just claiming to have noticed, what is manifestly not the case, that every assertive utterance which is to any extent intelligible falls unequivocally into one or other of these two mutually exclusive and together exhaustive categories. He is, rather, insisting that it is always possible and often necessary to force ourselves and others to decide which of these two utterly different sorts of assertion we are really wanting to make. This insistence was fundamental to the Logical Positivism of the Vienna Circle, formed shortly after the end of World War I, and dispersed when National Socialist Germany enforced its Anschluss with (annexation and incorporation of) Austria. Logical Positivism, as thus defined, is not to be confused with the Positivism unqualified of Auguste Comte and his nineteenth-century followers.

1 Logical necessity, logical possibility, and logical impossibility

Several further possible occasions of confusion call for brief attention before we can begin to put Hume's Fork to use. First, in speaking of the relations of ideas Hume is concerned with the logical relations between concepts rather than with likenesses and unlikenesses between mental images. It is not a matter of psychological fact but of what follows or does not follow, what is or is not incompatible with what.

Second, both the two fundamental catch-all categories include both true and false propositions. Since it is intolerably paradoxical to say that something is both a matter of fact and yet not the case, it is best to think, on the one hand, of propositions stating *or purporting to state* the relations of ideas, and, on the other hand, of propositions stating *or purporting to state* matters of fact.

Third, in the present context, the word 'possible', along with such associated terms as 'necessary' and 'impossible', are all employed in senses less familiar than those previously explained and characterized as practical or physical. To say that some suggestion is logically possible is to say that it is coherent, that it makes sense, that making it involves the maker in no self-contradiction, that what is suggested is conceivable. Even if it cannot be pictured, it can at least be intelligibly described.

(i)

Propositions stating the true relations of ideas are said to be necessarily true or to express necessary truths. If this proposition can be validly deduced from that, then this proposition is said to follow necessarily from that. And a valid deductive argument is, by definition, an argument such that to assert the premises while denying the conclusion is to contradict yourself. What a proposition means is thus the sum of all that can be immediately deduced from it, while both 'valid deduction' and 'logical necessity' are similarly defined in terms of meaning and of self-contradiction. So, for anyone who is serious about attempting to think soundly about anything, it is essential both to master these several notions and to appreciate their interconnections.

The key notion is self-contradiction. Where contradiction occurs it is – pace G. W. F. Hegel and all his direct and indirect disciples – a feature not of the non-linguistic world but of language. It is statements and propositions which may be in contradiction one to another. Material things are (sometimes) under tension, while people are (often) in conflict. Self-contradiction has to be an intolerable scandal to all, but only, those who – like Bertrand Russell's pedant – prefer their statements to be true. Such persons cannot endure to hear p simultaneously both asserted and denied. For, above all, we want to know, now and always, what truly is the case.

Deduction being what deduction is, definable in terms of self-contradiction, it follows that valid deductive argument can never reveal anything which was not already implicit in its premises. One mildly interesting corollary is that the explanation of a series of facts can never be deduced from any set of statements simply recording the facts to be explained. Any such 'explanans' would have to be dismissed on the grounds

*Mao Tse-tung's lecture 'On Contradiction', originally delivered in 1937 at the Yenan Anti-Japanese Military and Political College, constitutes a curious combination of practical revolutionary politics with complete theoretical confusion about contradictions supposedly inherent in the universe around us.

that it told us no more than we knew already, that it was at best only a partial or perhaps complete restatement of the explanandum. In this sense, if only in this sense, the explaining of facts cannot but be an essentially creative activity.

Because to contradict any true proposition stating only the relations of ideas is to contradict yourself, to assert such a proposition is not to assert anything substantial about the Universe around us. It would therefore seem – though this is, of course, disputed – that all the necessarily true propositions of formal logic and of pure mathematics must be, at bottom, tautologies. The reason why they do not all look as empty and as obvious as textbook examples of tautologies is that even the best of us humans are endowed with rather poor powers of reasoning and of logical intuition.

(ii)

It is as easy to confound the two senses of 'necessary' and of its associates as it is important that they should not be confounded. Hume employed his Fork first in order to establish that anything may be the cause of anything; in the sense that it is not logically necessary for any thing or sort of thing to be the cause of any other thing or sort of thing. Unfortunately he was so keen to defend this insight – an insight which, as we have seen, is essential to the progress of the social sciences – that he refused to allow that we all have experience of a second sort of necessity, the practical or physical or contingent.

It is also tempting and common to make the mistake of thinking that, when one proposition follows necessarily, as a matter of logic, from another proposition, then either the former or the latter or both must themselves be making some assertion about necessities, in either the second or the first sense of 'necessity'. This is what was going on, and going wrong, in all those arguments which purported to deduce the massively substantial conclusion of a universal, physically necessitating determinism from tautological premises stating only the logically necessary relations of ideas. It is the same vicious yet seductive move which is made whenever anyone infers what will in fact be done from premises making no claims about physical necessity; and then, falsely, takes it that they have shown that the persons concerned will not be able to behave in any but the predicted ways.

Arguments of the first of the two sorts just distinguished are at least as old as Book IX of Aristotle's *On Interpretation*. Let us, however, work here with a specimen familiar to an earlier generation of filmgoers. It comes in a theme song sung by Miss Doris Day beginning: "Che sarà, sarà. Whatever will be will be"; and concluding that there is nothing which anyone can do to stop anything. Spell this out in a clarificatory notation and it becomes obvious that the tautological premise is that, for all values of X, from X *will be* it follows necessarily that X *will be*. Indeed it does. But it does not follow necessarily that X *will necessarily be*. It simply does not follow: neither if the second 'necessarily' is construed, as in its new context is natural, in the physical sense; nor if it is construed, much less naturally, in the same logical sense as the first.

It is much more difficult to spot that and how things are going wrong when the premise or premises are not tautological but substantial; and when other words of the sort which Immanuel Kant (1724–1804) loved to call apodeictic are employed, as well as 'necessarily'. That was the pedagogic reason why, in the previous paragraph, we began with a cartoon-simple textbook example, dissecting the invalid argument in order to display its nerve in a clarificatory notation. (By the way: 'apodeictic' is an adjective referring to logically compulsive demonstration: such expressions as 'must be' and 'cannot but be' therefore score as apodeictic.)

(iii)

We have just considered one type of fallacious move, by which usually false conclusions about inexorable practical necessities may be invalidly derived from insufficient premises. There is another similar mistake, equally persistent and with an equally ancient ancestry. This consists in failing to distinguish causal from criterial senses of the word 'make'; and then, mistakenly, assuming that having the criteria is the cause of all the phenomena which satisfy those criteria. People notice that it is the law which makes crimes and, hence, criminals; in the sense that certain sorts of behaviour, and hence certain kinds of behaver, are correctly describable as crimes, and criminals, only and precisely because they are by the criminal law so defined. In this criterial sense of 'make', the law does indeed make both crimes and criminals.

But, thus understood, this is a pretty pedestrian truism. How much more dashing it is to suggest, or even outright to say, that the same sentence still expresses a truth when the 'makes' is construed in the causal sense. In this interpretation the claim is being made that it is the criminal justice system itself, or perhaps only the criminal justice system of "capitalist society", which is the ultimate cause of all the behaviour which it defines as criminal; that, if only we could get rid of the whole system, then there would – the Revolution accomplished – be no rapes, no muggings, no assault and battery, no robbery, no murder; nothing, nothing but idyllic sweetness and light.

Once again, once the nerve of the fallacious argument is thus clearly displayed, it becomes difficult to believe that anyone could, sincerely and with a straight face, either argue so outrageously or assert such nonsense. But, of course, the distinction between these two senses of 'make' has to be made. Even Plato himself, without making it, spoke of the Form or Idea or Essence of Justice as it if might be – must be – both the criterion and the cause of whatever is in fact just. Nowadays those who are still committing the same fallacy wrap it up both with empirical material and with other confusions. They argue, for instance, and just as wrongly, that whatever is legally defined as criminal must be so defined quite arbitrarily, or in the interests solely of the class enemy (Quinney 1970, pp. 1–14, 204–50 and 316; and compare S. Cohen 1972 passim).

The same ruinous failure to distinguish causal from criterial senses of the word 'make' is also found in widely circulating and strongly recommended works in the sociology of education. As in the criminological case the conclusion of the fallacious argument is supported, and its fallaciousness to some extent concealed, by further falsehoods and confusions. In Young 1971 (Ch. 5), for instance, we find Nell Keddie apparently believing that, since (of course) pupils do not differ in their actual abilities, the differences supposedly revealed by IQ tests and other kinds of categorization are merely apparent. (By the way: how do those many atheists so certain that there can be no natural differences in abilities between members of different racial sets, or even between different individuals, think that they know that things actually are as no doubt they would have been had the Universe been created and had the Creator taken their advice? It is a question which should be pressed more often than it is!)

Another example of this common collapsing of the distinction between two senses of 'make' was provided by Bernard Coard, a man who later played a leading role in the rise and fall of the Communist 'New Jewel' regime in Grenada. In a book recommended by ILEA in documents circulated during 1983 to all its employees, Coard undertook to explain *How the West Indian child is made educationally sub-normal in the British School System*. Here the differences allegedly made are real not apparent, while the conclusion that they are so caused is also supported both by the general assumption of environmental omnipotence and by a more particular belief that pupils are creatures of the expectations of their teachers. (If only this were true we should all of us be able to become 100 per cent successful teachers by an easy adjustment of our expectations!)

2 Putting Hume's Fork to use

In Act I Scene 5 of *Hamlet* the hero responds to a question about the ghost by saying:

> There's ne'er a villain dwelling in all Denmark
> But he's an arrant knave.

To this uninformative information Horatio very reasonably responds with a complaint:

> There needs no ghost, my lord, come from the grave,
> To tell us this.

There needs no ghost, because Hamlet's utterance is of the first Humian kind: it is a proposition stating only the relations of ideas. In another terminology it is analytic, its truth-value knowable apriori. To say this is to say that we can tell whether it is true or false – in this case that it is necessarily true – simply by analysing the meanings and hence the implications of the various symbols employed in its expression, and without any appeal to extra-linguistic experience.

It is, perhaps, just worth emphasizing what sort of appeal to experience is *not* required. For the author of *Anti-Dühring* was certainly not the last to believe that he could dispose of the contention that pure mathematics and abstract economic analysis consist in universal apriori truths by pointing out, perfectly correctly, that the concepts employed could not themselves be acquired without experience (Engels 1878, pp. 46ff.; and compare pp. 103 and 134ff.). A similar misconception of the nature of mathematics has apparently become established orthodoxy in British secondary education (North 1988, pp. 63–83). Yet Her Majesty's Inspectors of Schools would presumably be as surprised to learn that they had been anticipated by Engels, as he might have been to find that in this at least he was at one with John Stuart Mill (1806–73).

(i)

What Horatio wanted was a proposition of the second Humian sort; synthetic, with its truth-value knowable only aposteriori. Had Hamlet claimed, unpoetically and anachronistically, that all Danish villains are the products of maternal deprivation, then his proposition would have been both synthetic and aposteriori. It could be known to be true or – much more likely – false only by reference to some actual empirical study of the home background of Danish villains.

The distinction embodied in Hume's Fork has already been employed in our examination, in Chapter 7, of Popper's candidates for the diploma title 'Law of Nature in the social sciences'. But it has a much wider application. In the first place, as was hinted during that examination, people who have offered some generalization about supposed matters of social fact will often, under the pressure of falsifying counter-examples, so amend their too bold generalizations that these come to express nothing but made-to-measure tautologies. That all concerned shall appreciate exactly what is going on, and going wrong, the resolute and persistent application of Hume's Fork is most strongly indicated. In the second place, we frequently find one and the same form of words interpreted ambiguously: on some occasions as expressing a necessary truth; and on others as purporting to state a matter of fact. To the extent that Hume's Fork is not applied to these manoeuvres, resolutely and repeatedly, it will appear that the second proposition is both as necessary and as true as the first. Sometimes what are in fact tautologies are offered either as explanations of facts or as fresh factual findings from empirical research. Harassed by Opposition MPs during Prime Minister's question time, James Callaghan once opined that the reason why increased employment in British industry had resulted in no increase in output might be low productivity. Werner Sombart – another person capable of better things – even ventured the suggestion that the rise of capitalism might be attributed to the growth of the Spirit of Capitalism – something which cannot be identified except as epitomizing the phenomena to be explained.

(ii)

Such standing-start presentations of tautology are relatively rare, and can be recognized and discredited with little difficulty. For, though tautologies do not contain substance, they are analytic and do at least have a sense. Much more troublesome is the production of whole paragraphs leaving

the reader at a loss to divine what, if any, determinate meaning the author wishes to convey. Andreski's *Social Sciences as
Sorcery* is a very rich secondary source of such material.

Here the most important warning is against misplaced
humble-mindedness. Confronted by a piece of specialist
writing in any of the natural sciences, intelligent and literate
laypersons will, typically, have little or no understanding
of what is being said. That is because we do not know
the first thing about the subjects under discussion, and are
not masters of the required technical vocabularies. With
studies of human conduct and human affairs, however,
our situation is entirely different. All of us have a great
deal of knowledge and experience, although there are also
enormous differences between the amounts of that knowledge and the width of that experience. That is why we
should expect to understand not only history books written
for a general public but also most historical papers published
only in the specialist journals. The serious difficulties to be
expected are with accounts of the application of sophisticated
research techniques and, in particular, of statistical analyses.
The same, surely, should hold for most of the other social
sciences; certainly for anthropology and sociology, as well as
for policy studies and political science.

This point made we should recall two others mentioned
earlier. First, by far the most effective tactic for bringing
out what, if anything of substance, actually is being asserted
is to discover what would have to have happened or to be
happening or to be going to happen to require the asserter
to concede that the original assertion was false. Since not
not p ($\sim\sim p$) is equivalent to p, a proposition which denies
nothing about the Universe around us asserts nothing either
(Flew 1955). In the gnomic words of the *Tractatus Logico-
Philosophicus*: "The propositions of logic are tautologies. The
propositions of logic therefore say nothing. (They are the
analytical propositions)" (Wittgenstein 1922, 6 and 6.11).

Second, remember that Maxim of the Marquis de Vauven
argues: "For the philosopher clarity is a matter of good faith."
So it is for the social scientist, and for everyone else as well.

All those who prefer their statements to be true, and in particular everyone who is investigating in good faith, wants it to be clear to all what is being asserted. How else can those assertions be criticized and, if false, shown to be false? For all such persons, as above all for the Socrates of Plato's *Apology*: "The unexamined life is for a human being not worth living" (38 A 5).

The continually neglected truism embodied in that Maxim gives us the key to understanding our failure to understand a crucial paragraph in Nicos Poulantzas. He was, in 'The Problem of the Capitalist State', labouring to maintain a central Marxist doctrine; which, as a believing and practising Leninist, if for no other reason, he must himself at some level have realized to be untrue. He was, that is to say, trying, no doubt unconsciously, to ensure that neither he nor his readers should be forced to attend to the falsity of the contention that wielders of political and military and bureaucratic power are always and everywhere completely the creatures of class interests outside the state machine.

We have, therefore, to suffer this painful piece of near meaningless mystification: ". . . although the members of the state apparatus belong, by their class origin, to different classes, they function according to a specific internal unity. Their class origin – *class situation* – recedes into the background in relation to that which unifies them – their *class position* – that is to say, the fact that they belong precisely to the State apparatus and that they have as their *objective function* the actualization of the role of the State. This in turn means that the bureaucracy, as a specific and relatively 'united' social category, is the 'servant' of the ruling class, not by reason of its class origins, which are divergent, or by reason of its personal relations with the ruling class, but by reason of the fact that its internal unity derives from its actualization of the objective role of the State. The totality of this role itself coincides with the interests of the ruling class" (Blackburn 1972, pp. 246–7).

(iii)

Although tautologies and other utterances empty of determinate (would be) factual content are often launched from,
as it were, a standing start, it is more common to discover
that what certainly began as a hefty empirical generalization
has, under the pressure of falsifying counter-examples, been
so qualified as to become now emptily tautological. Perhaps
someone starts by contending, in the context of a discussion
of religious education, that those who have been raised to
be Christians will be better citizens than the rest. Then
an objector points out that those claiming to have been
raised as and to be Roman Catholics have long been heavily
over-represented in British prisons and Borstal institutions.
One possible but deplorably evasive response is to make the
No-*true*-Scotsman Move (Flew 1975, 3.1–3.7, 3.13–3.15 and
4.1): 'No *true* Roman Catholic becomes a criminal.'

Again we are, or at least until the admitted collapse of all
the Soviet Type Economies (STEs) at the end of the eighties
we used to be, bombarded with assurances that under full
socialism all manner of things would be well. To the objection
that in the existing fully socialist countries all manner of
things were far from well, and in many cases much further
from well than the corresponding things in countries not yet
fully socialist, the pat reply was all too often that precisely
this is what made those failed paradises not *truly* socialist.

The key point to seize is that if any general proposition
– All such and suches are so and so – is to be satisfactorily
substantial, then such and suches have to be identifiable
entirely independently of so and sos, and the other way
about. For instance, the *Communist Manifesto* asserts: "The
ruling ideas of each age have ever been the ideas of its ruling
class" (Marx and Engels 1848, p. 102). In so far as this is put
forward as a contribution to social science, we cannot begin
to determine its truth-value until and unless we have been
provided, or have provided ourselves, with objective and
independent criteria for identifying the ruling ideas and
for doing so without either implicitly or explicitly assuming
that these just are, by definition, the ideas of whoever we are

proposing to pick out as members of the ruling class. Once thus clearly stated, the present point, like almost all the others made in this chapter, will appear too obvious to merit our labouring. Yet all are being overlooked all the time, not only in popular but even in professional social thinking.

(iv)

Another kind of occasion for the employment of Hume's Fork is where we find one and the same form of words ambiguously interpreted, sometimes expressing a necessary truth, at other times purporting to state a matter of fact, and where the truth of the necessary truth is then mistaken to prove the truth of the more substantial proposition. One favourite token of this type of fallacy is the popular putative demonstration of the demoralizing conclusion that there can be no such thing as a genuinely unselfish action. In a made-to-measure sense of 'want', every action is defined as done solely because the agent wanted to do it. But that is not, of course, the everyday sense in which you can properly be credited with unselfishness for giving up your Saturday afternoon to sick-visiting; although that was in truth just about the last thing you wanted to do.

A currently important sub-class of this type of fallacy takes off from the logically necessary connections between correlative terms. It is, for instance, only in so far as something can be (said to be, relatively,) large that anything can be (said to be, relatively,) small; only in so far as there is (actual or possible) development that there can be (said to be) underdevelopment; and so on. The temptation is, through failing to distinguish either the criterial from the causal sense of 'make', or tautological from substantial interpretations of key utterances, fallaciously to conclude that the richer must everywhere be responsible for the absolute levels achieved by the poorer, the more developed for the absolute levels achieved by the less developed, and so on. But, if ever or wherever any of this is in fact the case, it has to be shown to be so: not by apriori and fallacious argument; but by citing hard and particular empirical evidence. To attempt anything else is like assuming that mice can be smaller than elephants only because the elephants have eaten all the food which would otherwise have fattened the mice.

A major reason why so many people, while deploying little if any relevant evidence, are so apt to be persuaded that poverty and underdevelopment are always and everywhere the results of exploitation by the less poor and the more developed is that they insist that what has to be explained is why so many people, and so many countries, have so little, and are so backward. They thus presuppose, as a socio-economic analogue of the First Law of Motion, that the natural condition of humanity, all deviations from which demand explanation in terms of anti-social forces, must be one of sustained economic growth, in which everyone enjoys a high and rapidly rising standard of living. Yet this, as the slightest acquaintance with world history should teach us, is the opposite of the truth.

The whole approach is, in the most literal construction, preposterous. It was looking-glass logic to argue "that in the self-same relations in which wealth is produced, poverty is produced also; that in the self-same relations in which there is a development of the productive forces, there is also a driving force of repression" (Marx 1847, p. 104).

(v)

For another collection of occasions for the strenuous employment of Hume's Fork we turn to Robert Michels' *Political Parties*. This is the source of the supposed Iron Law of Oligarchy. The first edition was published in 1911, an English translation from the 1915 edition appeared in the same year, while the most recent republication seems to have been in 1959 and by a New York firm specializing in reprints of classics of science and mathematics. It is called "a classic of sociology". It would be as well described, or as ill, as a classic of political science.

The most disappointing feature of an over-long and rather

wretched book is that we are offered no straightforward statement of the thesis proposed; no straightforward statement of
what it is which, according to the supposed law, is supposed
to be practically necessary, and what practically impossible.
So there simply is no official formulation, provided by its
eponymous discoverer, of Michels' Iron Law of Oligarchy.
In so far as the claim is that, in any centralized and hierarchical organization, those occupying positions of power and
influence must always be a minority, then all we have is a
logically necessary truth; on all fours with the modest and
unadventurous assertion that the winners of races involving
more than two competitors must always remain, among all
the runners, a minority. If the claim is that the same people
tend to stay in positions of power and influence, and that,
once they are in, it is often very hard to get them out,
then this is perfectly true. But it is not a truth with the
semantic force and the implications of a law of nature. If
the claim is that no one is ever got out of any such position
by pressures from below, or that, even if they are, successors
always maintain all the policies and practices of predecessors;
then these claims are simply false.

"As long as any organization is loosely constructed",
we are told, "no professional leadership can arise. The
anarchists ... have no regular leaders" (Michels 1959,
p. 36). But if the Michels thesis is to be applied only to
hierarchical and centralized organizations, then it is tautological. He proceeds to proclaim "the *logical impossibility*
of the 'representative' system" (p. 36: italics supplied).

Having offered Rousseauian reasons for saying this,
Michels goes on to suggest that it is a matter of fact
that representatives always take their own lines, ignore
the actual wishes of their electors, and cannot be by those
electors effectively replaced. But these would-be factual
assertions are then tacitly admitted to be less than universal truths. Britain, for instance, is accused of being an
untrustworthy ally because of changes in party control
(p. 103)! So some representatives can, after all, be replaced
by others, pursuing different policies? Sometimes too

representatives do, it seems, change course, in deference to the wishes of their constituents. This concession also is dismissed as of no account. For, Michels argues, they do this *only because* they do not want to be replaced by rivals (pp. 164–5).

It is, by the way, remarkable how many people will, like Michels here, attempt to show that something is not the case by offering their own account of why it is! So let us take a tip now from the notoriously pessimistic Arthur Schopenhauer (1788–1860), while discounting his nasty, false assumption that defections from ideal rationality are always intentional: "It would be a good thing if every trick could receive some short and obviously appropriate name, so that when a man used this or that particular trick, he could be at once reproached for it!" (Schopenhauer 1896, p. 18). Michels may thus be reproached, not at once but posthumously, for responding with 'The It-is-not-*only-because*-it-is-Riposte'.

Eventually we get around to considering socialism and, in particular, syndicalism: "All that the syndicalists have written upon political parties in general . . . applies to themselves as well, because it applies to all organizations as such, without exception" (Michels 1959, p. 347). This universal truth is, of course, the original tautology. But that is, almost immediately, granted superfluous support from a proposition which might plausibly be put forward as a sociological nomological. For this proposition makes a claim about the supposedly inevitable consequences of actions, which cannot be themselves necessary. However, both it and the reasonings from which it is derived are, with acknowledgement, borrowed from the neglected writings of Gaetano Mosca (1858–1941): ". . . social wealth cannot be satisfactorily administered in any other manner than by the creation of an extensive bureaucracy. In this way we are led by an inevitable logic to the flat denial of the possibility of a state without classes. The administration of an immeasurably large capital, above all when this capital is collective property, confers upon the administrator influence at least equal to that possessed by the private owner of capital . . . always and necessarily there

springs from the masses a new organized minority which
raises itself to the rank of a governing class" (Michels 1959,
pp. 390–1; and compare, for instance, Andreski 1975 and
Djilas 1958).

Michels finally concludes by repeating what he still does not
see to be a mere tautology: "Who says organizations says oligarchy" (p. 401). It was, surely, too harsh a judgement upon
either of those disciplines to describe such an uninformative
and misinformative shambles as a classic of either sociology
or political science.

3 A literary–sociological case study

Nowadays innumerable courses are taught and taken under
rubrics such as 'Sociology of Literature', 'Social History as
seen through the Contemporary Novel', 'Drama and Society
in the Age of So and So', and the like. Unfortunately these
courses almost never draw on the latest and best work of the
relevant specialists in economic and social history; while those
specialists themselves either complacently believe that their
findings are getting through or, irresponsibly, do not care
whether they are or not (Hayek 1954).

The consequence of these mutual withdrawals is that the
pictures of past periods usually presented to pupils have been
shaped not by actual historical evidence but by prejudices,
and, inevitably, by prejudices applied to a relatively small
selection of all the productions of those periods (Jefferson
1974). All such selections must be arbitrary too in so far as
they are made on the basis of literary merit, or of anything
else but an assessment of the evidential value of works cited.
And here, as properly everywhere, the word 'prejudice' is
being employed to describe views which, whether correct
or incorrect, were formed prior to and independent of any
scrutiny of the evidence.

Another pervasive methodological fault in such activities
calls for emphatic comment. For too many writers and readers,
having examined what may or may not be faithful portraits

of the miseries of life in the industrial cities of the UK during
the first half of the nineteenth century, then proceed immediately to infer that these miseries were consequent upon and
caused by the industrial revolution achieved under a regime
of capitalist laissez-faire.

But these, as a moment's thought should be sufficient to
show us, are not conclusions which could be validly drawn
by such immediate inference. It is necessary to enquire why
people crowded into those towns and were eager to obtain
employment in those factories. What was the alternative:
what would have been their fate had they stayed in their
villages; or had the industrial revolution never occurred?
The true answers to these crucial questions are suggested
by the answers to similar questions about those who today
crowd into the ever-growing cities of the Third World. Those
concerned presumably believe, or believed – and who are we
to say that they are, or were, wrong? – that, frightful as are,
or were, the conditions in those cities, they themselves, had
they survived at all, would have been even worse off staying
in their villages.

(i)

Many of those teaching these courses and, to a greater or
lesser extent and in one interpretation or another, Marxist.
They are therefore, and reasonably, committed to maintaining some sort of physical or metaphysical priority of stuff
over consciousness, of the material over the ideological.
But then, much more questionably, they construe this as
sustaining the contention that ongoings in the ideological
superstructure must always, even if only *ultimately* and *in the
last analysis*, be determined by prior or simultaneous ongoings
in the material foundations; and, hence apparently, that any
representations in the former must, albeit often in much
distorted forms, *reflect* the latter.

This is a movement of thought which many – including,
let it be confessed, at one time and many years ago the
present writer – have found compelling. Its most influential

formulation is in the obituary address which Engels gave at the grave of Marx: "Just as Darwin discovered the law of evolution in organic nature, so Marx discovered the law of evolution in human history; he discovered the simple fact . . . that man must first of all eat and drink, have shelter and clothing, before it can pursue politics, science, religion, art, etc; and that, *therefore*, the production of the immediate material means of life and consequently the degree of economic development . . . form the foundation on which the forms of government, the legal conceptions, the art and even religious ideas of the people have been evolved, and in the light of which these things must therefore be explained" (emphasis added).

But, of course, it was not left to Marx to discover that "simple fact", while the inference which he drew from thus "Rediscovering America" (Andreski 1972, Ch. 6) is manifestly fallacious. For the fact that there are various necessary preconditions for being able to engage in all sorts of other activities by no means guarantees that the forms which those activities take or even the fact that they are engaged in at all "must therefore be explained" by reference to those preconditions. For the search for explanations involves the search for sufficient not merely necessary conditions.

This is a necessary condition of that, if you cannot have that without this; whereas this is a sufficient condition of that, if you are bound to have that wherever you have this (Flew 1975, 2.15–2.19 and 2.23–2.26). Enthusiastic controversialists are, in the nature of our case, tempted to pretend that the opponent who is in fact maintaining only that some condition is necessary has instead rashly asserted that it is sufficient. The second, more comprehensive contention is, of course, much easier to refute.

For example: until very recently, when it ceased any longer to be possible seriously to deny the actual failures of their allegedly ideal system, those with pretensions to being democratic rather than revolutionary socialists were apt to dismiss with a snide, irrelevant reference to Chile, the contention that a pluralist, democratic politics – defined not by the facts of prior election but by the possibilities of 'voting the scoundrels *out*' – can be maintained only on the basis of a pluralist and largely private economy. (See Hayek 1944 and 1979; and contrast, for instance, *New Society* for 13 November 1980, p. 307). In Chile at that time soldiers who had seized power from a democratically elected regime proceeding to establish an irremovable Leninist despotism had yet to hand over that power to truly democratic, civilian politicians popularly chosen in a freely contested election (Moss 1973 and Labin 1982).

Again, suppose someone makes so bold as to suggest that genetics has some part to play in explaining the differences between human individuals or human sets, and that not every infant or every set of infants is, even given the most ideal environment, able to reach the topmost levels of achievement. Then such dissidents may expect to be met, or rather not met, with the true but irrelevant counter-contention that genetics cannot hope to explain all or even most of those differences. Thus in *Race Culture and Intelligence* (Richardson and Spears 1972) we can find two contributors, one from a School of Education and the other from a Division of Behavioural Sciences, proudly presenting what they see as a knock-down refutation: "... if 80 per cent of adult performance is directly dependent on genetic inheritance, how have the styles of our lives and the patterns of our thinking changed to the extent that they have?" A little later they repeat their failure to distinguish sufficient from necessary conditions in a different context: "It is hard to see how the grading system can be retained when a guarantee of job opportunity can no longer be given" (pp. 74 and 78). So, if ever there were more qualified surgeons than surgical jobs, one would no longer care whether the surgeons who operated on us were or were not qualified?

(ii)

A curious example of sociological work misguided by an invalid inference from a necessarily true, tautological proposition to a conclusion in which the same form of words is construed, if not quite as a nomological then at least as a substantial universal generalization, is provided by *Fact in Fiction* (Rockwell 1974). This book was issued by the leading sociological publishers, and was well received. It propounded a very untentative hypothesis: "To say that writers necessarily reflect their own time, which I must repeat is the justification for using their fictions to study the facts of their society, is to say that they are bound to do so, and cannot choose to do otherwise" (p. 119).

Certainly as a hypothesis this has to be construed as implying that all writers of historical fiction, of science fiction, or of fantasy are bound to give themselves away: the well-girded sociologist will always be able to discern marks of the lurking bourgeois beast in all the works of any writers whom she is putting down as such; while writers of historical fiction are bound to reveal, presumably through the admission of anachronisms, the actual periods of their compositions. A moment's thought reveals both that there is a very simple and straightforward way to test and, presumably, to falsify this claim. It is therefore, distressing, indeed alarming, that neither Joan Rockwell herself nor any of her sociologist or 'cultural studies' reviewers seems to have had a moment to spare for such thought.

The simple and straightforward way is this: first, to work out the principles on which we are supposed to be able to infer contemporary social facts from fiction of every kind; and, second, to apply these detective principles to a variety of works the actual social background of which is known, but not to the appliers. Suppose that the principles were found to work. Then they could be employed to achieve definitive solutions to several famous problems: when, for instance, and perhaps where the Homeric poems were composed; and so on. The reason why the Rockwell hypothesis is implausible is that any detective principles discovered or discoverable by sociologists could presumably be either communicated to or discovered by the authors themselves, and then employed by them to cover their sociological tracks. We have here, therefore, one more example of the importance in the social sciences of what has been named most aptly the Oedipus Effect: "the influence of an item of information upon the situation to which the information refers" (Popper 1957, p. 13; and compare Hume 1748, p. 94).

Fact in Fiction illustrates the claim in *Social Sciences as Sorcery* that this is an area "where anybody can get away with anything" (Andreski 1972, p. 16). Thus the authoress asserts: "The assumption in fiction that a given institution exists may be supported by other evidence ... but the deductions may justifiably be made even in the absence of this support ..." (Rockwell 1974, p. 122). She then proposes to show what might, she thinks, be thus reliably deduced from "the following group of fictional and personal accounts: *The Life and Times of Frederick Douglass; Uncle Tom's Cabin; Huckleberry Finn*; various works of William Faulkner; *Gone with the Wind*; and the recent *Confessions of Nat Turner*".

The first of these, however, does not belong to a study of *Fact in Fiction* at all. It is the autobiography of an escaped slave who became active in the Abolition Movement, and it has long been recognized as an invaluable primary source. About the rest the important point is "that they were written over a period of a hundred years by writers ... living up and down the Eastern seaboard from Maine to Mississippi". So, if Rockwell's detective principles were correct, the times which those of these writers who belong to our century "necessarily reflect" must be our times, and not those of "the USA in the first half of the nineteenth century" (p. 122). Slavery, therefore, must have survived into the early nineteen-thirties, to be 'reflected' in the writing of *Gone with the Wind!*

Fact in Fiction also provides us with a further example of a single form of words being interpreted without distinction in two different ways: expressing on one occasion a necessary truth; and, on another, a would-be factual falsehood – a falsehood believed to be true primarily on account of the confounding of these two interpretations. Not being equipped with and trained to handle Hume's Fork, the authoress moves easily; and without observing any difference of substance: from saying, in one sentence, that a society's literature "is an integral part of it and should be recognized as being as much so as any institution, the Family for instance, or the State"; to saying, in the next, and as if this were an equivalence or a logical consequence, that "Narrative fiction is an indicator, by its form and content, of the morphology and nature of a society, just as the structure and function of the family in a society will be an indicator of how that society differs from others" (pp. vii–viii).

4 Deductive conceptual schemes: (i) economic analysis

The motto quotations at the head of the present chapter 5 are drawn from Hume's first *Enquiry*. Later in the same part of the same Section IV Hume discusses how the calculi of pure mathematics, and, in particular, that of (Euclidean) geometry, can be and are applied in the natural sciences. All the propositions of pure mathematics belong, of course, to the first of Hume's two fundamental categories; whereas some of those in what we would call applied but what he described as "mixed mathematics" must fall into the second. "Every part of mixed mathematics proceeds", Hume says, "upon the supposition that certain laws are established by nature in her operations; and abstract reasonings are employed . . . to determine their influence in particular instances, where it depends upon any precise degree of distance and quantity. Thus, it is a law of motion, discovered by experience, that the moment or force of any body in motion is the compound ratio or proportion of its solid contents and its velocity . . . Geometry assists us in the application of this law, by giving us the just dimensions of all the parts and figures which can enter into any species of machine; but still the discovery of the law itself is owing merely to experience, and all the abstract reasonings in the world would never lead us one step towards the knowledge of it" (Hume 1748, p. 31).

(i)

Although he does seem to have the heart of the matter in him, Hume's formulation here is – putting it gently – unsteady and a shade crude. It is, nevertheless, sufficient to point what has to be, for us, the main moral. The validity of deductive arguments passing through calculi of pure mathematics constitutes no guarantee of the truth either of any supposedly factual premises from which those arguments begin, or, therefore, of any supposedly factual conclusions derived therefrom. Nowadays both the most important and the most frequent occasions for keeping this moral in mind are when we are told 'that the computer says'; that the final results in the elections in which the count has just begun will be such and such; that, on the NIESR or the Treasury of whoever else's model, GNP will next year increase by something point something percent; and so on.

It is most unlikely, although not altogether impossible, that there will have been any sort of computer failure: what the computer has in fact 'deduced' from its programmed input will, almost certainly, have been 'deduced' validly. What is much more likely is that there was something wrong with that input: that the model employed by the NIESR or the Treasury does not, after all, faithfully and adequately represent the economy which it is supposed to represent; that false assumptions were built into the original programme, or that false information was supplied later. The computer-wise whizz-kids have a slogan: "Garbage produces garbage." There is also the acronym GIGO – which, being explicated, becomes "Garbage In, Garbage Out".

(ii)

Towards the end of his *Logic* J. S. Mill disclaims any attempt "to decide what other hypothetical or abstract sciences, similar to Political Economy, may admit of being carved out of the general body of the social science" (Mill 1843, VI, (ix) 4: II, pp. 497–8). The insight revealed in this disclaimer is the more remarkable in that the previous discussion had not brought out at all clearly that economic analysis is a kind of pure mathematics, a deductive conceptual scheme which may or may not find application. This is, of course, true only of economic analysis, and not of many other activities pursued in Departments of Economics and of Economic History.

Nor is it any the less true for the fact that the basic notions have been abstracted and refined from some of those employed in the very concrete and down-to-earth business of producing and exchanging goods and services. For it is notorious that much the same holds of arithmetic and geometry. Most of us learn to collect and to count physical things, as well as to sum such collections together or subtract one from another, before we manage to compass any abstract numerical calculations; while it appears to be certain that Egyptian surveyors had discovered that in a rectangular field with sides as 3 to 4 the diagonal would be 5 well before Pythagoras – if it was Pythagoras – proved the Theorem of Pythagoras. Whereas the logical progression, both in mathematics and in economics, is from pure to applied, in the history of the race, and in the biography of individuals, this order is reversed.

In that previous discussion Mill lays it down that "Political Economy considers mankind as occupied solely in acquiring and consuming wealth . . ." (1843, VI (ix) 3; and II, p. 492). In the following year, in his *Outlines of a Critique of Political Economy*, Engels gives another and less sober account: "Political Economy – the science of how to make money – was born of the mutual envy and greed of the merchants. It bears on its brow the mark of the most loathsome selfishness" (Engels 1844, p. 148).

This furious misdiscription suggests that the classical economists were all trying to write the sort of book which might have been marketed as *How to Make your First Million* or *Getting Rich: a Guide for Everyman – and Every Woman*! But the full title of Smith's economic masterpiece was significantly different, *An Inquiry into the Nature and Causes of the Wealth of Nations*. Not for nothing was what we now call economics known traditionally as political economy. For Smith was investigating: not how he and his readers might become millionaires; but the political arrangements needed if "the natural effort of every individual to better his own condition" is to lead to self-sustaining economic growth, the increase of wages, and general prosperity. The findings of this kind of inquiry, making no strident demands for state-to-state charitable handouts but speaking only of unhindered self-help and self-reliance, should interest and appeal: not to would-be plutocrats, though it is surely no sin either to be or to want to be rich; but rather to all those, both in the Third World and out of it, who really do long to see poor countries climbing out of their poverty (Bauer 1976, 1981 and 1984).

(iii)

Where Mill and Engels were both wrong, however, was in limiting economic analysis to the acquisition and consumption of wealth. It is this limitation which provides purchase for, though it can scarcely justify, John Ruskin's dismissal of Adam Smith as "the half-bred and half-witted Scotchman" who taught "the deliberate blasphemy . . . : 'Thou shalt hate the Lord thy God, damn his laws, and covet his neighbour's goods'" (Ruskin 1876, pp. 516 and 714). Earlier Thomas Carlyle too had had a lot to say on the same lines, and in a similar tone of voice: one or two of his choicest phrases were even adapted and adopted by authors of the *Communist Manifesto*.

The truth, as Lionel Robbins made clear in his masterly *Essay on the Nature and Significance of Economic Science*, is that the key notion is not wealth but scarcity. Both are essentially relative: nothing can be either scarce or "valuable in itself . . . any more than a thing can be distant in itself without reference to another thing" (Robbins 1949, p. 56). It is, however, human wants and human needs in relation to which things are scarce or valuable. Earlier we quoted John Watkins as saying: "Whereas physical things can exist unperceived, social 'things' like laws, prices, prime ministers and ration-books, are created by personal attitudes. (Remove the attitudes of food officials, shopkeepers, housewives, etc., towards ration-books and they shrivel into bits of cardboard.)" The same is true of such social 'qualities' as scarcity. "Value", as Robbins puts it, "is a relation, not a measurement" (p. 56). So much, therefore, for the Labour Theory of Value; which maintains that the value of any good is the (measured) quantity of labour needed for its production.

Economic analysis is relevant wherever four conditions are satisfied. First, several different ends must be desired. Second, these ends must not all be equally important to those who cherish them. Third and fourth, the time and the other means required for attaining these ends must be both limited and capable of alternative applications. "But when time and the means for achieving ends are limited *and* capable of alternative application, *and* the ends are capable of being distinguished in order of importance, then behaviour necessarily assumes the form of choice. Every act which involves time and scarce means for the achievement of one end involves the relinquishment of their use for the achievement of another. It has an economic aspect" (Robbins 1949, p.14).

Once this is appreciated it becomes obvious that economic analysis may find application in areas remote from those which would be considered to be economic either by the contemporary layperson or by the classical economists and their critics. This was observed well before World War I by the logician father of the more famous Lord Keynes (J. N.Keynes 1904, p. 300). Yet it seems to have been only in World War II that people trained as economists began to play a part in Operational Research teams attached to the staffs of various very senior military commanders. Again, what is called in Britain *The Economics of Politics* and in the USA the study of Public Choice did not really begin to flourish before the late fifties (Seldon 1978). James Buchanan and Gordon Tullock, however, and other leading figures of that flourishing, are scrupulous to give due credit: both to anticipations in Adam Smith, and in other British classical economists; and to Machiavelli, as well as to several Italian successors in the tough-minded study of the workings of state machinery (Buchanan and Tullock 1962; and compare Radnitzky and Bernholz *Economic Imperialism: The Economic Method Applied Outside the Field of Economics*).

5 Deductive conceptual schemes:
(ii) economic imperialism

Mill was, as we have seen, reluctant to commit himself on the question whether "other hypothetical or abstract sciences ... may admit of being carved out of the general body of the social science". The most promising candidate to emerge in the years between is the mathematical theory of games, although some might want to disqualify this as constituting no more than a fresh branch of Political Economy. By far and away the most exciting application of any part of this theory is the work of Robert Axelrod on *The Evolution of Cooperation*. For this shows how cooperation can evolve without requiring, either self-sacrificing altruism, or machinery for making and enforcing contracts. Hume, and the other Founding Fathers considered in Chapter 5 would have loved this book.

(i)

The particular game which Axelrod examines is Prisoner's Dilemma. The two players are supposed to have been charged with a crime which they have in fact committed. Both are urged to confess, and neither is allowed to communicate with the other. If neither either confesses or implicates the other, then neither will be convicted and punished: this is winning through cooperation, and each scores three. If each confesses and implicates the other, each gets a 'punishment' score of one. If one confesses, implicating the other, whereas the other – the 'sucker' – does neither, then the latter scores zero whereas the former scores five – the 'temptation' payoff. The aim is to develop a strategy which enables the player to score high in a run of games, when the score in every game is revealed to both players at the end of every game, but when neither is ever able to communicate with the other.

What Axelrod did actually involved almost no mathematical theory: perhaps the further development of this will, as in other cases mentioned earlier, have to follow practice. For he asked assorted theoreticians how they would over a long series play Prisoner's Dilemma. He then set a University of Michigan computer to calculate which of these more than seventy-five suggested strategies would be most successful. TIT FOR TAT, submitted by Canadian psychologist Anatol Rapoport, won out against all comers.

This strategy begins on the first round by cooperating; that is, by neither confessing nor implicating the other. After that, it always does what the other player did in the previous round. If the other player cooperated on the previous round, TIT FOR TAT cooperates. If the other player defected, TIT FOR TAT 'punishes' the other player by defecting on the next round – but *only* the next round. And so on.

TIT FOR TAT thus has four fundamental characteristics. First, it is, as Axelrod puts it, "nice"; or, perhaps it would be better to say, optimistic. That is, it never betrays first, preferring to assume good intentions until proved wrong. Second, it is retaliatory: it does not ignore betrayals, but retaliates at once. Third, although retaliatory, it is not vengeful. It extracts only an equal amount of vengeance for each betrayal. (The principle of "an eye for an eye, a tooth for a tooth" was originally established to limit vengeance: it is only much later that some have come to think it too severe!) Fourth, it is easy to understand: many of the others failed because they conveyed no intelligible message to the other player.

This optimistic and generous yet never foolishly self-sacrificing strategy, neither spiteful nor exploitative, is, surely, that of Hume's "Two men who pull the oars of a boat", and "do it by an agreement or convention, tho' they have never given promises to each other". It is, it seems, in this way that "recognitions of common interest will lead to the regulation of conduct in ways which are not, and often could not be, derived from prior contracts." What Axelrod calls "niceness" the altogether English George Orwell would have commended as common sense and simple decency.

Analysing his computer printout, Axelrod made further discoveries. For example, when played against each other in lengthy computer tournaments, the strategies quickly separated themselves into two categories. The first was that of those called "nice" − the ones that assumed goodwill on the part of the other player and did not betray first. The second was the "not nice" strategies, which were generally built around a plan for *not* cooperating, but shrewdly trying to betray the other player.

The former always did better. With only one exception (which turned out to be a kind of anomaly), the "nice" strategies were all bunched at the top, while the "not nice" strategies formed a separate sub-class at the bottom. Moreover, when played over an evolutionary time sequence, the "not nice" strategies eventually faded into extinction, while the "nice" strategies all survived.

Actual games with and among his students revealed something else. Both Axelrod and his students found that they were strongly tempted to behave as if Prisoner's Dilemma were a zero-sum competitive game, which it was in fact deliberately designed not to be. They were strongly tempted, that is to say, to assume that, in order to do better for yourself, you had to do better than the other fellow; and, hence, that any gain on his side had to be at the expense of a loss on yours. But, of course, if they succumbed to this temptation, then their 'betrayals' provoked 'counter-betrayals'; and so both players, until and unless this spoiling strategy was reversed, proceeded to do progressively worse. Axelrod draws the moral that in Prisoner's Dilemma the first rule is to eschew envy: "Envy is self-destructive." (Compare here Schoek's classic treatise, *Envy*; also Flew 1981.)

(ii)

The important moral for Political Economy depends on the
logical truths that, while commercial competition has to be,
precisely as competition, a zero-sum game, the uncoerced
exchange of goods or services is not. It is as wrong as it
is common to say or to assume that "Whenever material
gain follows exchange, for every plus there is a precisely .
equal minus" (Ruskin 1899, p. 131). No one makes such
an uncoerced exchange save in so far as they believe that
they will be, in their own eyes, and by their own standards,
better off if it is made than they would be if it were not. Each
party, therefore, must, in consequence of the exchange, be
taken to be better off than they would have been otherwise. If
this is to be called exploitation, then both parties are equally
guilty. For both have made themselves better off through the
willingness of the other to cooperate in the exchange. In this
sort of social cooperation for one party to envy the gains of
the other is indeed paradigmatically self-destructive.

Another similar but perhaps less common because more
obviously outrageous mode of misrepresentation is to urge
that anyone who points some similarity between this and that
thereby identifies the two terms of the analogy: they must be
asserting or implying that this *is* that, and nothing else; or
that this is *merely* that. Perhaps because of the high degree
of abstraction involved in economic analysis, this mode seems
to be a favourite with those hostile either to economics in
general or to particular economic writings. Thus a correspondent to *The Times*, provoked by a leading article which
"compared the labour of a human being with a commodity
such as butter", immediately, yet quite invalidly, infers: that
the leader-writer was by this committed to maintaining that
the analogy obtains in all respects; and that he "has accepted
that human lives can be evaluated *simply* as 'goods' to be
bought in the marketplace with the bananas and the butter"
(5 July 1977: emphasis added).

One doubts whether the correspondent from whose letter
these passages are drawn was aware that she had been anticipated in this kind of objection by such eminent Victorians as

Carlyle and Marx, Engels and Ruskin. Thus Marx, attacking Ricardo in *The Poverty of Philosophy*, writes: "To put the cost of manufacture of hats and the cost of maintenance of men on the same plane *is to turn men into hats*" (Marx 1847, p. 44: emphasis added).

9   Facts and Values

In every system ... which I have hitherto met with,
I have always remark'd, that the author proceeds for
some time in the ordinary way of reasoning ... when
of a sudden I am surpriz'd to find, that instead of the
usual copulations of propositions, *is* and *is not*, I meet
with no proposition that is not connected with an *ought*,
or an *ought not*. This change is imperceptible, but it is,
however, of the last consequence. For as this *ought*, or
ought not, expresses some relation or affirmation, 'tis
necessary that it should be observ'd and explain'd; and
at the same time that a reason should be given, for what
seems altogether inconceivable, how this new relation
can be a deduction from others, which are entirely
different from it.

> David Hume, *A Treatise of Human Nature*,
> III (i) 1, p. 469.

Euclid has fully explained all the qualities of the circle,
but has not in any proposition said a word of its beauty.
The reason is evident. The beauty is not a quality of the
circle ... It is only the effect which that figure produces
upon the mind, whose peculiar structure renders it
susceptible of such sentiments.

> David Hume, *An Enquiry concerning the Principles
> of Morals*, App. 1, pp. 291–2

The interdict indicated in the first of the two motto passages
above has come to be called Hume's Law. What is by this law
ruled out as illegitimate is any attempt strictly to deduce conclusions about what ideally *ought* to be so from any premise
or premises stating only what, it is supposed, actually and
already *is* the case. Any neutral and non-partisan assertion
about what in fact has been, is or will be can, therefore,
without self-contradiction be conjoined with any contention,

whether positive or negative, dealing only with the supposedly ideal.

Some interpreters betray themselves by missing Hume's
irony. As in dealing with Hume's Fork, considered in Chapter
8, so here, they mistakenly think that he was maintaining
– what is quite obviously not true – that this fundamental
distinction is always made, and that it was left to him only
to notice the practice and to point the moral. This does
scant justice to Hume. The truth is that he was insisting
that, although it very often is not, the distinction always can
and often should be drawn, and is "of the last consequence"
(Hudson 1969, pp. 135–43).

Once this is understood, it becomes obvious that claims
that some favourite guru has 'resolved Hume's supposed
dichotomy' or has 'transcended this positivist distinction'
must be preposterous. For these supercilious pretensions
are now revealed as euphemistic and evasive alternatives to
a forthright and impious admission that your guru either
wholly failed to make, or else collapsed, a distinction which
it is scarcely possible to deny to be both fundamental and
indispensable (Popper 1945, II, pp. 394–5).

Invalidly to deduce an *ought* conclusion from *is* premises
is to commit what G.E. Moore christened the Naturalistic
Fallacy. This is a good name, notwithstanding that Moore's
own account of the matter is curiously constipated. Most
remarkably, that account neither quotes the now hackneyed
passage from which our first motto is drawn nor makes any
reference to Hume. By contrast Hume himself had at once
gone on to show that equivocations upon the word 'nature'
constitute the nerve of many tokens of that particular fallacy
type. For instance, though this is not one of his instances, we
need to distinguish – as many of the wise and good have
not – prescriptive from descriptive understandings of such
expressions as 'natural law' or 'law of nature'. It must be
absurd to hold that anything determined by a descriptive law
of nature could sensibly be either prescribed or proscribed by
a law of the moral or legal kind. Such prescriptions are bound
to be redundant, and such proscriptions futile. They cannot

but be, because everything determined by a descriptive law of nature occurs by physical necessity.

Another thing for which Moore's *Principia Ethica* became at first famous and later notorious was his contention that goodness is a simple, non-natural quality like, and yet at the same time very unlike, yellowness. In default of any explanation of what it might be for a quality to be non-natural, other than the one which Moore himself later dismissed as "utterly silly and preposterous", the adjective 'non-natural' has to be construed as *alienans*: non-natural qualities are no more qualities than non-tauroid bulls would be bulls. A more sophisticated philosophical objection is that, whereas of two otherwise identical objects one may be red and the other yellow, one cannot be good and the other not. This is because things are (said to be) good solely in virtue of their (other) good-making characteristics.

Thus in the case of beauty, which may perhaps be regarded as the aesthetic kind of goodness, and in those of virtue and vice, the moral forms of good and evil, Hume sees the actual characteristics of what is (called) beautiful or virtuous or vicious as causing our reactions to it. But the beauty or the virtue or the vice itself somehow consists in those same reactions. Thus, he argued, "morality consists not . . . in any *matter of fact*, which can be discover'd by the understanding . . . Take any action allow'd to be vicious: Wilful murder, for instance. Examine it in all lights and see if you can find that matter of fact, or real existence, which you call *vice* . . . The vice entirely escapes you, as long as you consider the object. You can never find it, till you turn your reflexion into your own breast, and find a sentiment of disapprobation, which arises in you towards this action" (Hume 1739–40, III (i) 1, pp. 468–9).

Both here, in his explanation of the nature of value characteristics, and elsewhere, in his parallel account of what he took to be the misconception of causal necessity, Hume's model was the treatment in the great natural scientific works of the previous hundred years of such supposedly secondary qualities as colour. Thus in the *Opticks* Newton had written:

"The . . . light and rays which appear red, or, rather, make objects appear so I call rubrific or red-making . . . And, if at any time I speak of light and rays as coloured or endued with colours, I would be understood to speak, not philosophically and properly, but grossly, and according to such conceptions as vulgar people in seeing all these experiments would be apt to frame. For the rays, to speak properly, are not coloured. In them there is nothing else than a certain power and disposition to stir up a sensation of this or that colour" (Newton 1704, I, (ii), Definition to the second theorem under the second Proposition, pp. 124–5). These sensations, as our private experiences, really are in our minds only; or, as Newton himself preferred to say, our sensoria. But we, vulgarly, project such private sensations out onto a public world which is in itself altogether colourless.

1   What is meant by 'value-freedom'?

It is in the Humian perspective, sketched in the immediately preceding paragraphs, that we can best consider the issues so clearly and so forcefully raised in Weber's classic paper 'The Meaning of "Value-Freedom" in Sociology and Economics' (Weber 1917, pp. 1–47). In deference to him the German 'Wertfreiheit' is in such discussions frequently employed rather than the English 'value-freedom'. He maintained two theses here.

(i)

The first was substantially that of Hume. There is, that is to say, an unbridgeable logical gulf between partisan prescription and non-partisan description, between assertions that something actually *is* the case and insistences that it ideally *ought* to be. Since the values which we put on things are not in truth qualities of those things, sciences concerned to describe what actually happens, and to explain why, cannot truly report that things have such intrinsic qualities, which they do not and cannot have. Of course sciences can and must take note of what individuals and groups do in fact value. But they cannot, in the nature of things, truly record that this or that *is* intrinsically valuable, and therefore categorically *ought* to be valued.

Confessing himself "quite unable to understand how it can be conceived to be possible to call this part of Max Weber's methodology into question", one leading economist enforced the crucial point with a homely yet historically contentious example: "We can", he urged, "ask people whether they are prepared to buy pork and how much they are prepared to buy at different prices. Or we can watch how they behave when . . . exposed to the stimuli of the pig-meat markets. But the proposition that it is *wrong* that pork should be valued . . . is a proposition which we cannot conceive being verified at all in this manner." He concludes, in words which may have been adapted from Hume, yet probably were not: "Propositions involving the verb 'ought' are different in kind from propositions involving the verb 'is' (Robbins 1949, pp. 148–9).

(ii)

Weber's second thesis was frankly prescriptive. He never claimed that values were either dispensable or unimportant. Nor did he assert that everyone, or even that all social scientists, should always and everywhere eschew value-judgements. On the contrary. What he insisted was that the difference between fact-stating and evaluation should be neither concealed nor blurred. When anyone expresses a value-judgement, they must not pretend that it is scientifically warranted; because it cannot be. If scientists, and in particular social scientists, make recommendations for action – and they are as much entitled and indeed obliged to do this as any other citizen – then they should be scrupulous to make plain, what in what they are saying is put forward as a scientific finding, and what has the very different status of a policy proposal. This is an imperative of intellectual honesty and respect for truth.

2   Repudiations of value-freedom

No wonder, surely, that the future Lord Robbins was at a
loss to understand how people wishing to be accounted social
scientists could bring themselves to challenge either of these
two proposals. Those who have in our day dismissed all talk
of value-freedom with confident contempt appear either not
to have studied Weber, or not to have understood him, or
perhaps to have chosen to misunderstand. He himself had to
complain of "the constantly recurring and almost incredible
wrong-headed misunderstanding of those who think it is
being maintained that empirical science cannot treat men's
'subjective' value-judgements as objects (whereas the whole
of sociology and, in economics, the whole theory of marginal
utility are based on the opposite assumption)" (Runciman
1978, p. 78).

(i)

Many examples of such egregious wrong-headedness can be
found in the widely circulating Penguin Educational Specials
of the early seventies. These remain important since much
of their doctrine apparently has continued to be taught,
especially in institutions for the training of schoolteachers.
For instance: in a volume offered as a 'Handbook for Course
Criticism', in a contribution entitled 'Class Struggle among
the Molecules', the author informs us that "The employees of
a chemical company . . . include research chemists. Nobody
pretends that the chemistry they do is value-free" (Pateman
1972, p. 212). His sole, preposterously irrelevant reason for
saying this is that their employers hope that some of their
discoveries can be made "useful (i.e. profitable)".

A more complicated example, but potentially more instructive, can be found in another Penguin Education Special,
Academic Freedom. The fiercely Radical author begins with an
understandably grudging concession to "objectivity, in the
sense of respect for facts, and a certain standard of honesty in the treatment of evidence". This, he is ungraciously
prepared to allow, "is an obviously desirable quality for

education to cultivate". But then, with enthusiasm now, he goes on to list what he sees as unacceptable consequences of what is denounced as "the quite mistaken belief that value-judgements could be eliminated" from the social sciences. He says: " . . . neutrality, or impartiality, in the sense of a demand that teacher, and students do not take sides and do not allow interpretation or opinion (or bias, or prejudice – call it what you will) to contaminate the pure stream of facts is an absurdity. The role of theory, or hypothesis, and interpretation is now generally accepted to be an irreducible element in even the most dispassionate and factual sciences" (Arblaster 1974, p. 17).

There is no room here to re-establish all the distinctions which this outburst collapses, and all the subtleties which it blunts. The essential is to recognize that "theory, or hypothesis, and interpretation" too, all belong to the world of facts rather than to that of values. So to show that these are "an irreducible element in even the most dispassionate and factual sciences" is not to show that those cannot be value-free.

That this is so becomes manifest the moment that we get down to concrete cases. The theories or hypotheses of historians, for instance, are theories and hypotheses about what in fact happened, and how, and why. Certainly matters of opinion are sometimes contrasted with matters of fact. But in these contrasts the former involve opinions about what was or is or will be the case. The opposition is between belief and knowledge rather than between value and fact: there are (disputatious) matters of opinion; which are contrasted with (established, known) matters of fact. So to show that the social sciences must accommodate some of the former as well as some of the latter would not be to show that, in any understanding obnoxious to Weber, they either are or ought to be value-laden.

Before moving on to a third example of the ignorant and hasty dismissing of Weber it is worth protesting briefly against refusals to recognize any distinctions between prejudices, biases and points of view. Earlier we took issue with the slovenly practice of abusing all disfavoured beliefs as prejudices, instead of reserving the word for convictions formed prior to any examination of the evidence. A prejudice in this strict sense is not at all the same as a bias. With both this latter term and the expression 'a point of view' we should do well to bear in mind the literal meanings.

Thus a bias in a bowl is built-in and permanent; although it can, of course, be recognized and regularly offset by a skilful player. A bias in thinking should be regarded in the same way: it is a disposition to underestimate or to overestimate in one particular direction. As such, a bias can be recognized and systematically compensated for; just as prejudices can be and will be identified and open-mindedly examined by all those who prefer their beliefs to be, even if uncomfortable, well-evidenced and, hopefully, true.

Literally construed the expression 'a point of view' refers to a position and a direction of observation. What is or is not visible from a particular point of view, while looking in a particular direction, is not subject to the control of the persons in that position, while looking in that direction. There is, therefore, nothing irredeemably subjective about differences between observations made by observers observing from different points of view. Again, while everyone is at every moment bound to have some point of view, and while it is no doubt practically impossible to dispose of absolutely every prejudice, we are not, surely, all subject to strong biases which we cannot possibly recognize and for which we are genuinely unable to compensate.

(ii)

In both the 'Handbook for Course Criticism' mentioned above, and in another volume of Radical essays from a different publisher, professional historians refer to what is supposed to have been established by E.H. Carr's *What is History?*. In the first of these books were are told: "It is now generally realized that the claim to record facts and reconstruct the past 'as it actually happened' is not tenable. Carr . . . argues that 'facts' are defined as worth recording at all, in terms of some model in the historian's mind" (Pateman 1972, p. 284). The Editor of the second promises that Gareth Stedman Jones, a Cambridge historian, will show that "the assumption that there exists a realm of facts independent of theories which establish their meaning is fundamentally unscientific." Jones himself writes: "Carr attacked the notion that 'facts' and 'interpretation' are rigidly separable. Pointing out that all writing of history involves a selection from the sum of facts available, he demonstrated that any selection of facts obeys an implicit evaluative criterion. 'Facts' are thus inseparable from 'interpretations', which in turn are determined by 'values'" (Blackburn 1972, pp. 10 and 113).

Chapter 3 quoted a preposterous passage propounding a fashionably secularized version of the philosophical idealism of George Berkeley (1685–1753). In this the Honoured Society of the sociologists usurps the creative and sustaining role of Berkeley's God: " . . . it is not an objectively discernible, purely existing external world which accounts for sociology; it is the methods and procedures of sociology which create and sustain that world" (Young 1971, p. 131). To this anyone wanting true scientific knowledge, rather than factitious "informal understandings negotiated among members of an organized intellectual collectivity" (p. 177), has to respond that, on the contrary, there is "an objectively discernible, purely existing external world which accounts for sociology". It cannot be, and it is not, "the methods and procedures of sociology which create and sustain that world".

A similar response is required when professional historians dare thus slightingly to dismiss the great Leopold von Ranke. For it was he who claimed, famously and truly, that his and their professional business was to discover and to tell, "wie es eigentlich gewesen" [how it actually was]. Anyone who truly believes that it is, necessarily and in all cases, impossible "to reconstruct the past 'as it happened'", and who nevertheless accepts employment as a historian should ask himself, and tell us, what reason he has left us for believing anything which he chooses to say about the past.

Nor is it compatible with any sort of science, whether social or other, much less less required by it, to deny "that there exists a realm of facts independent of theories". For if it was not possible – as of course it is – to describe experimental and other data in ways logically independent of rival theories offered to explain such data, then no one could ever show that any theories are inconsistent with the facts, and, therefore, false. Significantly Jones covers his Marxist embarrassment about real wages rising when Marx's theory required them to be falling with bluster, sneering and abuse (Blackburn 1972, pp. 107–9).

(iii)

The more immediately relevant objection to what is alleged to have been established in *What is History?* is that nothing of this sort follows from the proposition "that all writing of history involves a selection from the sum of facts available". Certainly such selection is always involved: not only in "all writing of history"; but also in all other descriptive discourse, both written and oral. For there is no limit on the number of true propositions which could be formulated and asserted about anything. This is, perhaps, what Lenin and others have had in mind when maintaining that the properties of matter are infinite.

It does not, however, follow: either that every statement of the facts in the case must be more or less viciously selective and misleading; or that every such statement and every interpretation put upon it has to be either equally value-loaded or – what is often, though wrongly, thought to be a further implication – equally arbitrary. When, for instance, you are as a witness sworn to tell "the truth, the whole truth, and nothing but the truth" you have not undertaken the impossible task of uttering an infinite collection of truths. What the court wants, and what in this and in other cases is meant by 'telling the whole truth', is that you should reveal everything which you know, *which is relevant to the business in hand*.

Notice well that here, as everywhere, both relevance and

importance are essentially relative. But we must not succumb to the temptation to hold that what is relative is, necessarily, also subjective; and hence, it is thought, arbitrarily determinable.

Many people find this temptation too strong to resist. It is, for instance, common to take it that, if what is right or wrong is relative to time and place, then it will follow that there is nothing right or wrong but each particular individual's (entirely arbitrary) thinking makes it so. Whether this common conclusion is true or false it certainly does not follow. For motion too is essentially relative. Yet from this we cannot infer that the question whether this is now in motion relative to that is a question not of objective physical fact but of the psychology of possible observers. Even some of the classical philosophers, however, have made fallacious inferences of this form: " . . . *great* and *small*, *swift* and *slow*, are allowed to exist nowhere without the mind; being entirely relative . . . " (Berkeley 1710, Bk I 11, p. 263).

A big mouse – a mouse, that is, which is bigger than the usual run of mice – will be very small when compared with even a small hippopotamus – a hippopotamus, that is, which is small relative to the usual run of hippopotami. In the same way what is relevant and important relative to one set of interests may be unimportant or altogether irrelevant relative to another, different set of interests. Nevertheless, given any one particular set, what is relevant and important is just as much a question of objective fact as any of those otherwise very different questions about the bigness or smallness of mice or hippopotami.

Certainly, what interests we are to have, and when, is a matter for our individual choice. Such choices may or may not be arbitrary; meaning that there may or may not be good reason to make them in one sense rather than another. Conventions too may or may not be arbitrary, and at two levels: there may or may not be good reason for having some convention; and there may or may not be good reason for having one particular convention and not another. It is not 'a *mere* matter of convention' but, literally, a matter of life and

death that we should have some 'rule of the road'. Yet, if we
were starting from scratch, the choice between 'Keep left' and
'Keep right' might indeed be arbitrary.

Again and equally, social scientists, like the rest of us, must
decide for themselves what questions they wish to answer. So
too the selection of points of view from which to take their
photographs is something for photographers to decide. But
then, as in a better moment Berkeley went on to say, "When
in broad daylight I open my eyes, it is not in my power
to choose whether I shall see or no, or to determine what
particular objects shall present themselves to my view: and so
likewise to the hearing and other senses; the ideas imprinted
on them are not creatures of *my* will" (1710, Bk. I 29, p. 273).

In the light of what has just been said of both the objectivity and the relativity of both relevance and importance,
it becomes easy to appreciate that, although every account
of anything can constitute only an infinitesimal selection
from the infinity of true statements which conceivably could
have been formulated and uttered, still there is never either
need or excuse for that kind of selectivity which truly is
scandalous.

There is – to add a rather old-world illustration to the more
recent instances cited in Chapter 2 – no excuse for certain
professing and pretending historians who have written and
published scandalously selective biographies of Jesuit mis-
sionaries martyred during the reign of Queen Elizabeth I.
They have managed not to mention that these had all sworn
obedience to the Pope: who had both declared that anyone
assassinating her, "with the pious intention of doing God
service . . . not only does not sin but gains merit"; and who
was all the time giving full support to Spain in its ongoing
war with her kingdom (Trevor-Roper 1957, pp. 108–18).

Certainly historians have to choose what periods they are
going to study, into what aspects of those periods they want
to inquire, and what questions they are trying to answer. So
we might say that, by choosing in whatever sense they do
choose, they are also choosing what is going to be relevant
to and important in their inquiries. But, if we do choose to

say this, then we must be more than ever resolved to insist that what actually is relevant or important relative to some given set of interests is so relevant or important *altogether independent of the will of persons who have chosen to pursue those interests*. We also need to be aware that, since historians even of the same periods may be and often are pursuing very different sets of interests, two very different history books may both contain equally sound and objective history. The fact that historians have to choose what they will investigate "is no reason whatever . . . why historians at different times, but possessing the same information, should answer the same question differently" (Hayek 1948, p. 75).

Nor is this fact, which is just as much the fact about both other social scientists and all other investigators, any reason for holding that their investigations cannot be value-free, or have always to be corrupted by a sort of subjectivity both peculiar to history and the other social sciences, and vicious. Sir Lewis Namier, therefore, misled when he argued that "History is . . . necessarily subjective and individual, conditioned by the interest and the vision of the historian" (Namier 1952, p. 7).

Weber himself, who demanded Wertfreiheit both in socio-logical investigation and in the presentation of findings, was, quite consistently, just as strongly committed to Wertbezie-hung – value-relevance – in the choice of subjects for inquiry. Another of his classic articles deals with '"Objectivity" in Social Science and Social Policy'. It is entirely right and proper that sociologists should choose those questions to which the true answers, whatever these turn out to be, will in their view be most important practically. What concepts they find applicable in so doing will then be determined by those interests; although those concepts should not by them – at least not in their working hours – be defined in even partially prescriptive or evaluative terms. "In the mode of their use," Weber concludes, "the investigator is obviously bound by the norms of our thought just as much here as elsewhere. For scientific truth precisely is what is *valid* for all who *seek* the truth" (Weber 1904, p. 84).

3   Are all cultures equal?

It would seem that it is nowadays widely believed either that
the social sciences must presuppose, or even that they have
discovered, that all cultures are equally good or equally valid.
Thus in *Race, Culture and Intelligence* the sociologically trained
Professor of Education in the Open University concluded:
"And finally we cannot accept quality distinctions between
cultures" (Richardson and Spears 1972, p. 156; and compare
Sarup 1986, p. 14, where the value-neutrality proper to
the scientist as such is characteristically confounded with a
commitment to the equal value of all cultures.)

Again, presumably after receiving some such academic mis-
guidance, the Education Committee of the London Borough
of Brent, in a document entitled *Book I: Education for a
Multicultural Democracy*, issued a ukase to all its teachers: "The
recognition that all peoples and cultures are inherently equal
must be a constant from which all educational practice will be
developed" (p. 7). It is obvious that acceptance is thought to
be essential to a total rejection of racism; which is, presumably, why the Committee at once goes on to insist that this "is
not a negotiable principle" (p. 7). That ukase, fairly typical
of the whole of what the satirist Peter Simple would call the
race relations industry, is more particularly characteristic of
the programmes now so widely and so strenuously promoted
in the name of 'Anti-racist, Multi-ethnic and Multicultural
Education' (Flew 1991c).

(i)

The first point about this insistence upon the equality of
all cultures is that it reveals a failure to appreciate the
enormous difference between racial and cultural identification. Certainly there are many social sets all of whose
members share what sociologists and anthropologists would,
in their extremely broad and comprehensive sense, count as
a culture, and all or almost all of whose members happen
to have skins of roughly the same colour. But if and where
any culture is racially exclusive, and cannot be shared by

members of any but the most favoured race, there we have a culture which truly is, and is surely to be condemned as, paradigmatically racist. For, as the activists of the race relations industry so often need to be reminded, racism just is, and is to be unreservedly abominated precisely and only in so far as it consists in, the advantaging or disadvantaging of individuals for no other or better reason than that they happen to belong to some favoured or disfavoured racial set.

The distinction between race and culture is here crucial. For many people would like to explain all inter-set differences in economic or educational success or failure by referring to hostile discrimination against members of the sets which in the event prove unsuccessful. Certainly there has been, and is, plenty of hostile discrimination against members of disfavoured racial sets; and of that any at all is too much. But, as we saw in Chapter 4, there is now a vast accumulation of evidence of often very extensive inter-set differences in performance which cannot honestly be attributed to either friendly or hostile discrimination (Sowell 1981 and 1990).

This abundance of contrary evidence is not, of course, enough to overcome the more resolute and interested prejudices. One illustrative treasure from my files is an article from *New Society* for 21 August 1987. This reviews statistics, mentioned already in Chapter 7, of performance in independently assessed public examinations. These reveal wide variations between different racially defined sets, with some Asian sets performing much better than whites, and blacks from Africa doing better than the Afro-Caribbeans. But the writer is a Professor of Sociology serving in a senior capacity on the Commission for Racial Equality. He therefore insists on believing: both that a well-nigh incorrigible form of racism is endemic in the UK; and that racism is primarily if not exclusively hostile discrimination by whites against non-whites. So he sees all these figures: not as legitimizing doubts about his own cherished assumptions; but as "raising fascinating puzzles about the impact of racism on children" – the supposedly differential impact, that is, as between different non-white racial sets!

The second point to be made here, about what for Brent Education Committee "is not a negotiable principle", is that it is flat inconsistent with their own crusading commitments. For there certainly are cultures – in the relevant, most comprehensive sense – which are both racist and sexist: indeed the Brent Committee-persons would themselves bring both charges against that of, or against some of those of, contemporary Britain. So how can they, how can anyone, say that male chauvinist macho cultures and racist cultures are equally good or "equally valid" (p. 10), when compared with cultures sexually egalitarian and wholly colour-blind?

(ii)

These attempts to marry a pretence that everything is equally good with insistence that some things are very definitely better than others may be instructively, but ruefully, compared with the combination in so much of the criminal justice world of a pretence to be working for the reform and rehabilitation of offenders with a horrified rejection of any desire "to impose our values on them" (Morgan 1978, Ch. 9).

If the word 'impose' is felt to be too harsh and too authoritarian, then it can without much loss be jettisoned. But if the Probation Officers and others involved in this business are not even trying somehow to bring it about that offenders come to prefer a non-criminal to a criminal way of life – come, that is, to value the one and to disvalue the other – then why do we as taxpayers have to go on employing these 'public servants'; and why do they have no scruples against accepting their salaries, and repeatedly asking for more? The fact is that Brent Education Committee actually is, and the Probation Officers ought to be, trying to get those under its, or their, charge to accept certain values: anti-racist and anti-sexist in the one case; and anti-criminal in the other.

It is only very recently that any educational researcher has become ready to argue – against a consensus of colleagues persistently identifying outcome with opportunity and inequality with injustice – that efforts socially to engineer an equal enthusiasm for higher education into the Registrar General's lower social classes constitute a costly, illiberal and almost wholly ineffective attempt to impose middle class values (Murphy 1990).

(iii)

It is rare for those who proclaim that all cultures are of equal value to state the source from which they derive this revelation. In the two cases cited so far it was presumably derived, by way of some confusing of culture with race, from a doctrine of racial equality; and that probably a doctrine construed as in the first instance descriptive rather than prescriptive (Flew 1976, Ch. 5). But where no question of race is involved the source or sources must be different. Perhaps one is the jurisdictional claim that the scope of the social sciences embraces all societies, everywhere and at all times. It was this general claim which, in maintaining that "Every age is equal in the sight of God", Ranke was making for history in particular.

Once this picturesque utterance is duly demythologized there is little temptation to read it as either constituting or entailing any claims about the equal goodness or 'validity' of all cultures. A somewhat more persuasive suggestion is that we have here another case of something quite often found in the history of ideas; namely, the transformation of a methodological rule into a metaphysical assertion – an assertion, that is, about ultimate reality.

Back in Chapter 5 we quoted Malinowski's explanation of Functionalism: "in every type of civilization, every custom, material object, idea and belief fulfils some vital function, has some task to accomplish, represents an indispensable part within a working whole." Now it is one thing to urge, as a methodological maxim, that the anthropologist – like the biologist – should always search for such vital functions. It is quite another to maintain, as a piece of metaphysics, that these are, ultimately and in the last analysis, always there to be found. The temptations are: both to offer the metaphysics as unsupported support for the maxim; and illicitly to replace the maxim by the metaphysics. So the suggestion is that at least in some cases the doctrine of the equal goodness of all cultures may be an illegitimate derivation from functionalist methodology. If every feature of every culture "has some task to accomplish, represents an indispensable part within a working whole", then every culture, as an efficiently working whole, must be equally 'valid'. Of course this does not follow. Yet someone might well think that it did.

4   And all languages and dialects?

The most influential current particular application of this general doctrine seems to be in Linguistics. Thus, in an Open University setbook on *Accent, Dialect and the School*, we read: "During the past several decades, people working in linguistics have studied a good proportion of the world's languages . . . From this study it has emerged that there are no linguistic reasons for saying that any language is superior to any other. All languages, that is, are equally 'good'" (Trudgill 1975, p. 24).

Notice first that the word 'good' in the passage quoted is wrapped in what have to be read as sneer or disclaimer quotes. Presumably these were introduced to indicate the distaste of the value-free, professionally neutral scientist for all such normative notions. But this distaste should have led him to say: not that all languages are equally good, or equally (sneer) 'good'; but that no such normative terms are to be found in the vocabulary of the (properly value-free) science of Linguistics. Instead he appears to have fallen – like so many others – into the error of holding that, while to say that this is superior to that is, to say that this and that are of equal worth is not, a value-judgement.

Notice, second, and perhaps more surprising, that, although Trudgill speaks at the beginning of extensive empirical studies, and although he says there that his con-clusion "emerged . . . from" these studies, and although he later tells us that we "have already seen that there is no way in which one variety of language can be considered superior to any other" (p. 27); still he never either gives his own account of or otherwise specifically refers to any of those particular pieces of more or less esoteric work by which this conclusion is supposed to be sustained. The truth is, surely, that it has no such foundation. Instead, in so far as it has any basis it all, this is in invalid derivations from methodological maxims, an uncomprehending commitment to value-freedom, and some manifesto of the comprehensive scope of Linguistics.

Another relevant error is to hold that a value-free social science has to disown all consideration: not only of absolute but also of instrumental good; not only of categorical but also of hypothetical imperatives. Failing to make and to appreciate the importance of such distinctions Trudgill, like too many of his colleagues, feels he has to avoid admitting as relevant what are undeniable facts of Comparative Linguistics. It is not to the point, he has to insist: that a speaker of Eskimo (Inuit) is far better equipped to make nice distinctions between different kinds of snow than a speaker of Arabic; that such highly inflected languages as Lithuanian require complex machinery to do jobs which are more economically done in English and Chinese; or that to become literate is more of a feat in Chinese or Japanese than in such a phonetically spelt language as Italian; and so on. (Anyone who, like the present writer, once laboured long to achieve a miserably low level of literacy in Japanese has to be amazed by Japanese educational achievement. All done – be it noted – with class sizes averaging forty or more. See, for instance, Lynn 1988.)

Again, like too many of his colleagues, Trudgill, through failing to employ these distinctions, becomes committed to denying the vital instrumental importance for anyone proposing to make their life in Great Britain of a mastery of Standard English (Honey 1983). Certainly other dialects and other languages might have served us equally well. But Standard English is what we actually have, and not Urdu or Creole or Japanese or anything else at all. So, although these others might or might not have been or be equally good or equally 'valid', this is what anyone wanting to become British now has to learn.

An absolute good is something which is (thought to be) good in itself and independent of consequences. An instrumental good is one which is an effective means of securing something else (thought to be) good in itself.) The distinction between categorical and hypothetical imperatives was first drawn by Immanuel Kant. A categorical imperative rules that something categorically must be done, quite regardless of the possibly different or even contrary desires of the agent. A hypothetical imperative asserts that, if the agent wants this, then, in order to get it, he must do that. It is, therefore, obvious that both propositions asserting that this is instrumentally good, that this is an efficient means to get that, and propositions asserting hypothetical imperatives, that if you want this then in order to get it you must do that, must be, in Humian terms, propositions belonging in the *is* category rather than the *ought*; that they describe or purport to describe our actual world, rather than recommend actions which (it is thought) would make it more ideal.

10 Subjective or Objective: Relative or Absolute?

There is nothing good and nothing bad absolutely speaking; everything is relative, this is the only absolute statement.

Auguste Comte, *L'Industrie*, III, 2;
quoted in Hayek 1979, pp. 238 and 389.

What in fact has been missing from so much recent controversy in religion, science and other fields, is the notion of 'objectivity' – of things being the case whether people recognize them or not. This gives point to arguments which otherwise, if they were possible at all, would merely appear to result from clashes of different personalities or different social structures.

Roger Trigg, *Reason and Commitment*, p. 168.

Often nowadays it is said or suggested that in the areas of social science and social policy – indeed perhaps in other areas too – there can be no such things as objective knowledge; knowledge, that is, of "how it actually was", or is. It is also urged, in support of this conclusion, that everything is always and necessarily in some way relative; and that this results in an inescapable subjectivity. Although these are sometimes presented as philosophical implications of work in the social sciences – in particular the sociology of knowledge, anthropology and the history of science – practitioners tend to respond with petulant impatience when confronted with the obvious yet devastating objection: namely, that this is to make the whole enterprise self-refuting. For it is to say, on the basis of supposed findings of social scientific investigations, that no such findings are to be relied on as constituting authentic knowledge; which is, by definition, justified *true* belief.

Since any sincerely truth-seeking inquirers, fully persuaded of the impossibility of attaining knowledge in their chosen field, would presumably construe this conviction as a decisive reason for frankly abandoning the quest, we are forced to infer that those who do not react in this forthright and realistic way either have a commitment to truth-seeking which is something less than total and overriding, and/or cannot entirely persuade themselves that these alleged implications are true. Yet even a half-belief in the hopelessness of the whole enterprise is demoralizing. If objectivity is anyway impossible, and the truth forever undiscoverable, then why bother to be strenuously and painfully self-critical? Anything goes; or, rather, nearer to the bone, anything sitting comfortably with our own values and interests is quite acceptable.

To appreciate just how demoralizing such a half-belief in such conclusions can be, consider again the response which Margaret Mead made when she was confronted with the evidence proving that all her main claims about Samoa in the period of her visit were false. *Coming of Age in Samoa*, she insisted, "must remain, as all anthropological works must remain, exactly as it was written, true to what I saw in Samoa and what I was able to convey of what I saw, true to the state of our knowledge of human behaviour as it was in the mid 1920s; true to our hopes and fears for the future of the world."

Many of the weapons needed for dealing with those challenges to the possibility of social scientific knowledge which are being considered in the present chapter have been deployed already on various occasions in its predecessors. The first and almost always neglected essential is to insist that anyone proposing to employ any of the various key terms must begin by making clear what usage they propose, and must then stick to that usage. This is essential because, although they sound like established technical terms the words 'subjectivist', 'objectivist' and 'relativist' possess in fact only whatever meanings may be supplied for them ad hoc in some particular context. We have therefore to demand to be told what precisely it is which is being said to be subjective or objective, and exactly what it is which makes it count as such.

Again, what is it which is supposed to be relative to what, and in what way?

Once that first fundamental is seized, we are positioned to grasp a second. Notwithstanding widespread assumptions to the contrary, to say that this is necessarily relative to that is by no means to imply that the relation between this and that is only in the minds of observers, or is determinable by their arbitrary fiat. To maintain, for instance, that what anyone ought to do must depend upon time, place and circumstance is not at all the same thing as maintaining that there is no right or wrong about it, and that it is entirely a matter of individual or even collective taste. The general maxim, 'Do in Rome as the Romans do' is not a licence to please yourself alone; unless, of course, the particular place and period in question is that of *La Dolce Vita*, in which precisely that is what the Romans do do! Again, motion is everyone's paradigm case of the essentially relative. Yet, once both the moving body and the reference point have been specified, nothing, surely, could be more a matter of mind-independent objective fact than whether and in what direction, and how fast, that body is in motion.

A third fundamental concerns the concepts employed in articulating our beliefs, and us as the subjects of those beliefs. It is, certainly, true: that we understand and have to understand whatever we do understand in terms of whatever concepts we have; that it is, and cannot but be, we who believe or who know whatever we do believe or know, and who possess whatever concepts we do possess; and, consequently, that facts of both these two unexciting sorts are facts about ourselves as subjects. But from all this, when presented in an unfevered fashion, it does not even seem to follow that propositions involving our concepts cannot constitute, and be by us known to constitute, statements of objective, mind-independent truth.

1   Subjective idealism and the sociology of knowledge

Much as already been made of *Knowledge and Control* (Young

1971). This collection has been and apparently remains enormously influential in what Tom Lehrer taught some of us to call Edbiz. In it, according to the Editor, "sociology of education is no longer conceived as an area of enquiry distinct from the sociology of knowledge" (p. 3). So, apparently, we must "explore the implications of treating knowledge, or 'what counts as knowledge', as socially constituted or constructed", insisting that "the subversion of absolutism by sociology is of crucial importance for the sociology of education" (pp. 5 and 6).

(i)

The key contention, the misguiding thread, is never formulated in a properly terse, explicit, or completely categorical form. It is, nevertheless, perfectly clear what it is: namely, that the mere possibility of developing some sociological account of the desires and interests supporting the making of some kind of discrimination constitutes a sufficient demonstration that there is no objective basis for anything of the kind; that there are, that is to say, no corresponding differences 'without the mind'.

Thus the Editor faults the authors of "an otherwise excellent paper" for "drawing on a *metaphysical* 'out there' in terms of which, they claim, we must check our theories against our practice" (Young 1971, p. 43n). Again, Nell Keddie, one of his favourite contributors, after noting that "teachers differentiate . . . between pupils perceived as of high and low ability", forthwith dismisses the very idea that corresponding differences might actually subsist between those teachers' pupils: "The origins of these categories are likely to lie outside the school and within the structure of the society itself in its wider distribution of power" (p. 156). Finally, in Blum's own commended contribution, we have, as we have seen twice already, a reckless manifesto of total subjective idealism: " . . . it is not an objectively discernible, purely existing external world which accounts for sociology; it is the methods and procedures of sociology which create and sustain that world" (p. 131).

It should be obvious that the doctrines of *Knowledge and Control* are educationally subversive. For they foreclose on the possibility that distinctions made by examiners may correspond to actual differences in the quality either of the work or of the candidates examined. In *New Society* (24 February 1977) this implication was exultantly proclaimed by a couple of senior teachers of intending schoolteachers at Chelsea College: "The point is fundamental. There are no universal standards; there are only people's perceptions of standards." But what are teachers supposed to be trying to produce if it is not real improvements in the capacities and performances of their pupils? Our immediate concern here, however, is not with the educational or anti-educational implications. It is, rather, with the reasons which have been offered or suggested for reaching these obscurantist and preposterous conclusions.

Take Blum first. In a key sentence he concludes that "if objective knowledge is taken to mean knowledge of a reality independent of language, . . . then there is no such thing as objective knowledge" (p. 128). It is embarrassingly clear that Blum fails utterly to appreciate that and how large differences in the meaning of English sentences can result from small changes in word order. He might perhaps benefit from the exercise of inserting the word 'only' at various positions in Marghanita Laski's exemplary sentence: "The peacocks are seen on the Western hills."

Here there is a crucial difference: between, on the one hand, "knowledge of a reality independent of language"; and, on the other hand, knowledge, independent of language, of a reality. It is just plumb grotesque to maintain that – say – the stars in their courses are in any way dependent on what we say or do not say; and it is not for any sociologist to deny the claims of the natural scientists to know that this earth existed long before it bore any language-using creatures. If, on the other hand, Blum really intended to deny only propositional knowledge independent of language, then this is unexceptionable. Or, rather, it is unexceptionable so long as it is not mistaken to imply that the truths which we have to express in a particular form of words would not be true at all until and unless someone had formulated those truths in these or equivalent words. The crucial distinctions are: first, between knowing, and the truths which are known; and, second, between knowledge of a reality which is independent of language, and knowledge which is itself independent of language.

It is one thing, and scarcely disputatious or exciting, to say that the extent of our knowledge must be limited by, among other things, the quality and quantity of the conceptual equipment which happens to be available to us. It is quite another and, as we have been reminding ourselves, utterly paradoxical and preposterous to hold that every reality of which we can have knowledge must be dependent upon our presence, and our activities, and our "observer's procedures", and our having the concepts required to possess and to express that knowledge. Embarrassing though the observation is, it does appear to be true that the shamefully simple confusions removed in this and the two previous paragraphs have been and remain perennial chief sources of the demoralizing dogma that any knowledge which we do possess must be, in some depreciatory and emasculating sense, essentially and only relative and subjective opinion; the dogma – to put it in a brief, brutal and straightforward way – that there really neither is nor can be any such thing as, without prefix or suffix, knowledge.

(ii)

Certainly there are several other sources, and some of these are more particularly concerned with the fields of social science and social policy, and with the alleged impossibility in these of "objective knowledge"; knowledge, that is, and not merely perceived knowledge, of mind-independent realities.

The first of these other sources is the identification of investigator-produced pseudo-phenomena; the identification, that is, of what has been mnemonically nicknamed The Buggery in Bootle Effect. Young begins: "It is a statistical truism that . . . half a population of kidney beans will be of shorter than average length . . . despite efforts of breeders to produce longer beans . . . " (pp. 9–10).

It is an unauspicious beginning. For if the word 'average' is to be interpreted in its ordinary sense, in which it is equivalent to the 'arithmetic mean' of mathematicians, then it is not necessarily true, but plain false, that half of any population must be below average. Where one is a mere five foot and everyone else is a six-footer, there all but the first must be above the arithmetic mean height. It is the median, not the arithmetic mean, which (nearly) half of any population has to be at or below.

Young proceeds: "the methodical character of marriages, divorces and suicides is seen and made possible by the organized practices of sociologists: likewise . . . the regular 50–60 per cent of passes in General Certificate are seen and made possible by the organized activities of . . . examiners" (p. 10).

The initial ill omens are thus fulfilled. For these cases are different. The activities of marrying, divorcing and suiciding were, surely, all going strong long before there were any sociologists available to make them possible. But the other does seem to constitute an example of an investigator-produced pseudo-phenomenon. For, as we saw in Chapter 2, examiners for the General Certificate of Education have apparently been obeying an instruction from the whilom Secondary Schools Examinations Council to ensure that in every year in each subject roughly the same proportions of all candidates are awarded the various different grades.

A little later Young refers approvingly to a "discussion of how 'official statistics' on crime are produced" (p. 25). He suggests, though he does not outright say, that crime is another investigator-produced pseudo-phenomenon. Certainly everyone with a sophisticated interest in the subject knows that some, though not of course all, increases or declines in the recorded numbers of offences may refer rather to features of the system of reporting than to actual variations in the popularity of these offences. Thus, in the bad old pre-Wolfenden days, a sudden jump in the number of successful prosecutions for homosexual offences in – say – Bootle might have indicated, not a real explosion of unnatural vice, but the appointment of what would now be called a homophobic Chief Constable. Young and his associates, with the over-enthusiasm of the freshly initiated, are inclined to see everywhere nothing else whatever but this Buggery in Bootle Effect.*

(iii)

It is, as has been emphasized before, a fundamental fact about the peculiar subject-matter of the social sciences that as near as makes no matter all distinctively human activities are concept-guided, in the sense that they can be performed only by persons possessing the relevant concepts. This carries two important consequences. First, all social scientific explanation must accept as fundamental the reasons which agents themselves had for acting. Hence, second, whatever further concepts and explanations social scientists find it necessary or possible to introduce, they must always begin by mastering the action-guiding concepts employed by the subjects of their studies.

In part no doubt it was a badly focused appreciation of these truths which, with the help of the three kinds of intellectual malpractice reviewed in the preliminary paragraphs of the present chapter, led Blum to maintain that "the methodical character of marriage, war and suicide is only seen, recognized and made possible through the organized practices of sociology" (Young 1971, p. 131). But, surely, another part of the story is that many notions originally

This should, by the way, be carefully distinguished from the England Expects Effect identified above. This is itself a special case of the more general Oedipus Effect. For, surely, Nelson by issuing his most famous signal actually made some difference to morale in the British fleet?

devised by social scientists, slipping out of their sometimes strikingly uncloistered cloisters, have been adopted as action-guiding by what Blum would call "societal members". This is the less surprising since so many of the leaders have, like Smith and Malthus, combined and sometimes confused quests for theoretical understanding with commitments to practical policies.

Thus, for instance, a Weberian ideal type, originally offered primarily or purely as an instrument of neutral and non-participatory understanding of some society, may become the normative ideal of some members of that society and may in this way guide both their social activities and their understanding of these activities: this surely happened with Smith's ideal picture of a dynamic, private, pluralist and competitive economy. Again, consider a characteristic statement by Lenin: "The history of all countries shows that the working class, exclusively by its own effort, is able to develop only trade-union consciousness . . . The teachings of socialism, however, grew out of the philosophic, historical and economic theories elaborated . . . by intellectuals" (Lenin 1902, p. 80; and compare Hayek 1952 on the concurrent development of sociological science and socialist ideals).

Nevertheless, whatever the present and future influence of notions devised by social scientists, we cannot accept any Revised Version of Genesis 1:27: "And sociologists created societal members in their own image . . . male and female societal members created they them." What we can do is take emphatic note of the Oedipus Effect: "the influence of an item of information upon the situation to which the information refers" (Popper 1957, p. 13). For there have been, and certainly will be more, important cases in which the publication of social scientific findings to the people to whom those findings refer has drastically affected the future behaviour of many of those people. The most familiar and most discussed examples are of the influence of the publication of opinion poll findings upon the electoral behaviour of the populations (sample) polled. Thus in the 1948 US Presidential election it was thought that polls suggesting that

Dewey would win in a landslide led a lot of lazy Republican
voters to stay at home, letting Truman scrape back. But
then there was also reason to believe that the samples had
been unrepresentative. The clearer cases are from British
by-elections – notably at Orpington in 1962 – where published polls showing how many electors really preferred a
third-party candidate have encouraged them to plump for
that first preference, instead of settling for their second best
'for fear of wasting their vote'.

(iv)

Everyone always concedes or insists that the sociology of
knowledge is not directed specifically and exclusively at
Real McCoy knowledge. It is not, that is to say, concerned
always and only with rationally justified true belief. Indeed
the author of one unusually powerful essay, although himself
privately persuaded that all positive religious beliefs are at
best false and at worst incoherent, nevertheless commends as
a model "Durkheim's classic study 'The Elementary Forms of
the Religious Life'": this, it is asserted, "shows how a sociologist can penetrate to the very depths of *a form of knowledge*"
(Bloor 1976, p. 2: italics supplied).

Although the treatises and the textbooks usually begin by
disclaiming concern with knowledge as such, sociologists of
knowledge are stubborn in their resistance to proposals to
rename their discipline, truthfully, sociology of belief. The
maximum concession which most of them will allow is: either
actually to put such key words as 'reality' and 'knowledge'
between quotation marks; or else, and more often, to admit
that perhaps this is what they ideally ought to do, but not
to do it (Berger and Luckmann 1971, Introduction). The
significance of the inverted commas here would be to indicate
that the sociologists are dealing only with perceived reality
and believed knowledge. They are dealing, that is to say,
with whatever their subjects think is the case and whatever
they believe that they know; altogether without prejudice to

the questions whether what they believe is true and whether they really do know.

This said, it should at once be interjected that social scientists who insist on obeying this perverse self-denying ordinance thereby prevent themselves from raising exciting questions and discovering what are likely to be revealing answers. How do so many generally sensible people continue to harbour so many beliefs which it should be obvious to them are, and could by them be known to be, untrue? But the more immediately relevant and widely important need is to attack the irresponsible insouciance of employing the word 'knowledge' when what you are supposed to be meaning is, without prejudice, belief. This objection – like another, earlier objection – may be met with complaints about merely verbal purism and sneers at Linguistic Philosophy. Yet it is in truth an objection which social scientists ought to be peculiarly well fitted to appreciate.

For they of all people should be most aware of the enormous strength of long and firmly established habits. But the habits of association formed in mastering the established usage of a term, and hence its established meaning, habits strengthened by then following that established usage, and understanding the term in that sense, such verbal and semantic habits are no less habits than all other habits. It is, therefore, wildly unrealistic to expect to be able to change your own and other people's actual usage of a word, and hence your own and other people's understanding of it, even if only in one limited context, by simply saying that this is what you propose to do, and want the others too to follow you in doing.

Consider, for example, a similar project from another area of sociology. Thorstein Veblen (1857–1929) insisted upon introducing into *The Theory of the Leisure Class* what is, given his and our established habits of association, the heavily offensive expression 'conspicuous waste'. He then immediately and perhaps somewhat disingenuously protested that, since what and all he was doing was value-free social science, this phrase from now on was to be read as a detached and

evaluatively non-committal description. No one should be
surprised, however, to find that his own actual usage is not
consistent with this stated intention; while his readers have
always in fact construed that key phrase as an expression
of emphatic, and often well-warranted, disapproval (Veblen
1899, pp. 97ff.).

It should not be surprising, therefore, that much confusion
and many misconceptions have been, are, and will be generated by such irresponsible abusages. In the present particular
case confusion is the worse confounded in two other ways. In
the first place, most people only begin to seek possible social
or psychological causes for (what are always other people's)
beliefs after they have already somehow satisfied themselves
that these beliefs are either false or at least held with a degree
of conviction disproportionate to the evidencing reasons
available to the believer. The temptation, therefore, is to
infer that any belief for which some sociological explanation
is offered or sought is thereby revealed to be: not what
Milton once called "real and delightful knowledge"; but,
rather, rationally unjustified false belief. This temptation
is further strengthened by the fact that it has been only
in comparatively recent years that sociologists of belief have
in fact addressed themselves to the hard sciences and to
mathematics. (See, for instance, Bloor 1976 and Barnes 1974;
and compare Flew 1982.)

The second reinforcing temptation is provided by the
inverted commas around such words as 'reality' and 'knowledge'; when, that is, rather rarely, anyone remembers that
these are supposed to be there. It is all too easy to misread
them as indicating that what is being talked about is: not,
without prejudice, perceived reality and believed knowledge;
but beliefs which are already unequivocally discredited.

(v)

These, surely, are the main reasons why contributors to
Knowledge and Control reach the remarkable and altogether

devastating conclusions which they do reach. Thus they assume that what they still insist on calling the sociology of knowledge is an essentially subversive activity, necessarily discrediting every belief to which it can be applied: "the subversion of absolutism by sociology is of crucial importance" (Young 1971, p. 6). Still more remarkable, and still more devastating, is the conclusion that it is by this same discipline revealed that we do not and cannot have any objective knowledge; any knowledge, that is, of mind-independent realities. On no account is there to be any "drawing on a *metaphysical* 'out there' in terms of which . . . we must check out our theories . . ."

The false assumption that the sociology of knowledge must be essentially subversive is supported by another common misconception, that to criticize is necessarily to disparage. The assumption about sociology is false, since we can consistently say: both that Jones has an interest, maybe even a social class interest, in making that distinction or asserting this proposition; and that he knows both that the proposition asserted is true and that there are actual differences being thus distinguished. The short though in the longer run insufficient way with the common misconception about criticism is to ask whether, in order to qualify as a Shakespearian critic, you have systematically to condemn his collected works.

"Much research in education", we are told, "starts from an absolutist view of cognitive categories such as 'rational' and 'abstract'. This view in effect prevents these categories from being treated as themselves socially constructed and therefore open to sociological enquiry" (Young 1971, p. 11). Certainly, if the word 'absolute' is to be construed thus, as precluding sociological inquiry, then the absolutist is indeed exposed as an obscurantist. Whatever the merits or demerits of these or any other concepts, it should be obvious that there is room for questions about how we in fact come to have and to use those which we do have and use.

So far, which is not very far, so good. But then, a little later on, we meet a general objection to the work of philosophers of education – Paul Hirst in particular. "The problem with this kind of critique" apparently is that, since it neither begins nor ends by rejecting, it is not truly critical; and, hence, that it is, but now in a quite new sense, absolutist. Hirst himself has "an absolutist conception of a set of distinct forms of knowledge which correspond closely to the traditional areas of the academic curriculum and thus justify . . . what are no more than the socio-historical constructs of a particular time" (Young 1971, p. 23).

The word 'absolutist' is thus no longer employed in the original sense. For Hirst is being faulted: not for obstructing sociological investigation of how we come to make the distinctions; but for concluding that the distinctions made do in fact refer to actual differences. Not having noticed this crucial shift in meaning, Young has omitted to offer any reason for his own confident insistences: that the various concepts under discussion "are no more than the socio-historical constructs of a particular time"; and hence, presumably, that they do not correspond to any actual, objective differences.

The fallacious move made here is extremely common in all areas, although no doubt it is eased here by some of the more particular muddles and misconceptions examined previously. The heart of the matter is that, while it is one thing to say that certain notions are "the socio-historical constructs of a particular time", it is quite another to add that they are *no more than* "the socio-historical constructs of a particular time". It cannot be right to proceed from a premise stating only that this is that, direct to the richer conclusion that this is *merely* that, that this is *nothing but* that, that this is that *and nothing else*. Let us, therefore, introduce the appropriately shaming nickname 'The Debunker's Fallacy'.

That is the fallacy committed when anyone moves direct from 'That is your opinion' to 'That is *nothing but* your opinion'; with the implication that the proposition asserted has no other and better evidential support than your own bold, bald asserting. It was committed in, for example, a polemic entitled 'Popper's Mystification of Objective Knowledge'. This maintained that: "To appraise an argument for validity is to apply the standards of a social group. It cannot be other, *or more*, than this because we have no access to other standards" (Bloor 1974, p. 75: italics supplied). This is preposterous. For it is: from the fact that, although by applying the only available standards, we have determined that the argument is valid; to infer the conclusion that in truth it cannot actually be so!

Elsewhere in *Knowledge and Control* Pierre Bourdieu, who does not share the peculiar convictions common to the Editor and his most approved contributors, quotes a relevant passage from the psychologist Kurt Lewin: "Experiments dealing with memory and group pressure on the individual show that what exists as 'reality' for the individual is, to a high degree, determined by what is socially accepted as reality . . . 'Reality' therefore, is not an absolute. It differs with the group to which the individual belongs" (Young 1971, p. 195).

This is both true and important. But it is true only when read correctly with a proper appreciation of the significance of the inverted commas embracing the word 'Reality'. What Lewin is saying is: not that reality is not an absolute, because it differs with the group to which the individual belongs; but that 'reality' — that is to say what someone believes about reality — is not an absolute, because it differs with the group to which that individual belongs.

The distinction between reality and 'reality' or, if you prefer, between reality as it objectively is and perceived or believed reality, is, though often perversely collapsed, manifestly fundamental. While it is, therefore, all very well to speak of our concepts and categories "as themselves socially constructed"; it is very far from very well to slide from this to saying that the realities to which those concepts refer and which those categories categorize are created and sustained similarly. So Berger and Luckmann were both asking for and making trouble when they gave their bestselling textbook the title *The Social Construction of Reality*, and then proceeded to compound that initial fault by defining the words 'reality' and 'knowledge' in terms of our (subjective) recognitions and our (subjective) feelings of certainty (Berger and Luckmann 1971, p. 13).

2 *Anthropology, the relative and the rational*

Sometime in the fifth century BC Darius, Great King of what would now be described as the Iranian Empire, staged a dramatic confrontation to show the extreme diversity of the norms to which different social sets are committed, often equally strongly. He summoned "those Greeks who were with him and asked them what sum of money would induce them to make a meal of their dead fathers. And they said that nothing would induce them to do this. Darius then summoned the . . . Callatian Indians, who do eat their parents and, in the presence of the Greeks . . . asked them how much money they would take to burn their dead fathers in a fire. And they raised a great uproar, telling him not to speak of such a thing" (Herodotus III 38, p. 229).

(i)

From Plato's generation onwards facts of this sort, or in our own day – as in the case of Mead's bestselling books about Samoa – often only supposed facts of this sort, have led many to adopt positions about values of the kind indicated in our motto quotation from Comte. Although there have always been some who have wanted to extend such relativism to embrace not only values but facts and truths also, this desire seems to have become much more widespread in recent years, and to have captivated many of those working in the social sciences, and even the natural. Upstanding and forthright formulations are, nevertheless, hard to find. Presumably this is because clear and unequivocal formulation is bound to reveal relativistic claims to be either truistic or preposterous.

To claim, for instance, that one and the same proposition – let it be christened, conservatively, *p* – is true for me (and my associates) but not for you (and yours) is to contradict yourself. For it is to say that one and the same proposition is both true and false. This catastrophic claim presumably arises from a confusion: between what is true of Smith but not of Jones; and what is thought to be true *for* Smith but not *for*

Jones. But, of course, nothing is true *for* anyone; or, if you prefer, everything which is true at all is true for everyone, and hence for no one in particular. It may in some election be true of Smith that he voted Conservative and true of Jones that he voted Labour. Since, however, Smith and Jones are different people the proposition 'Smith voted Conservative' does not contradict the proposition 'Jones voted Labour (and not Conservative)'. (Compare Hollis and Lukes 1982, pp. 106–22.)

Slightly more complicated formulations rely on confusing some of the fundamental distinctions laboured earlier. What can by me be known to be true is in part a function both of my spatio-temporal position and of my intellectual equipment; while all knowledge presupposes a knowing subject. But none of this even begins to show that the truth of any truths which may or may not be known in any way depends upon or is somehow relative to anyone's particular spatio-temporal position or intellectual equipment; or that what actually is or is not true is always determined more or less arbitrarily at the will of some subject or set of subjects.

Again, perceived knowledge and hence perceived truth are totally different from, without prefix or suffix, knowledge and truth; while there is, similarly, a great gulf between truths about 'reality' and truths about reality. So to show that and how the former are socially constructed or essentially relative is not at all to show – what most surely cannot be shown – that the same is true of the latter.

(ii)

Various writings by Peter Winch have, since the publication in 1958 of *The Idea of a Social Science*, attracted an extraordinary amount of attention. Winch, as becomes a professional philosopher, propounds a somewhat more sophisticated reading of relativism. This starts by emphasizing the fundamental importance here of 'Our Reasons for Acting', the subject of Chapter 3. In consequence rationality becomes a key concept in all the social sciences. So far, so excellent.

But then, in a paper disquietingly entitled 'The Reality of Magic', Winch proceeds to raise "certain difficulties about Professor E.E. Evans-Pritchard's . . . classic *Witchcraft, Oracles and Magic among the Azande*" (B. Wilson 1970, p. 78). These involve Winch faulting Evans-Pritchard for wanting to say "that the criteria applied in scientific experimentation constitute a true link between our ideas and an independent reality, whereas those characteristic of other systems of thought – in particular, magical methods of thought – do not" (pp. 82–3). Poor culture-bound Evans-Pritchard was, apparently, in error when he maintained that in their beliefs about witchcraft the Azande "attribute to phenomena supra-sensible qualities . . . *which they do not possess*" (quoted p. 85: Winch's italics).

In a second part, on 'Our Standards and Theirs', Winch tries to justify this conclusion: "Something can appear rational to someone only in terms of *his* understanding of what is and is not rational. If *our* concept of rationality is a different one from his, then it makes no sense to say that anything either does or does not appear rational to *him* in *our* sense . . . MacIntyre seems to be saying that certain standards are taken as criteria of rationality because they *are* criteria of rationality. But whose?" (pp. 97–8).

First, enough has been said already about the wrongheadedness of this move: that is, from the necessarily true premise that whatever I sincerely assert must be my opinion; to the conclusion that those assertions must therefore be, if not false, at any rate not known to be true. Yet it is perhaps worth underlining one disturbing consequence of the collectivist version of this invalid reference. If "to appraise an argument for validity" and to assess a proposition for truth or falsity really is "to apply the standards of a social group", and if it really "cannot be other, or more, than this"; then, no doubt, "the objectivity of knowledge resides in its being the set of accepted beliefs of a social group" (Bloor 1974, pp. 75–6).

To say this, however, is to imply that there neither is nor could be any standing ground for dissident individuals.

Given such absolute collectivism it becomes doubtful whether Orwell's Winston Smith could without self-contradiction even muse privately over his doubts about the truth of the historical revisions authorized by Minitrue. For whatever was by due process of collective decision – applying the standards of a social group – tossed down the memory holes must, necessarily, have been false. That, after all, is what under Ingsoc (or English socialism) 'true' and 'false' are supposed to mean (Orwell 1950).

Second, two people, or two cultures, can have two different concept(ion)s of this or that only in so far as there is considerable coincidence between one and the other. For the mere fact that the same vocable – 'rationality' say – is found to be used in two radically distinct ways indicates the subsistence, not of two concept(ion)s of rationality, but of two senses of the word 'rationality'. So if there really are different concept(ion)s of rationality, then the differences between these cannot be either as total or as unbridgeable as Winch assumes.

We are here, it has to be interjected, observing a useful distinction between the concept of such and such and a conception of it. The concept of – say – justice is given when we have been equipped with some traditional definition of 'to do justice'; such as "to live honourably, to wrong no one, and to allow to each their own"; which is to say their several, and presumably often different, deserts and entitlements (Flew 1981, Chs. III–IV). But people who share that concept, and accept a definition on those lines, may, and sometimes do, have very different conceptions of justice – very different ideas, that is, both about what different people's deserts and entitlements are, and about the proper grounds of desert and entitlement.

Third, Winch continues: "MacIntyre seems to be saying that certain standards are taken as criteria of rationality because they *are* criteria of rationality." Why, please, is this thought to be heinous? Suppose we discover that the Kachin word previously rendered as 'rationality' in fact refers to a wholly different concept, then this merely shows that we have been mistranslating. Suppose that the two terms are perfectly equivalent, then we have no alternatives to choose between. It is only if, though they are not perfectly equivalent, they do have a great deal in common that we are warranted to speak of two concept(ion)s of rationality.

Suppose, for example, that a member of the tribe under investigation utters words which we are initially inclined to render into English as 'I am a macaw'. And suppose too that, not greatly to anyone's surprise, they do not act as we should expect a rational person to act if they genuinely believed that they had been transformed into something non-human. (Anyone requiring here some imaginative stimulus is recommended to reread Kafka's nightmare novelette *Metamorphosis*). The moral which the anthropologist should draw is: not that this tribe is, by the making of such strange utterances, shown to harbour a different conception of rationality; much less that, since its members are not rational animals, they are by Aristotelian standards not human at all. Instead, and more modestly, he should recognize that he has misunderstood the utterance rendered as 'I am a macaw'. Presumably it ought to have been construed as an idiomatic way of identifying with the macaw totem. (Compare, perhaps, the restaurant idiom in which diners are said or claim to be their chosen dishes. If I say, in such a context, 'I am a turkey and mushroom pie', then I am neither reporting an unprecedented metamorphosis nor – for that matter – claiming membership of a totem.)

Fourth, we must be cautious about following Winch and others in accepting extensive and intractable disagreements as evidence that those who differ thus must have different concepts, or even different conceptions falling under the single concept of rationality. We should remember that people may be awkward or careless in their handling of a concept which they do in fact share with others more careful or more competent. The fact, for instance, that I get nearly all the logical exercises wrong is not good evidence that I am master of an alternative concept of deduction. If in the end we have nevertheless to conclude that the Kachins or the Azande or whoever else have a different conception of rationality, then we certainly do not, whether for that or for any other reason, have to accept that 'our standards and theirs' are equally good or equally bad; and hence that 'their' witchcraft, oracles and magic are cognitively on all fours with 'our' science.

Consider, for example, some of the doctrinally infatuated sayings of one of those currently applying 'A Strong Programme for the Sociology of Belief' to the natural sciences. At the beginning of Chapter 2 of *Scientific Knowledge and Sociological Theory* the author writes: "If due weight is given to the preceding arguments, no particular set of natural beliefs [= beliefs about Nature] can be identified as reasonable, or as uniquely 'the truth'" (Barnes 1974, p. 22; and compare Flew 1982). If the passage from which that sentence is drawn stood alone then it might perhaps be construed in some alternative more charitable way. But before the chapter ends Barnes brings ridicule upon himself by ridiculing a rival sociologist's claims to know what in my young day our elders used to pick out as 'the facts of life'. Poor Steven Lukes, who might for generational and other reasons have hoped for more gentle treatment, is put down for his "rampant inductivism". More outrageous still, "Lukes refers to the ignorance of physiological paternity among some people and their 'magical' notions of conception; he regards these notions as in violation of objective rationality criteria without making any attempt to show why" (Barnes 1974, p. 36).

I imagine that Lukes, like most contemporary adults, knows them to be not so much "in violation of objective rationality criteria" as plain false. That is why he does not propose to insult his readers by suggesting that they are, unlike him, still infantile innocents; that they need someone else to spell out for them that, and how, these 'facts of life' are indeed, objectively and absolutely, known to be true.

3   The primacy of the untheoretical language of public description

Winch seems never to have asked himself how the first

anthropologists to take the field acquired their knowledge
of the languages peculiar to the peoples they wished to
study. Of course most of the earliest anthropologists, like
most of their successors today, began by employing bilingual
or multilingual helpers. But then the question to press is
how these helpers first acquired their knowledge of a second language. Certainly the *English-Zande* or *English-Nuer
Dictionary* did not descend immaculate from heaven, miracu-
lously endowed with inexpugnable authority. Someone had
somehow to master these to them foreign languages before
anyone could be in a position to compile such dictionaries
of equivalents. And presumably that someone would have
started, and indeed would have had to start, by establishing
an elementary vocabulary of terms for ostensible objects and
ostensible operations; a sort of Basic Zande or Basic Nuer.

(i)

All this is fundamental, and carries equally fundamental
implications. Let us assume that the would-be language
learner is an anthropologist, or would-be anthropologist;
and, since he or she will be the foreigner, let us call
the persons whose language is to be learnt the natives.
Now to understand native utterances the anthropologist
has to relate them not only to one another but also to
the non-linguistic world. For by simply discovering logical
relations between utterances he is not discovering what any
of these thus related utterances itself actually means. Suppose
that he learns that *p* implies *q* is incompatible with *r*, and
so on. Then he has learnt to operate what is for him still
only an uninterpreted calculus. To establish the bridgehead
indispensable for further advance the anthropologist has to
discover the meanings of some native sentences. He has, that
is to say, to discover what it is that these sentences are used
to assert, or to ask, or to command, as the case may be.

To achieve this the anthropologist does not necessarily
have to find any equivalent in his own language, much less
any straightforward and not too unwieldly equivalent. After

all, when he originally learnt his own mother tongue he had no other language into which to translate anything. What is essential is that the first sentences to be mastered must in some way refer to something which is observable by all concerned, the natives and the anthropologists both. And if we had really been from the beginning born into a world other than that of our parents and teachers, if we had been altogether unable to perceive anything of what is around us and to know truths about that shared environment, then we could never have even begun to learn what is for us our mother tongue.

Maybe there are no widgets where the anthropologist comes from, and maybe his own language previously lacked a single word for these devices. But, unless both he and the natives are able to identify widgets if and when these do make their appearance, then the native equivalent of 'He is carrying a load of widgets round the kraal' cannot serve as one of their bridgehead sentences. Once a bridgehead has been established, however, a whole new world of communicational possibility opens up. Any number of additional notions can be explained either in terms of those already mutually understood and/or by reference to other common or potentially common experience – experience, of course, always and only in what was earlier distinguished as the everyday or public sense.

We can even come to understand statements about our own or someone else's experience – in that more artificial and private sense in which a person's dreams are elements in their experience. Yet, here as everywhere else, we can only know that we mean by the words we use what others mean by these same words in so far as there is a permanent possibility of a cross-check. When they report that they are having yellow after-images do they mean the same as I mean by 'yellow'? Yes, surely; but only if they apply that word to describe substantially the same collections of publicly observable objects as I do (Flew 1961, Ch. II).

The implications of all this are of the last importance, both for philosophy in general and for the philosophy of social science in particular. In general, and for a very big start, they must render any non-solipsistic form of philosophical idealism untenable. We just cannot, consistent with these implications, communicate, and know that we are communicating, any disbelief in or sceptical doubt about the mind-independent existence of what philosophers since Descartes have dubbed 'the External World' – what M.F.D. Young and his associates dismiss as "a *metaphysical* 'out there'". For, as we have argued, it is only and precisely in so far as we are able genuinely to perceive (and not merely seem to perceive) and truly to know (and not simply claim to know) truths about objects and ongoings in 'the External World' that we can master any language in which to communicate with one another; or perhaps any language at all (Flew 1989b, Chs. IX–X).

It is also notably prejudicial and perverse to describe the situation as represented by such philosophical scepticism about 'the External World' as *our* cognitive predicament. For, for each of us, everyone else must be an inhabitant of that "*metaphysical* 'out there'"; hence, putatively, forever inaccessible. But, once we know that other people share our predicament, then already we must know, both that there really is, and quite a lot else about, that not merely perceived but also actual reality (Lenin 1908; and compare Flew 1978, Ch. 10).

Furthermore, and much more immediately relevant, all the basic notions of logic are and cannot but be involved from the beginning in any learning of a language. Even before we have words for all these ideas we have to be ready to make some distinctions between the true and the false, between the equivalent and the non-equivalent, between what follows necessarily and what is incompatible. So to insist upon logical propriety, rejecting contradiction and requiring validity in proposed deductions, is not arbitrarily to impose some external authority. For to tolerate contradiction in utterance is: not only to speak incoherently, by taking away what you have said out of one side of your mouth by what you are now saying out of the other; but also to reveal your indifference to truth, since you do not scruple to assert both the true and the false indifferently. 'Deduction' is itself defined in terms of contradiction; in as much as a valid deductive argument is one in which it is impossible, without self-contradiction, simultaneously to assert the premises and to deny the conclusions.

It was, therefore, an outrageous violation of the presuppositions of honest communication and truth-seeking inquiry when Herbert Marcuse borrowed a motto from his fellow Frankfurters Adorno and Horkheimer – "The general concept which discursive logic has developed has its foundations in the reality of domination" – and went on to contend that we have to be emancipated, apparently willy-nilly, from the allegedly artificial and oppressive doctrine that "contradictions are a fault of incorrect thinking" (Marcuse 1964, Ch. 5; and compare MacIntyre 1970, pp. 75–9). No wonder that that Modern Master's sympathies were more with *Soviet Marxism* than with the "repressive tolerance" contradictorily attributed to liberal societies!

All the fundamental notions of elementary logic are necessary to the learning of any language because the anthropologist, or any other language-learner, does not know what he can correctly say except in so far as he also knows what he cannot correctly say. That is why his progress is so much faster when he has the help of a particular native speaker than it would be if he had to try to pick everything up by simply observing the linguistic behaviour of native speakers in general. The crux is that the learner can put questions to the helper: 'Have I got it right; and, if not, what should I have said?'

So our conclusion must be that, if our anthropologists really are confronted with different conceptions of rationality, then the common element which makes them all conceptions of rationality must be or include whatever is essential for learning any language, and without which no one could ever know what anyone was saying about anything.

(ii)

The relativism presented by Winch in *The Idea of a Social Science* and later writings refers in the first instance only to those sciences, and to anthropology in particular. Thomas Kuhn, in his enormously influential book *The Structure of Scientific Revolutions* and in later papers, has presented a similar doctrine in the context of the natural sciences. But Kuhn's contentions have been welcomed by many people working in the social sciences, and applied there too. It will, therefore, be both relevant and rather piquant to conclude by bringing out that and why Kuhn himself, as an historian of ideas – and thus under our wide definition a social scientist – cannot consistently maintain the characteristic contentions put forward as fruits of that study.

Giving his 'Reflections on my Critics' Kuhn writes: "Granting that neither theory of a historical pair is true, they nonetheless seek a sense in which the later is a better approximation to the truth. I believe that nothing of that sort can be found." Like Young and his associates, and like other sociologists of belief, he believes that it is (nearer to) the objective truth to deny that there is any such truth; and so, like them, he derides those who "wish . . . to compare theories as representations of nature, as statements about 'what is really out there'" (Lakatos and Musgrave 1970, p. 265).

But, of course, while Kuhn is actually doing historical work he has to recognize that some scientists offer more or less good reasons for or against even what he calls paradigms, and that some paradigms are either more fruitful of discoveries or are themselves nearer the truth than others. Thus, in discussing paradigm changes – shifts of allegiance, that is, from one to another of two supposedly incommensurable theoretical structures supposedly not susceptible of any independent critical appraisal – Kuhn tells us: "Because scientists are reasonable men, one or another argument will ultimately persuade many of them. But there is no single argument that can or should persuade them all" (p. 157).

Here a first caveat has to be interjected. Kuhn is, like so

many others, collapsing the distinction between proof and persuasion. Certainly all reasonable people should, and to the extent that they are both reasonable and equipped to deal with the particular field will, be persuaded that a valid proof does indeed constitute a valid proof. But the fact that someone, and that someone an otherwise reasonable and relevantly well-equipped person, refuses to be persuaded by some material is not a sufficient reason for concluding that that material does not constitute a valid proof. It is, therefore, always wrong to argue direct from the fact that people are not persuaded to the conclusion that no valid proof has been presented to them; and doubly wrong to speak neither of proving something nor of persuading someone but of proving or failing to prove something *to* someone. What you should say is that you have failed to persuade them, perhaps through no fault either of yours or in your proof.

The second necessary caveat is that, even where "there is no single argument that can or should persuade them all" there may well be, especially in human affairs, accumulations so overwhelming that the reasonable man has no alternative but to concede that the case is proved to the hilt. Abundant illustrative examples are ready to hand both in the Law Reports and in the writings of historians.

Again, in the same 'Reflections' Kuhn writes: "Something must make at least a few scientists feel that the new proposal is on the right track . . . " (p. 157). How odd it is that he never asks himself: 'On the right track for where? What are the scientists trying to do?' Kuhn is here like those who tell us – oh so knowingly – that science is not concerned to discover truth, because scientists commend certain theories as fruitful rather than as true. Yet what is this good fruit if it is neither truth nor some better approximation to it?

Yet again, Kuhn writes: "The . . . comparison of two successive theories demands a language into which at least the empirical consequences of both can be translated without loss or change . . . that theories can be compared by recourse to a basic vocabulary consisting entirely of words which are attached to nature in ways that are unproblematic and, to the extent necessary, independent of theory." Indeed it does. For, if there really was no available vocabulary uninfected by either of the rival theories, then neither could be tested by reference to theory-independent facts, and maybe falsified. Kuhn, however, denies that any "such vocabulary is available . . . Successive theories are thus incommensurable" (pp. 206–7).

But now, in what vocabulary does Kuhn or any other historian of science begin to describe one of these paradigm changes? Obviously he begins by employing only the ordinary untechnical and untheoretical vocabulary of whatever language he himself is working in. Nor does he find it impossibly difficult to describe the crucial observations and experiments in neutral terms, even though the protagonists perhaps relied on their own loaded technicalities.

They may, in writing up their own experiments, have mentioned gains or losses of phlogiston, or the chemical combinations of oxygen and carbon, whereas the historian can and will describe the scenes in their laboratories in the sorts of ways in which these might have been described by acute but innocent persons totally ignorant of any chemical theory at all. When he wants to introduce any of the theoretical notions of either of the rival paradigms he will do this, as the original sponsors of these paradigms must at some stage themselves have done, by explaining these novelties in the untheoretical and untechnical terms of the vernacular – supplementing his explanations in words with various sorts of showing as and when necessary.

Suppose someone now suggests that even an ordinary, untechnical vocabulary must be itself theoretically loaded. Then the reply has to be that it can be, and is, at least "to the extent necessary, independent of theory". The favourite example here used to be talk about the sunrise, the suggestion being that all such talk is necessarily loaded with pre-Copernican astronomical theory. This example was especially popular in debates about the so-called Ordinary Language philosophy, spokespersons for which frequently employed it to bring out that they were not, in insisting that it is sound, idiomatic, untechnical English to describe a sunrise as a sunrise, committing either themselves or anybody else to any theory for explaining the observed phenomena. Such talk is purely observational rather than explanatory. Its terms can be, and are, defined ostensively.

Yet opponents who had been exposed to Ordinary Language philosophy in its Oxford homeland were wont to brandish this same sunrise example in triumph, just as if their exultant objection had never been pre-empted. But nowadays it is usual, in urging the thesis that the vocabulary of even the most concrete and down-to-earth vernacular cannot but be theory-loaded, to offer somewhat more sophisticated grounds. The key idea is that observers, by applying any of these terms in reporting their observations, cannot help making claims which go far beyond the provision of a narrowly non-committal record of their own private experience. To say, for instance, that you can see a glass of milk on the table is to say something which carries a load of implications: both about the origins of the substance in the glass; and about what would or will happen if various things were or are done to or with it. So, it is argued, even this most innocent and detached of observer's reports really involves the application of an elaborate theory; theory necessary in order to classify and thus to some extent to explain that observer's private experience, his sense-data.

The key idea here is perfectly sound, albeit misemployed. For in reporting, for instance, that you can see a glass of milk, you are certainly asserting much more than in claiming to have just had the peculiarly philosophical experience (private) of enjoying a glass-of-milkish sense-datum. But there is nothing controversially speculative about this assertive move. Instead it is firmly grounded in your lifetime of common experience (public). Nor was it 'theories' at this most fundamental level which Kuhn and others have been discussing. So even the more sophisticated objection constitutes no sufficient reason to withdraw the crucial contention: "that theories can be compared by recourse to a basic vocabulary consisting entirely of words which are attached to nature in ways that are unproblematic and, *to the extent necessary*, independent of theory" (Italics supplied).

(iii)

Finally, let it be in summary emphasized once again that Kuhn and others, both in presenting their findings and in finding them, make assumptions which they themselves claim that they have found to be false. Some will be reminded of how Sir Karl Popper – a far, far greater man, who was later to publish a book entitled *Objective Knowledge* – apparently became in *The Logic of Scientific Discovery* committed to the intolerably paradoxical, grossly false conclusion that there is no such thing: " . . . we must not look upon science as a 'body of knowledge', but rather as . . . a system of guesses . . . of which we are never justified in saying that we know that they are 'true' or 'more or less certain' or even 'probable'" (Popper 1934, p. 317; and compare pp. 280–1).

In *Scientific Knowledge and Sociological Theory* we are supposed to have been shown "how the culture of natural science may be made intelligible without recourse to externally based 'objective' assessments of the 'truth' of its beliefs or the rationality of its activities" (Barnes 1974, p. 69). But if, truly, "the sociologist cannot single out beliefs for special consideration because they are *the* truth" (p. 22), then what does Barnes himself think he is doing in thus presenting to a wider public this particular collection of beliefs about the subject of his book. Are these thus recommended beliefs, too, no more than "the informal understandings negotiated among members of an organized intellectual community" – one particular Edinburgh sept of the sociological clan?

The truth is, as we have seen, that the anthropologist has to start by establishing some vocabulary shared with his tribe. It is only upon this basis that he can begin to ask his distinctively anthropological questions. In the same way the historian of science investigating paradigm changes has to have some vocabulary shared with both his two tribes if he is to begin to understand what the conflict was about, and perhaps to hope to appreciate its development better than its participants did. If the rival systems really were irredeemably opaque to one another they would both, presumably, be equally or more opaque to the latter-day historian. But no, he and "we are suitors for agreement from everyone else, because we are fortified with a ground common to all" (Kant, 1790, I, mom. 4, sec. 19; p. 82).

References

This list is intended to include all, but only, those works mentioned in the text. For an obvious reason, works by authors who died before 1900 (and, exceptionally, for some others), the date given in the text is the date of original publication. Where page numbers are given, however, these refer to the more accessible editions detailed in the reference list. Both dates are given in the reference list, the date of original publication in square brackets and the date of the edition used in round parentheses.

Anderson, D. (ed.) (1980) *The Ignorance of Social Intervention* (London: Croom Helm).

Anderson D. (ed.) (1981a) *Breaking the Spell of the Welfare State* (London: Social Affairs Unit).

Andreski, S. (1972) *Social Sciences as Sorcery* (London: Deutsch; later Pelicanned).

Andreski, S. (ed.) (1975) *Reflections on Inequality* (London: Croom Helm).

Arblaster, A. (1974) *Academic Freedom* (Harmondsworth: Penguin).

Aristotle (1) (1950) *The Constitution of Athens*, translated by K. von Fritz and E. Kapp (New York: Hafner).

Aristotle (2) (1963) *On Interpretation*, in *Aristotle's Categories and de Interpretatione*, translated by J.L. Ackrill (Oxford: Clarendon).

Aristotle (3) (1926) *Nicomachean Ethics*, translated by H. Rackham (London: Heinemann and New York: Putnam).

Aristotle (4) (1948) *The Politics of Aristotle*, translated by E. Barker (Oxford: Clarendon).

Austin, J.L. (1961) *Philosophical Papers*, edited by J.O. Urmson and G.J. Warnock (Oxford: Clarendon).

Austin, J.L. (1962) *Sense and Sensibilia*, reconstructed from manuscript notes by G.J. Warnock (Oxford: Clarendon).

Axelrod, R. (1984) *The Evolution of Cooperation* (New York: Basic).

Bacon, F. (1905) *Philosophical Works*, edited by J.M.
Robertson (London: Routledge).

Barnes, B. (1974) *Scientific Knowledge and Sociological Theory*
(London: Routledge and Kegan Paul).

Bauer, P. (1976) *Dissent on Development* (Cambridge, Mass:
Harvard UP, Revised Edition).

Bauer, P. (1981) *Equality, the Third World and Economic
Delusion* (London: Weidenfeld and Nicolson).

Bauer, P. (1984) *Reality and Rhetoric: Studies in the Economics
of Development* (London: Weidenfeld and Nicolson).

Berger, P.L. and Luckmann, T. (1971) *The Social
Construction of Reality* (Harmondsworth: Penguin).

Berkeley, G. [1710] (1901) *A Treatise concerning the Principles
of Human Knowledge*, in the *Works*, edited by A.C. Fraser
(Oxford: Clarendon).

Berlin, I, [1953] (1969) 'Historical Inevitability', in his *Four
Essays on Liberty* (Oxford: OUP).

Blackburn, R. (ed.) (1972) *Ideology in Social Science* (London:
Collins/Fontana).

Blaug, M. (1970) *An Introduction to the Economics of Education*
(London: Allen Lane/Penguin Press).

Block, W. (1976) *Defending the Undefendable* (New York:
Fleet Press).

Bloor, D. (1974) 'Popper's mystification of objective
knowledge', *Science Studies*, IV, pp. 65–76.

Bloor, D. (1976) *Knowledge and Social Imagery* (London:
Routledge and Kegan Paul).

Bohm-Bawerk, E. von [1896] (1975) *Karl Marx and the Close
of his System* (Clifton, NJ: Kelley).

Borger, R. and Cioffi, F. (eds) (1970) *Explanation in the
Behavioural Sciences* (Cambridge: CUP).

Bosanquet, N. and Townsend, P. (eds) (1980) *Labour and
Equality* (London: Heinemann).

Bottomore, T. (1984) *Sociology and Socialism* (Brighton:
Wheatsheaf).

Boudon, R. (1969) *The Logic of Sociological Explanation*
(Harmondsworth: Penguin).

Boudon, R. (1974) *Education, Opportunity and Social Inequality* (New York: Wiley).

Brewer, C. and Lait, J. (1980) *Can Social Work Survive?* (London: Temple Smith).

Broadway, F. (1976) *Upper Clyde Shipbuilders* (London: Centre for Policy Studies).

Bruce-Gardyne, J. (1978) *Meriden: Odyssey of a Lame Duck* (London: Centre for Policy Studies).

Buchanan, J.M. and Tullock, G. (1962) *The Calculus of Consent* (Ann Arbor, MI: Michigan UP).

Buckle, H.T. (1903) *History of Civilization in England* (London and New York: Longmans Green).

Burnet, J. (Lord Monboddo) (1774) *The Origin and Progress of Language* (Edinburgh).

Burton, J. (1978) 'Private property rights or the spoliation of nature', in S.N.S. Cheung (ed.), *The Myth of Social Cost* (London: Institute of Economic Affairs).

Burton, J. (1979) *The Job Support Machine* (London: Centre for Policy Studies).

Carr, E.H. (1961) *What is History?* (London: Macmillan; later Pelicanned).

Chew, J. (1990) *Spelling Standards and Examination Results among Sixth Formers 1984–1990* (York: Campaign for Real Education).

Coard, B. (1971) *How the West Indian Child is made educationally sub-normal in the British School System* (London: New Beacon).

Cohen, G.A. (1972) 'Karl Marx and the withering away of social science', in *Philosophy and Public Affairs*, I 2 (Winter).

Cohen, S. (1972) *Folk Devils and Moral Panics* (London: MacGibbon and Kee).

Coleman, A. and others (1985) *Utopia on Trial: Vision and Reality in Planned Housing* (London: Shipman).

Comte, Auguste (1830) *Cours de philosophie positive* (Paris: Bachelier).

Conquest, R. (1967) *The Politics of Ideas in the USSR* (New York: Praeger).

Conquest, R. (1972) *Lenin* (London: Collins/Fontana).

Conquest, R. (1986) *The Harvest of Sorrow: Soviet Collectivization and the Terror-Famine* (New York and London: OUP).

Cox, C. and Marks, J. (1980) *Real Concern* (London: Centre for Policy Studies).

Cox, C. and Marks, J. (1982) 'Cause for concern: research on progress in secondary schools', in C. Cox and J. Marks (eds), *The Right to Learn* (London: Centre for Policy Studies).

Cox, C. and Marks, J. (1988) *The Insolence of Office* (London: Claridge).

Crosland, C.A.R. (1976) *Socialism Now* (London: Cape).

Darwin, C. [1859] (1968) *The Origin of Species*, edited by J.B. Burrow (Harmondsworth: Penguin).

Davie, R., Butler, N. and Goldstein, H. (1972) *From Birth to Seven* (London: Longman).

Dawson, G. (1981) 'Unfitting teachers to teach: sociology in the training of teachers', in D. Anderson (ed.), *The Pied Pipers of Education* (London: Social Affairs Unit).

Descartes, R. [1637] (1931) *A Discourse on the Method*, in *The Philosophical Works of Descartes*, translated by E.S. Haldane and G.R.T. Ross (Cambridge: CUP, Revised Edition).

Diels, Hermann (1906–10) *Die Fragmente der Vorsokratiker* (Berlin: Weidmannische Buchhandlung).

Dilthey, W. (1961) *Meaning in History* (London: Allen and Unwin).

Djilas, M. (1958) *The New Class* (London: Thames and Hudson).

Dray, W. (1957) *Laws and Explanation in History* (London: OUP).

Durkheim, E. [1895] (1964) *The Rules of Sociological Method*, translated by S.A. Soloway and J.H. Mueller and edited by G.E. Catlin (Glencoe, Illinois: Free Press).

Durkheim, E. [1897] (1967) *Le Suicide: étude de sociologie* (Paris: Presses Universitaires de France).

Durkheim, E. [1918] (1965) *Montesquieu and Rousseau:*

Forerunners of Sociology, translated by R. Mannheim (Ann Arbor: Michigan UP).

Eberstadt, N. (1988) *The Poverty of Communism* (New Brunswick, NJ: Transaction).

Engels, F. [1844] (1967) *Outlines of a Critique of Political Economy*, in W.O. Henderson (ed.), *Engels: Selected Writings* (Harmondsworth: Penguin).

Engels, F. [1845] (1971) *The Condition of the Working Class in England*, translated and edited by W.O. Henderson and W.H. Challoner (Oxford: Blackwell).

Engels, F. [1878] (1934) *Herr Eugen Dühring's Revolution in Science*, alias *Anti-Dühring*, translated by E. Burns and edited by C.P. Dutt (London: Lawrence and Wishart).

Engels, F. [1880] (1892) *Socialism: Utopian and Scientific*, translated by E. Aveling (London: Allen and Unwin).

Engels, F. [1884] (1940) *The Origin of the Family, Private Property and the State*, translated by A. West and D. Torr (London: Lawrence and Wishart).

Engels, F. [1888] (1934) *Ludwig Feuerbach and the End of German Classical Philosophy*, no translator named, edited by C.P. Dutt (London: Martin Lawrence).

Farrington, B. (1965) *Science and Politics in the Ancient World* (London: Allen and Unwin, Second Edition).

Felix, D. (1983) *Marx as Politician* (Carbondale and Edwardsville, IL: Southern Illinois UP).

Ferguson, A. [1767] (1966) *An Essay on the History of Civil Society*, edited by D. Forbes (Edinburgh: Edinburgh UP).

Ferguson, A. (1792) *Principles of Moral and Political Science* (London and Edinburgh).

Flew, A.G.N. (1961) *Hume's Philosophy of Belief* (London: Routledge and Kegan Paul).

Flew, A.G.N. (ed.) (1964) *Body, Mind and Death* (New York and London: Collier-Macmillan).

Flew, A.G.N. (1973) *Crime or Disease?* (London: Macmillan).

Flew, A.G.N. (1975) *Thinking About Thinking* (London: Fontana/Collins, 1975. Also as *Thinking Straight* (Buffalo, NY: Prometheus).

Flew, A.G.N. (1976) *Sociology, Equality and Education* (London: Macmillan).

Flew, A.G.N. (1978) *A Rational Animal* (Oxford: Clarendon).

Flew, A.G.N. (1981) *The Politics of Procrustes* (London: Temple Smith).

Flew, A.G.N. (1982) 'A strong programme for the sociology of belief', *Inquiry* (Oslo), XXV.

Flew, A.G.N. (1984) *Darwinian Evolution* (London: Granada/Paladin).

Flew, A.G.N. (1986) *David Hume: Philosopher of Moral Science* (Oxford: Blackwell).

Flew, A.G.N. (1987a) *Thinking About Thinking* (London: Fontana). Also as *Thinking Straight* (Buffalo, NY: Prometheus).

Flew, A.G.N. (1987b) *Power to the Parents: Reversing Educational Decline* (London: Sherwood).

Flew, A.G.N. (1989a) *Equality in Liberty and Justice* (London and New York: Routledge).

Flew, A.G.N. [1971] (1989b) *An Introduction to Western Philosophy: Ideas and Argument from Plato to Popper* Revised Edition (London: Thames and Hudson).

Flew, A.G.N. (1989c) *Self-improvement and Social Action* (London: Social Affairs Unit).

Flew, A.G.N. (1989d) 'The Philosophy of Schools Council History', in the *Journal of the Philosophy of Education* for 1989, pp. 113–21.

Flew, A.G.N. (1991a) *Educational Services: Independent Competition or Maintained Monopoly?* (London: Institute for Economic Affairs).

Flew, A.G.N. (1991b) 'Communism: The Philosophical Foundations' in *Philosophy* LXVI.

Flew, A.G.N. (1991c) 'Education: Anti-Racist, Multiethnic and Multicultural', in B. Carr and I. Mahalingham (eds.) *Logical Foundations: Essays in Honour of D.J. O'Connor* (London: Macmillan).

Flew, A.G.N. and Vesey, G. (1987) *Agency and Necessity* (Oxford: Blackwell).

Freeman, D. (1983) *Margaret Mead and Samoa: The Making*

and Unmaking of an Anthropological Myth (Cambridge, MA: Harvard UP).

Freeman, D, (1992) *The Hoaxing of Margaret Mead: A Cause Célèbre of 20th Century Anthropology* (Cambridge, MA: Harvard UP).

Friedman, M. and R. (1980) *Free to Choose* (London: Secker and Warburg).

Gardiner, P.L. (1952) *The Nature of Historical Explanation* (London: OUP).

Gellner, E.A. (1959) *Words and Things.* (London: Gollancz, later Pelicanned).

Gellner, E.A. (1973) *Cause and Meaning in the Social Sciences* (London: Routledge and Kegan Paul).

Gellner, E.A. (1985) *Relativism and the Social Sciences* (Cambridge: CUP).

Ginsberg, M. (1956) *The Diversity of Morals* (London: Heinemann).

Gould, J. and others (1977) *The Attack on Higher Education* (London: Institute for the Study of Conflict).

Grigg, J. (1980) *1943: The Victory that Never Was* (London: Hill and Wang).

Grimble, A. (1952) *A Pattern of Islands* (London: Murray).

Haldane, J.B.S. [1932] (1937) 'Scientific Calvinism', in *The Inequality of Man* (Harmondsworth: Penguin).

Halévy, E. (1928) *The Growth of Philosophic Radicalism*, translated by Mary Morris (London: Faber & Faber).

Hall, S. (1976) 'Violence and the media', in N. Tutt (ed.), *Violence* (London: DHSS).

Halmos, P. (1974) 'The moral ambiguity of critical sociology', in R. Fletcher (ed.), *The Science of Society and the Unity of Mankind* (London: Heinemann).

Halmos, P. (1976) Review article on the 'Ideology of welfare', *Times Higher Education Supplement*, 18 June 1976.

Hardin, G. (1977), 'The Tragedy of the Commons', in G. Hardin and J. Baden (eds), *Managing the Commons* (San Francisco: W.H. Freeman).

Hayek, F.A. (1944) *The Road to Serfdom* (London: Routledge and Kegan Paul).

Hayek, F.A. (1948) *Individualism and Economic Order* (Chicago: Chicago UP, 1948).

Hayek, F.A. [1952] (1979) *The Counter-Revolution of Science* (Indianapolis: Liberty).

Hayek, F.A. (ed.) (1954) *Capitalism and the Historians* (Chicago: Chicago UP).

Hayek, F.A. (1967) *Studies in Philosophy, Politics and Economics* (London: Routledge and Kegan Paul).

Hayek, F.A. (1978) *New Studies in Philosophy, Politics, Economics and the History of Ideas* (London: Routledge and Kegan Paul).

Hayek, F.A. (1988) *The Fatal Conceit: The Errors of Socialism* (Chicago, and London: Chicago UP, and Routledge).

Herodotus (1910) *The History of Herodotus*, translated by G. Rawlinson (London: Dent, and New York: Dutton).

Hoff, T.J.B. (1981) *Economic Calculation in the Socialist Society* (Indianapolis, IN: Liberty Press).

Hollander, P. (1981) *Political Pilgrims* (Oxford: OUP).

Hollis, M. and Lukes, S. (eds.) (1982) *Rationality and Relativism* (Oxford: Blackwell).

Hollis, N. and Nell, E. (1975) *Rational Economic Man* (Cambridge: CUP).

Honey, J. (1983) *The Language Trap* (London: National Council for Educational Standards).

Hook, S. (1943) *The Hero in History* (New York: John Day).

Housman, A.E. (1931) *Juvenalis Saturae* (Cambridge: CUP, Revised Edition).

Hudson, W.D. (ed.) (1969) *The Is/Ought Question* (London: Macmillan).

Hume, D. [1739–40] (1974) *A Treatise of Human Nature*, edited by L.A. Selby-Bigge with revisions by P. Nidditch (Oxford: Clarendon).

Hume, D. [1741–77] (1985) *Essays Moral Political and Literary*, edited by E.F. Miller (Indianapolis, IN: Liberty Classics).

Hume, D. [1748] (1975) *An Enquiry concerning Human Understanding*, in *Hume's Enquiries*, edited by L.A. Selby-Bigge with revisions by P. Nidditch (Oxford: Clarendon).

Hume, D. [1751] (1975) *An Enquiry concerning the Principles of Morals*, in the same.

Hume, D. [1779] (1947) *Dialogues concerning Natural Religion*, edited by N. Kemp Smith (Edinburgh: Nelson).

Huxley, A. (1936) *The Olive Tree* (London: Chatto and Windus).

Jarvie, I.C. (1973) *Functionalism* (Minneapolis: Burgess).

Jefferson, J.M. (1974) 'Industrialization and poverty: in fact and fiction', in N. Gash (ed.), *The Long Debate on Poverty* (London: Institute of Economic Affairs).

Jencks, C. and others (1973) *Inequality: A Reassessment of the Effect of Family and Schooling in America* (London: Allen Lane).

Jones, C. (1977) *The £200,000 Job* (London: Centre for Policy Studies).

Joynson, R.B. (1989) *The Burt Affair* (London and New York: Routledge).

Kafka, F. (1961) *Metamorphosis, and other stories*, translated by W. and E. Muir (Harmondsworth: Penguin).

Kant, I. [1790] (1917) *A Critique of Aesthetic Judgement*, translated by J.G. Meredith (Oxford: Clarendon).

Kautsky, K. [1918] (1964) *The Dictatorship of the Proletariat*, translated by H.J. Stenning (Ann Arbor: Michigan UP).

Keynes, J.N. (1904) *The Scope and Method of Political Economy* (London: Macmillan).

Kolakowski, L. (1978) *Main Currents of Marxism: Its Rise, Growth and Dissolution* (Oxford: Clarendon).

Kuhn, T. (1962) *The Structure of Scientific Revolutions* (Chicago: Chicago UP).

Labin, S. (1982) *Chile: The Crime of Resistance* (Richmond, Surrey: Foreign Affairs Publishing).

Lait, J. (1980) 'Central Government's ineptitude in monitoring local welfare', in A. Seldon (ed.), *Town Hall Power or Whitehall Pawn* (London: Institute for Economic Affairs).

Lakatos, I. and Musgrave, A. (eds.) (1970) *Criticism and the Growth of Knowledge* (Cambridge: CUP).

Lange, J. [1929] (1931) *Crime as Destiny: A Study of Criminal*

Twins, translated by Charlotte Haldane (London: Allen and Unwin).

Lavoie, D. (1985) *National Economic Planning: What is Left?* (Cambridge, MA: Ballinger).

Leach, E. (1970) *Lévi-Strauss* (London: Fontana/Collins).

Lenin, V.I. [1902] (1970) *What is to be Done?*, translated by S.V. and P. Utechin (London: Panther).

Lenin, V.I. [1908] (1952) *Materialism and Empirio-Criticism*, no translator named (London: Lawrence and Wishart).

Lenin, V.I. [1917] (1939) *State and Revolution*, no translator named (London: Lawrence and Wishart).

Lenin, V.I. [1918] (1934) *The Proletarian Revolution and the Renegade Kautsky*, no translator named (New York: International).

Lenin, V.I. [1922] (1947) 'Our Revolution', in *The Essentials of Lenin*, no translator named (London: Lawrence and Wishart).

Levin, M. (1988) *Feminism and Freedom* (New Brunswick, NJ: Transaction).

Lévi-Strauss, C. (1955) *Tristes Tropiques* (Paris: Librairie Plon).

Lewis, M. (1980) *The Culture of Inequality* (New York: New American Library, and London: New English Library).

Locke, J. [1690] (1975) *An Essay concerning Human Understanding*, edited by P. Nidditch (Oxford: Clarendon).

Lukes, S. (1974) 'Relativism: cognitive and moral', *Proceedings of the Aristotelian Society*, supp. vol. XLVIII.

Lundberg, G. (1963) 'The postulates of science and their implications for sociology', in M. Natanson (ed.), *Philosophy of the Social Sciences* (New York: Random House).

Lynn, J. and Jay, A. (1988) *The Complete Yes Minister* (New York, and London: Harper and Row, and British Broadcasting Corporation).

Lynn, R. (1988) *Educational Achievement in Japan: Lessons for the West* (London: Macmillan and Social Affairs Unit).

MacIntyre, A.C. (1970) *Marcuse* (London: Fontana/Collins).

Malinowski, B. (1922) *Argonauts of the Western Pacific* (London: Routledge).

Malinowski, B. [1944] (1960) *A Scientific Theory of Culture* (New York: OUP).

Malthus, T.R. [1798] (1970) *An Essay on the Principle of Population*, edited by A. Flew (Harmondsworth: Penguin) – The *First Essay*.

Malthus, T.R. [1802] *An Essay on the Principle of Population* (London: Sixth Edition, 1826) – the *Second Essay*.

Malthus, T.R. (1817) *1817 Appendix*. This is an appendix to what is presented as the Fifth Edition of Malthus [1798]. It is reprinted in the Sixth, the last to be revised by the author. This was in truth the Fifth Edition of Malthus 1802.

Malthus, T.R. [1824] (1953) 'A summary view of the principle of population', in D.V. Glass (ed.), *An Introduction to Malthus* (London: Watts).

Mandeville, B. de [1723] (1970) *The Fable of the Bees*, edited by P. Harth (Harmondsworth: Penguin).

Marcuse, H. (1961) *Soviet Marxism* (London: Routledge and Kegan Paul).

Marcuse, H. (1964) *One Dimensional Man* (London: Routledge and Kegan Paul).

Marks, J., Cox, C. and Pomian-Srzednicki (1983) *Standards in English Schools: First Report* (London: National Council for Educational Standards).

Marsland, D. (1988) *Seeds of Bankruptcy* (London: Claridge).

Marx, K. [1843] (1975) 'A contribution to the critique of Hegel's Philosophy of Law: Introduction', in K. Marx and F. Engels, *Collected Works* vol. III (London: Lawrence and Wishart).

Marx, K. [1844] (1964) *The Economic and Philosophical Manuscripts of 1844*, translated by M. Milligan and edited by D.J. Struik (New York: International).

Marx, K. [1847] (1936) *The Poverty of Philosophy*, no translator named (London: Lawrence and Wishart).

Marx, K. [1852] (1934) *The Eighteenth Brumaire of Louis Bonaparte*, no translator named (Moscow: Progress).

Marx, K. [1859] (1970) *A Contribution to the Critique of Political Economy*, translated by S.W. Ryazanskaya and edited by M. Dobb (Moscow: Progress).

Marx, K. [1867] (1961–2) *Capital*, translated by S. Moore and E. Aveling (London: Lawrence and Wishart).

Marx, K. [1875] (1969) *A Critique of the Gotha Programme*, in Vol. II of K. Marx and F. Engels *Selected Works* (Moscow: Foreign Languages Publishing House).

Marx, K. and Engels, F. [1845] (1975–) *The Holy Family*, translated by R. Dixon and C. Dutt, in K. Marx and F. Engels, *Collected Works* (London: Lawrence and Wishart), vol. IV, pp. 5–211.

Marx, K. and Engels, F. [1846] (1964) *The German Ideology*, edited by S. Ryazanskaya, no translator named (Moscow: Progress). Although this work was finished in 1846 it was first published, in the original German, in 1932.

Marx, K. and Engels, F. [1848] (1967) *The Communist Manifesto*, translated by Samuel Moore and edited by A.J.P. Taylor (Harmondsworth: Penguin).

Mayhew, H. (1861) *London Labour and the London Poor* (London: Griffin).

Mayhew, H. (1862) *The Criminal Prisons of London* (London: Griffin).

Mead, M. (1943) *Coming of Age in Samoa* (Harmondsworth: Penguin).

Merton, R.K. (1963) *Social Theory and Social Structure* (New York: Free Press).

Michels, R. (1959) *Political Parties*, translated by E. and C. Paul (New York: Dover).

Mill, J.S. (1843) *A System of Logic, Ratiocinative and Inductive* (London: Longmans Green). Also Sixth Edition 1865.

Moore, G.E. (1903) *Principia Ethica* (Cambridge: CUP).

Morgan, P. (1978) *Delinquent Fantasies* (London: Temple Smith).

Moss, R. (1973) *Chile's Marxist Experiment* (Newton Abbot, Devon: David and Charles).

Murphy, J. (1990) 'A most respectable prejudice: inequality

of educational research and policy', in the *British Journal of Sociology*, XLI, 1 (March 1990).

Murray, C. (1984) *Losing Ground: American Social Policy 1950–1980* (New York: Basic).

Murray, C. (1988) *In Pursuit of Happiness and Good Government* (New York: Simon and Schuster).

Murray, C. and others (1990) *The Emerging British Underclass* (London: Institute for Economic Affairs).

Namier, L.B. (1952) *Avenues of History* (London: Hamish Hamilton).

Neave, G. (1979) 'Sense and Sensitivity: The Case for Comprehensive Education', in the *Quantitative Sociology Newsletter*, No. 21.

Newton, I. [1687] (1962) *Principia Mathematica Philosophiae Naturalis*, translated by A. Motte, revised and edited by F. Cajori (Berkeley and Los Angeles: California UP).

Newton, I. [1704] (1952) *Opticks*, edited by I.B. Cohen (New York: Dover).

North, J. (ed.) (1987) *The GCSE: An Examination* (London: Claridge).

Oakeshott, M. (1966) 'Historical continuity and causal analysis', in W. Dray (ed.), *Philosophical Analysis and History* (New York: Harper and Row).

O'Neill, J. (ed.) (1973) *Modes of Individualism and Collectivism* (London: Heinemann).

Orwell, G. (1945) *Animal Farm* (London: Secker and Warburg).

Orwell, G. (1950) *Nineteen Eighty-Four* (London: Secker and Warburg).

Orwell, G. (1970) *Collected Essays* (Harmondsworth: Penguin).

Palmer, F. (ed.) (1986) *Anti-Racism – An Assault on Education and Value* (London: Sherwood).

Parkinson, C.N. (1981) *The Law* (Harmondsworth: Penguin).

Parsons, T. (1968) *The Structure of Social Action* (New York: Free Press).

Pateman, T. (ed.) (1972) *Counter Course: A Handbook for Course Criticism* (Harmondsworth: Penguin).

Plato (1) (1963) *The Republic*, translated by P. Shorey (London: Heinemann, and Cambridge, Mass: Harvard UP).

Plato (2) (1952) *The Laws*, translated by R.B. Bury (London: Heinemann, and Cambridge, Mass: Harvard UP).

Plekhanov, G. V. [1898] (1940) *The Role of the Individual in History* (London: Lawrence and Wishart).

Polanyi, G. and P. (1976) *Failing the Nation: The Record of the Nationalized Industries* (London: Fraser Ansbacker).

Popper, K.R. [1934] (1959) *The Logic of Scientific Discovery* (London: Hutchinson).

Popper, K.R. [1945] (1956) *The Open Society and its Enemies* (London: Routledge and Kegan Paul).

Popper, K.R. (1957) *The Poverty of Historicism* (London: Routledge and Kegan Paul).

Popper, K.R. (1963) *Conjectures and Refutations* (London: Routledge and Kegan Paul).

Popper, K.R. (1979) *Objective Knowledge* (Oxford: Clarendon).

Popper, K.R. (1982) *The Open Universe; An Argument for Indeterminism* (London: Hutchinson).

Price, R.H., Ketterer, R.F., Bader, B.C. and Monahan, H. (eds.) (1980) *Prevention in Mental Health: Research, Policy and Practice* (Beverley Hills and London: Sage).

Pryke, R. (1981) *The Nationalized Industries: Policies and Performance since 1968* (Oxford: Martin Robertson).

Quinney, R. (1970) *The Social Realities of Crime* (Boston: Little, Brown).

Radnitzky, G. and Bernholz, P. (eds.) (1986) *Economic Imperialism: The Economic Method Applied outside the Field of Economics* (New York: Paragon).

Randi, J. (1982) *Flim-Flam!* (Buffalo: Prometheus).

Rawls, J. (1971) *A Theory of Justice* (Cambridge, Mass: Harvard UP, and Oxford: Clarendon).

Redwood, J. (1980) *Public Enterprise in Crisis* (Oxford: Blackwell).

Richardson, K. and Spears, D. (eds.) (1972) *Race, Culture and Intelligence* (Harmondsworth: Penguin).

Robbins, L. (1949) *An Essay on the Nature and Significance of Economic Science* (London: Macmillan).

Robertson, W. (1890) *The Works of William Robertson* (Edinburgh).

Rockwell, J. (1974) *Fact in Fiction* (London: Routledge and Kegan Paul).

Rosenberg, N. and Birdzell, L.E. (1986) *How the West Grew Rich* (New York: Basic).

Rottenberg, S. (ed.) (1973) *The Economics of Crime and Punishment* (Washington: American Enterprise Institute).

Runciman, W.G. (ed.) (1978) *Weber: Selections in Translation*, translated by E. Matthews (Cambridge: CUP).

Runyon, D. (1950) *Runyon on Broadway* (London: Constable).

Ruskin, J. (1876) Various letters in vol. XXVIII of *The Works of John Ruskin* (London: G. Allen, and New York: Longmans Green, 1903–12).

Ruskin, J. (1899) *Unto this Last* (London: G. Allen).

Sarup, M. (1982) *Education, State and Crisis: A Marxist Perspective* (London and Henley: Routledge and Kegan Paul).

Sarup, M. (1986) *The Politics of Multiracial Education* (London: Routledge and Kegan Paul).

Schelling, T. (1978) *Micromotives and Macrobehaviour* (New York: Norton).

Schoeck, H. [1969] (1990) *Envy: A Theory of Social Behaviour*, translated by M. Glenny and B. Ross (Indianapolis, IN: Liberty Press).

Schopenhauer, A. (1896) *The Art of Controversy*, translated and edited by T.B. Saunders (London: Sonnenschein).

Schwartzschild, L. (1948) *The Red Prussian* (London: Hamish Hamilton. Reissued by Pickwick in 1986).

Scruton, R. (1985) *Thinkers of the New Left* (London: Longman).

Seldon, A. (ed.) (1978) *The Economics of Politics* (London: Institute of Economic Affairs).

Seligman, E.R.A. (1907) *The Economic Interpretation of History* (New York: Columbia UP).

Senior, W.N. (1829) *Two Lectures on Population*, with the correspondence between the author and T.R. Malthus (London: Saunders etc.).

Sextus Empiricus (1955) *Works*, translated by R.G. Bury (London: Heinemann, and Cambridge, Mass: Harvard UP).

Shaw, B. (1983) *Comprehensive Schooling: The Impossible Dream?* (Oxford: Blackwell).

Skinner, A.S. and Wilson, T. (eds.) (1976) *Essays on Adam Smith* (Oxford: Clarendon).

Skinner, B.F. (1938) *The Behavior of Organisms* (New York: Appleton-Century-Crofts).

Skinner, B.F. (1971) *Beyond Freedom and Dignity* (New York: Knopf, and London: Cape).

Smith, A. [1776] (1979) *An Inquiry into the Nature and Causes of the Wealth of Nations*, edited by R.H. Campbell and A.S. Skinner (Indianapolis: Liberty).

Smith, K. (1951) *The Malthusian Controversy* (London: Routledge and Kegan Paul).

Snyderman, M. and Rothman, S. (1990) *The IQ Controversy: The Media and Public Policy* (New Brunswick, NJ: Transaction).

Solzhenitsyn, A. (1974–8) *The Gulag Archipelago*, translated by T.P. Whitney and H.T. Willets (London: Fontana/Collins).

Sowell, T. (1975) *Race and Economics* (New York and London: Longman).

Sowell, T. (1980) *Knowledge and Decisions* (New York: Basic).

Sowell, T. (1981) *Ethnic America: A History* (New York: Basic).

Sowell, T. (1983) *The Economics and Politics of Race* (New York: William Morrow).

Sowell, T. (1985) *Marxism: Philosophy and Economics* (London: Allen and Unwin).

Sowell, T. (1990) *Preferential Policies: An International Perspective* (New York: William Morrow).

Speake, J. (1984) *A Dictionary of Philosophy* (London: Macmillan and Pan).

Sumner, W.G. (1940) *Folkways* (Boston: Ginn).

Thouless, R.H. (1930) *Straight and Crooked Thinking* (London: Hodder and Stoughton).

Thurrow, L. (1969) *Poverty and Discrimination* (Washington, D.C.: Brookings Institution).

Trevor-Roper, H.R. (1957) *Historical Essays* (London: Macmillan).

Trigg, R. (1973) *Reason and Commitment* (Cambridge: CUP).

Veblen, T. (1899) *The Theory of the Leisure Class* (London and New York: Macmillan).

Weber, M. (1904) '"Objectivity" in social science and social policy', in *The Methodology of the Social Sciences*, translated by E.A. Shils and H.A. Finch and edited by E.A. Shils (Glencoe, Ill.: Free Press, 1949).

Weber, M. (1917) 'The meaning of "value-freedom" in sociology and economics', in *The Methodology of the Social Sciences*, as above.

Wesson, R.G. (1976) *Why Marxism? The Continuing Success of a Failed Theory* (London: Temple Smith).

Whately, R. [1832] (1855) *Lectures on Political Economy* (Oxford: Parker).

Wiles, P. (1974) 'Explaining Violence and Social Work Practice', in *The Lawbreakers* (London: BBC).

Williams, S. (1981) *Politics is for People* (Harmondsworth: Penguin).

Wilson, B. (ed.) (1970) *Rationality* (Oxford: Blackwell).

Wilson, J.Q. (1977) *Thinking about Crime* (New York: Vintage).

Winch, P. (1958) *The Idea of a Social Science* (London: Routledge and Kegan Paul).

Wittfogel, K.A. (1981) *Oriental Despotism: A Comparative Study of Total Power* (New York: Random House, Vintage Edition with a new Foreword by the author).

Wittgenstein, L. (1922) *Tractatus Logico-Philosophicus*, translated by C.K. Ogden (London: Kegan Paul, Trench, Trubner). As well as this Authorized Version there is also a Revised – more accurate but inferior as literature.

Wolfe, B.D. (1967) *Marxism: 100 Years of a Doctrine* (London: Chapman and Hall).
Young, M.F.D. (ed.) (1971) *Knowledge and Control* (London: Collier-Macmillan).

Index of Names

Index of Notions